I0660909

Alexander Johnston

The United States

History and Constitution

Alexander Johnston

The United States
History and Constitution

ISBN/EAN: 9783744704632

Printed in Europe, USA, Canada, Australia, Japan

Cover: Foto ©ninafisch / pixelio.de

More available books at **www.hansebooks.com**

THE UNITED STATES

THE UNITED STATES

ITS HISTORY AND CONSTITUTION

BY

ALEXANDER JOHNSTON

Late Professor of Jurisprudence and Political Economy
in Princeton College

NEW YORK
CHARLES SCRIBNER'S SONS
1889

TYPOGRAPHY BY J. S. CUSHING AND CO.
PRESSWORK BY BERWICK AND SMITH.
BOSTON.

PUBLISHERS' NOTE.

THE contents of the present volume, by the late Professor Alexander Johnston, first appeared as the article of the Encyclopædia Britannica on the history and Constitution of the United States. The narrative, it should be borne in mind, ends with the year 1887 — the last of the period entitled by the author "The Reconstructed Nation: 1865–1887." There are, however, few details which the events of the past two years have modified, and few which need to be supplemented. Some slight verbal changes, where evidently indicated, have been made in this sense, a note added with reference to the admission into the Union of Washington, Montana, and North and South Dakota, and the election of Harrison and Morton, and the prohibition of Chinese immigration chronicled. It has not been thought advisable, however, to change or supplement the text in two or three other instances in which statistics of 1889 might have been given, but in which the reader will perceive those of 1887 to have been retained as better preserving the consistency and significance of the passages in which they occur.

CONTENTS.

THE UNITED STATES.

I.

COLONIZATION.

1607–1750.

1. THOUGH the voyages of the Cabots (1497–98) along the coast of North America were the ground which the English finally adopted as a basis for their claims on that continent, no very effective steps were taken to reduce the continent to possession until after 1606. Martin Frobisher (1576) failed in an attempt to explore Labrador. Sir Humphrey Gilbert (1578) failed in a similar attempt on the con-

Early voyages and explorations.

tinent; and in a second effort (1583) he was lost in a storm at sea on his return. In 1584 his half-brother Raleigh took up the work under commission from Queen Elizabeth. He sent two small vessels under Amidas and Barlow. They explored the south-central coast of what is now the United States, and returned with such flattering reports that the courtly Raleigh at once named the country Virginia, in honor of the queen, and sent out a colony. It was starved out in a year (1585). He sent another to the same place, Roanoke Island (1587), but it had disappeared when it was searched for three years after. Gosnold (1602) found a shorter route across the Atlantic, and spent a winter on an island off the present coast of Massachusetts; but his men refused to stay longer. These are the official records of English explorations up to 1606; but it is pretty certain that fishing and trading voyages, of which no record was kept, were more common than has been supposed, and that they kept alive a knowledge of the country.

2. In 1606 James I. formed two companies by a single charter. To one, the London Company, he granted the North-American coast between 34° and 38° N. lat.; to the other, the Plymouth Company, whose membership was more in the west of England, he granted the coast between 41° and 45° N. lat. The intervening coast, between lat. 38° and 41°, or between the Rappahannock and Hudson rivers, was to be common to both, but neither was to plant a settlement within 100 miles of a previous settlement of the other. Each was to be governed by a council appointed by the king, and these councils were to appoint colonial councils of thirteen, with really absolute powers. Neither company did much in colonization : the London Company gave up its charter in 1624, and the Plymouth Company, after a complete change of constitution in 1620, surrendered its charter in 1635. But the London Company at least began the work of colonization, and the Plymouth Company parcelled out its grant to actual colonists. Above all, the charter of the two companies had granted the principle to which the colonists always appealed as the foundation of English colonization in North America, as the condition on which immigrants had entered it, irrevocable unless by mutual consent of

[margin note: London and Plymouth Companies.]

crown and subjects: "Also, we do, for us, our heirs and successors, declare by these presents that all and every the persons, being our subjects, which shall go and inhabit within the said colony and plantation, and every their children and posterity, which shall happen to be born within any of the limits thereof, shall have and enjoy all liberties, franchises, and immunities of free denizens and natural subjects· within any of our other dominions, to all intents and purposes as if they had been abiding and born within this our realm of England, or in any other of our dominions."

3. The London Company was first in the field. A ship-load of the adventurers then swarming in London was sent out under Christopher Newport. He found a fine river, which he named after the king, and on its banks, within the present State of Virginia, he planted the settlement of Jamestown[1] (13th May, 1607). Misgovernment, dissension, mismanagement, and starvation were almost too much for the infant colony, and several times the colonists were on the point of giving it up and going home. Twelve years were required to put Virginia on a sound footing. By that time the liberal element in the London Company had got control of it, and granted the colonists a representative government.

Settlement of Jamestown; of Virginia;

---

[1] The former settlement of Jamestown is now in James City county, Va., about 32 miles from the mouth of the James river. It was at first the capital of the colony, but began to decline when Williamsburgh was made the capital. Its death-blow was received when it was burned in 1676, during Bacon's rebellion. It was not rebuilt, and has now almost disappeared. " Nothing remains but the ruins of a church tower covered with ivy, and some old tombstones. The river encroaches year by year, and the ground occupied by the original huts is already submerged."

The year in which this house of burgesses met (1619) was the year in which African slaves were introduced into the colony from a Dutch vessel.

4. Separatists from the Church of England began the more northerly settlements. Driven from England, they found refuge in Holland. Thence returning for the moment to England, a company of 102 of them set sail for America in the " Mayflower," landing (December 21,

Settlement of 1620) at Plymouth, in the south-eastern part
Plymouth; of the present State of Massachusetts. The rigors of a new and cold country, combined with poverty and the payment of interest at 45 per cent., made the early years of the Plymouth colony a desperate struggle for existence, but it survived. It had no special charter, but a license from the Plymouth Company. Other little towns were founded to the north of this settlement, and in 1629 these were all embraced in a charter given by

of Massachu- Charles I. to the Governor and Company of
setts Bay; Massachusetts Bay. This was a Puritan venture, composed of men of higher social grade than the Plymouth Separatists; and was meant to furnish a refuge for those who dreaded the ecclesiastical policy of the crown. The next year the company took the bold step of transferring its organization to America, so as to be out of the immediate notice of the crown and its agents. Eleven vessels took more than a thousand colonists over, and the real colony of Massachusetts was begun.

5. The charter of the London Company was surrendered to the crown, as has been said, in 1624; and the king thereafter disposed of the territory which had been

of Maryland; granted to it as he pleased. In 1632 the new
colony of Maryland was carved out of it for Lord Baltimore. In 1663 the territory to the south of

the present State of Virginia was' cut off from it and called Carolina, covering the present States of Settlement of Carolina; North and South Carolina and Georgia. In 1729 Carolina was divided into North and South Carolina; and in 1732 the last of the colonies, of Georgia; Georgia, was organized. Five distinct colonies were thus formed out of the original London Company's grant.

6. When the Plymouth Company finally surrendered its charter in 1635, it had made one ineffectual attempt at colonization (1607) near the mouth of the Kennebec river, in Maine, and one complete colony, Massachusetts Bay, had arisen within its territory. Another colony, that of Plymouth, existed by license. Massachusetts settlers, without even a license, were pouring into the vacant territory to the south of Massachusetts, there to form the colonies of Connecticut and Rhode Island, of Connecticut and Rhode Island; afterwards chartered by the crown, 1662 and 1663. A few fishing villages to the north of Massachusetts, established under the grant of John Mason, were the nucleus of the colony of of New Hampshire. New Hampshire. The present States of Vermont and Maine were not yet organized. Out of the original Plymouth Company's grant were thus formed the colonies of Massachusetts, Connecticut, Rhode Island, and New Hampshire. The name New England was commonly applied to the whole territory from the beginning, having been first used by Captain John Smith in 1614.

7. Nine of the "old thirteen" colonies are thus accounted for. The remaining four fell in the territory between the two main grants, which was to be common to both companies, but was in fact never appropriated by

either.   The Spaniard had settled contentedly far to the south; and the Frenchman, still bound by too many of the ancient ecclesiastical influences to contest supremacy with the Spaniard, had settled as far to the north as possible, in Canada.   England had been so far released from ecclesiastical influences by the spread of the Reformation as to be prepared to contest supremacy with Spaniard, Frenchman, or any one else; but her lingering desires to avoid open conflict at any cheap rate had tended to fix her settlements on the very choicest part of the coast, in the middle latitudes, — a fact which was to color the whole future history of the continent.   The concurrent claims of the two English companies in the central zone seem to have deterred both of them from any attempt to interfere with the development of a colony there by the only other people of western Europe which was prepared

The Dutch settlements. to grasp at such an opportunity.   The Dutch (1609) sent out Henry Hudson, an Englishman in their service, and he made the first close exploration of this central region.   Dutch merchants thereupon set up a trading post at Manhadoes (the present city of New York), where a government under the Dutch West India Company was organized in 1621, when the Dutch states-general had granted the territory to it.   The territory was named New Netherland, and the town at the mouth of the Hudson river New Amsterdam.   Sweden sent a colony to Delaware bay in 1638; but the attempt was never thoroughly backed, and in 1655 it was surrendered to the Dutch.

8. By the time of the Restoration in England, the northern and southern English colonies had developed so far that the existence of this alien element between them had come to be a recognized annoyance and danger.   From

the Hudson river to Maine, from the Savannah river to Delaware Bay, all was English. Roads had been roughly marked out; ships were sailing along the respective coasts as if at home; colonial governments were beginning to lean upon one another for support; but between the two was a territory which might at any moment turn to hostility. There was an evidently growing disposition in New England to attempt the conquest of it unaided. When England and Holland found themselves at war (1664), the opportunity arrived for a blow at Holland's colonial possessions. An English army and fleet under Colonel Nichols touched at Boston, and, proceeding thence to New Amsterdam, took possession of the whole central territory. It had been granted by the king to his brother, the duke of York, and the province and city were now named New York in honor of the new pro- The colony of prietor. The duke, the same year, granted a New York; part of his territory to Berkeley and Carteret, and the new colony of New Jersey was the result. of New Jersey; In 1681 the great parallelogram west of New of Pennsyl- Jersey was granted to Penn and called Penn- vania; sylvania. In the following year Penn bought from the duke of York the little piece of territory which remained united to Pennsylvania until the revolution, then becoming the State of Delaware. The central of Delaware. territory thus furnished four of the "old thirteen" colonies, New England four, and the southern portion five.

9. If there was any governing idea in the organization of the colonial governments, it was of the The colonial rudest kind; and in fact each was allowed to governments. be so largely modified by circumstances that, with a general similarity, there was the widest possible diver-

gence. A general division of the colonial governments
The charter is into charter, proprietary, and royal govern-
colonies. ments. The charter governments were Massachusetts, Connecticut, and Rhode Island. In these the
colonial governments had charters from the crown, giving
the people, or freemen, the right to choose their own
governors and other magistrates, to make their own laws,
and to interpret and enforce them. Only Connecticut
and Rhode Island kept their charters intact. The Massachusetts charter was cancelled by the crown judges (1684)
under a *quo warranto;* and in 1691 a new charter was
granted. As it reserved to the crown the appointment of
the governor, with an absolute veto on laws and after
1726 on the election of the speaker of the lower house,
Massachusetts was thus taken out of the class of purely
charter colonies and put into that of a semi-royal colony.
The proprietary colonies were New Hampshire, New
The proprietary York, New Jersey, Pennsylvania (including
colonies. Delaware), Maryland, Carolina, and Georgia.
These were granted to proprietors, who, as inducements
to settlers, granted governmental privileges almost as
liberal as those of the charter colonies. Only Pennsylvania, Delaware, and Maryland remained proprietary
colonies down to the revolution, and in these the governor had a charter right of veto on legislation. Vir-
The royal ginia became a royal colony in 1620, and
colonies. New York as soon as its proprietor became
king; and other proprietors, becoming tired of continual
quarrels with the colonists, gradually surrendered their
grants to the crown. New Hampshire, New York, New
Jersey, North and South Carolina, and Georgia had thus
become royal colonies before the revolution. In the royal
colonies, commonly called provinces, the governors were

appointed by the crown, and had an absolute veto on legislation. There were thus at last three proprietary, seven royal, one semi-royal, and two charter colonies.

10. The two charter colonies were simple representative democracies, having the power *Representative systems.* to legislate without even a practical appeal to the crown, and having no royal governor or agent within their borders. Their systems were the high-water mark to which the desires and claims of the other colonies gradually approached. Massachusetts and the proprietary colonies were very nearly on a level with them; and the royal or proprietary governor's veto power was rather an annoyance than a fundamental difference. But in all the colonies representative governments had forced their way, and had very early taken a bicameral shape. In the charter colonies and Massachusetts the lower house was chosen by the towns and the upper house from the people at large, and the two houses made up the "assembly." In Pennsylvania and Delaware there was but one house. In the royal colonies and in Maryland the lower house alone was elected by the people; the upper house, or council, was chosen by the crown through the governor; and the assent of all three elements was essential to legislation. In the final revolution the charter colonies did not change their governments at all; they already had what they wanted. The revolution was consummated in the other colonies by the assumption of power by the lower or popular house, usually known as the "assembly," the governor or council, or both, being ousted.

11. All these governmental organizations take a prominent place in American history, *Town and parish.* and had a strong influence on the ultimate development of the United States; and yet they touched the life of

the people at comparatively few points. A more marked and important distinction is in the local organizations of the northern and southern colonies. All the southern colonies began as proprietary governments. Settlers went there as individuals connected only with the colony. To the individual the colony was the great political factor; his only other connection was with his parish, to which the colony allowed few political functions; and, where political power touched him at all, it was through the colony. In time it became necessary to allow political powers to the parish or county, but they were really more judicial than political. "The southern county was a modified English shire, with the towns left out." The whole tendency shows the character of the immigration in this part of the country, from English districts outside of the influence of the towns.

12. In New England local organization was quite different. A good example is the town of Dorchester. The town system. Organized (March 20, 1630) in Plymouth, England, when its people were on the point of embarkation for America, it took the shape of a distinct town and church before they went on shipboard. Its civil and ecclesiastical organizations were complete before they landed in Massachusetts Bay and came under the jurisdiction of a chartered company. Its people governed themselves, in their town government, in all but a few points, in which the colony asserted superiority. As the colony's claims increased, the town's dissatisfaction increased. In 1635 the town migrated in a body, with its civil and ecclesiastical organization still intact, into the vacant territory of Connecticut, and there became the town of Windsor. Here, uniting with other towns, which had migrated in a similar fashion, it formed

the new Commonwealth of Connecticut, in which the local liberty of the towns was fully secured in the frame of government. Rhode Island was formed in the same way, by separate towns; Vermont afterwards in the same way; and the towns of the parent colony of Massachusetts learned to claim a larger liberty than had been possible at first. Thus, all through New England, the local town organizations came to monopolize almost all ordinary governmental powers; and the counties to which the towns belonged were judicial, not political, units, marking merely the jurisdiction of the sheriff. In the annual town meetings, and in special meetings from time to time, the freemen exercised, without any formal grant, the powers of self-taxation, of expenditure of taxation, of trial by jury, and of a complete local government. Further, the lower houses of their colonial legislatures were made up of generally equal representations from the towns, while the upper houses were chosen from the colony at large. In this was the germ of the subsequent development of the United States senate, in which the States are equally represented, and of the house of representatives, representing the people numerically (§§ 104, 105, 109, 110).

13. The two opposite systems of the north and south found a field for conflict in the organization of the central territory after its acquisition (§ 8). The crown agents were strongly disposed to follow The middle colonies. the more centralized system of the southern colonies, though Penn, having organized counties and restricted his legislature to a single house, based it on the counties. In New York and New Jersey the Dutch system of "patroonships" had left a simulacrum of local independence, and a stronger tendency in the same direction

came in through immigration from New England. To encourage this immigration, the New Jersey proprietors gave town powers to many of them; and some of the New Jersey towns were merely transplanted New England towns. But the middle colonies never arrived at any distinct system; at the best, their system was a conglomerate. Much the same result has been reached in the new Western States, organized under the care of the Federal Government, where the New England immigration has brought with it a demand for local self-government which has resulted in a compromise between the two systems of town units and county units.

14. Ecclesiastical divisions were at first as strong as civil diversities. The New England colonies were Con-

Ecclesiastical systems. gregational, and these churches were established and supported by law, except in Rhode Island, where the Baptists were numerically superior. In the royal colonies generally there was a steady disposition to establish the Church of England, and it was more or less successful. In language there were striking dissimilarities, due to a most heterogeneous immigration. It was said that every language of Europe could be found in the colony of Pennsylvania. But, after all, this diversity had no indications of persistence; the im-

Immigration. migration in each case had been too small to support itself. Very little of the wonderful increase of American population between 1607 and 1750 was due to immigration; most of it had come from natural increase. After the first outflow from Old to New England, in 1630–31, emigration was checked at first by the changing circumstances of the struggle between the people and the king, and, when the struggle was over, by the better-known difficulties of life in the colonies.

Franklin, in 1751, when he estimated that there were "near a million English souls" in the colonies, thought that scarce eighty thousand had been brought over by sea. No matter how diverse the small immigration might have been on its arrival, there was a steady pressure on its descendants to turn them into Englishmen; and it was very successful. When Whitefield, the revivalist, visited America about 1740, he found the population sufficiently homogeneous for his preaching to take effect, all the way from Georgia to New England. The same tendency shows itself in the complete freedom of intercolonial migration. Men went from one colony to another, or held estates, or took inheritances in different colonies, without the slightest notion that they were under any essentially diverse political conditions. The whole coast, from Nova Scotia to the Spanish possessions in Florida, was one in all essential circumstances; and there was only the need of some sudden shock to crystallize it into a real political unity. Hardly anything in history is more impressive than this mustering of Englishmen on the Atlantic coast of North America, their organization of natural and simple governments, and their preparations for the final march of 3000 miles westward, unless it be the utter ignorance of the home Government and people that any such process was going on.

15. This ignorance had one singular effect in completing the difference between the new and the old country. An odd belief that European *Democracy.* plants and animals degenerated in size and quality on transplantation to the western continent was persistent at the time even among learned men in Europe, and Jefferson felt bound to take great pains to combat it so late as the end of the 18th century. That passage in

Thackeray's *Virginians,* where the head of the elder
Virginian branch of the family returns to England, to be
treated with contempt and indifference by the younger
branch which had remained at home, indicates the state
of mind among the influential classes in England which
bent them against any admission of Americans to the
honors or privileges of the English higher classes. A
few titles were given; entails were maintained in the
southern colonies; but there were no such systematic
efforts as are necessary to maintain an aristocratic class.
This may have been gratifying to the ruling class in
England; but it was in reality an unconsciously systematic effort to develop democracy in the English colonies
in North America. In combination with the free representative institutions which had taken root there, it was
very successful, and, when the final struggle between the
English ruling class and the colonists took shape, the
former had singularly few friends or allies in the colonies.
What the results might have been if efforts had been
made to build up a titled class in the colonies, with
entailed revenues and hereditary privileges in the upper
houses of the colonial legislatures, is not easy to imagine;
but the prejudices of the privileged classes at home
eliminated this factor from the problem. Every influence
conduced to make the American commonwealths representative democracies; and the reservation of crown influence in the functions of the governors or the appointment of the council was merely a dam which was sure
to be broken down as development increased.

16. Social circumstances had all the features of life in
a new country, aggravated by the difficulties
of inter-communication at that time. In the
southern and middle colonies there was a rude abundance,

Social conditions.

so that, however much the want of luxuries might be felt, there was no lack of the necessaries of life. The growth of tobacco, indigo, and rice in the southern colonies was so large a source of wealth that luxury in that part of the country had taken a more pronounced form than in, the others. The southern planter, trained in English schools and universities and admitted to the English bar, was more like an English gentleman in a condition of temporary retirement than an American colonist. The settler of the middle colonies was the ordinary agriculturist. The hardships of colonial life were the special lot of the New England colonist. For some reason — perhaps because the forests retained the snow on the ground — the New England winters were more severe than they are now. The rudely built house, with its enormous chimney attracting draughts of outer air from every point, was a poor protection against the cold. Travel, difficult enough at the best, became impossible in winter, unless the snow rose so high as to blot out the roads and permit the traveller to drive his sledge across country. Medical and surgical attendance was scarce in summer, and hardly dreamed of in winter. The religious feeling of the people was against amusements of all kinds, except going to funerals, an occasional dinner, and the restricted enjoyments of courtship. It was a point of honor or of religious feeling to exclude luxury from church equipment: stoves were not known in Connecticut churches until the beginning of this century, and yet new-born infants were taken to church for baptism in the bitterest weather.[1]

---

[1] An extract from a New England diary of 1716 will give some notion of social circumstances at that comparatively late period. "Lord's

17. Wealth in the southern colonies was sufficient to give the better classes there an education of a very high

Education. order; and they in turn, by virtue of their political and social leadership, imparted something of their acquisitions to those below them. In the middle colonies commercial pursuits and those interests which go to make men of affairs had something of the same influence on special classes. In New England education was more general, even though it had no such advantages for special classes as at the south. The first immigration into New England contained an unusually large proportion of English university men, particularly among the ministers. These fixed the mould into which their descendants have been run, and New England's influence in the United States has been due largely to them. The town system added to their influence. Owing to it the ebbing and flowing of population through New England was not blind or unorganized. Every little town was a skeleton battalion, to be filled up by subsequent increase and immigration; and the ministers and other professional men made a multitude of successors for themselves, with all their own ideas. Considering the execrable quality of school and college instruction in New England, as elsewhere at the time, it is very remarkable that, as the original supply of university-bred leaders died off, there was a full crop of American-bred men quite prepared to take their places and carry on their work. Here

Day, Jany. 15. An extraordinary cold Storm of wind and Snow. Blows much as coming home at Noon and so holds on. Bread was frozen at the Lord's table; Mr. Pemberton administered. Came not out to afternoon exercise. Though 'twas so cold, yet John Tuckerman was baptised. At six a-clock my ink freezes so that I can hardly write by a good fire in my wive's chamber. Yet was very comfortable at meeting. *Laus Deo.*"

were Harvard and Yale, the two leading colleges of the
country, which in 1760 had six : — Harvard College, in
Massachusetts (founded in 1636) ; William and Mary
College, in Virginia (1692) ; Yale College, in Connecticut
(1700) ; Princeton College, in New Jersey (1746) ; Pennsylvania University (1749) ; and King's, now Columbia,
College, in New York (1754).

18. Shipwrights had been sent to Virginia at an early
date ; but shipbuilding never made great head in the
southern colonies, in spite of the fact that
they had all the materials for it in abundance. Commerce.
At a later period ships were built, and it was not uncommon for planters to have their private docks on their
own plantations, where their ships were freighted for
Europe. But such building was individual : each planter
built only for himself. The first vessel built by Euro-
peans in this part of the continent was constructed by
Adrian Block at New Amsterdam (1614). Many small
vessels were built at the mouth of the Hudson river
under Dutch and English domination, but New York's
commercial supremacy did not fairly begin until after the
revolution. Perhaps the hardships of life in New England made its people prefer water to land ; at any rate
they took to shipbuilding early and carried it on diligently and successfully. Plymouth built a little vessel
before the settlement was five years old, and Massachusetts another, the "Blessing of the Bay" (1631). Before 1650 New England vessels had begun the general
foreign trade, from port to port, which combined exportation with a foreign coasting trade and mercantile business,
the form in which New England commercial enterprise
was to show itself most strongly. Before 1724 English
ship-carpenters complained of the competition of the

Americans, and in 1760 the colonies were building new ships at the rate of about 20,000 tons a year, most of them being sold in England.

19. The earliest manufactures in the colonies were naturally those of the simplest kind, the products of saw-

Manufactures mills, grist-mills, and tanneries, and home-
and mining. made cloth. The search for ores, however, had been a prime cause of immigration with many of the settlers, and they turned almost at once to mining and metallurgy. Most of their efforts failed, in spite of "premiums," bounties, and monopolies for terms of years granted by the colonial legislatures. To this the production of iron was an exception. It was produced, from the beginning of the 18th century, in western Massachusetts and Connecticut, in eastern New York, in northern New Jersey, and in eastern Pennsylvania. All these districts were about on a level, until the adaptation of the furnaces to the use of anthracite coal drove the New England and New York districts, which had depended on wood as fuel, almost out of competition (§ 210). Until that time iron production was a leading New England industry. Not only were the various products of iron exported largely; the manufacture of nails, and of other articles which could be made by an industrious agricultural population in winter and stormy weather, was a "home industry" on which New Englanders depended for much of their support.

20. The colonial system of England differed in no respect from that of other European nations of the time;

The English probably none of them could have conceived
colonial system. any other as possible. The colonies were to be depôts for the distribution of home products on a new soil; whenever they assumed any other func-

tions they were to be checked. The attempts of the Americans to engage in commerce with other nations, their shipbuilding, and their growing manufactures were, in appearance, deductions from the general market of English producers, and the home Government felt itself bound to interfere. Virginia claimed, by charter-right, the power to trade freely with foreign nations; and Virginia was notoriously on the side of the Stuarts against the parliament. In 1651 parliament passed the Navigation Act, forbidding the carrying of colonial produce to England unless in English or colonial vessels, with an English captain and crew. By the Act of 1661 the reach of the system was extended. Sugar, tobacco, indigo, and other "enumerated articles," grown or manufactured in the colonies, were not to be shipped to any country but England. All that was necessary to make this part of the work complete was to add to the "enumerated articles," from time to time, any which should become important colonial products. The cap-stone was placed on the system in 1663, when the exportation of European products to the colonies was forbidden, unless in vessels owned and loaded as in the preceding Acts and loaded in England. Virginia's commerce withered at once under the enforcement of the system. New England, allowed to evade the system by Cromwell for political reasons, continued to evade it thereafter by smuggling and bold seamanship.

The Navigation Laws.

21. In 1699, on complaint of English manufacturers that the colonists were cutting them out of their foreign wool markets, parliament enacted that no wool or woollen manufactures should be shipped from any of the colonies, under penalty of forfeiture of ship and cargo. This was the first fruits of the appoint-

Restrictive Laws.

ment of the Board of Trade and Plantations three years
before. From this time until the revolution, this body was
never idle; but, as its work was almost confined to schemes
for checking or destroying the trade and manufactures of
the plantations, it cannot be said to have done them any
great service. It was continually spurring on colonial
governors to turn their people to the production of naval
stores, or to any occupation which would divert them
from manufactures; and the governors, between fear of
the legislatures which paid their salaries and of the
Board which was watching them narrowly, had evidently
no easy position. At intervals the Board heard the complaints of English manufacturers, and framed remedial
bills for parliament. From 1718 the manufacture of iron
was considered particularly obnoxious; and, so late as
1766, Pitt himself asserted the right and duty of parliament to "bind the trade and confine the manufactures"
of the colonies, and to do all but tax them without representation. In 1719 parliament passed its first prohibition of iron manufactures in the colonies; and in 1750
it forbade under penalties the maintaining of iron-mills,
slitting or rolling mills, plating-forges, and steel-furnaces
in the colonies. At the same time, but as a favor to
English manufacturers, it allowed the importation of
American bar-iron into England, as it was cheaper and
better than the Swedish. Before this, in 1731, parliament had forbidden the manufacture or exportation of
hats in or from the colonies, and even their transportation from one colony to another. All these Acts, and
others of a kindred nature, were persistently evaded or
defied; but the constant training in this direction was
not a good one for the maintenance of the connection
between the colonies and the mother country, after the

interested classes in the colonies should become numerous and their interests large. Unluckily for the connection, the arrival at this point was just the time.when the attempt was first made to enforce the Acts with vigor (§ 38).

22. English imports from the North American colonies amounted to £395,000 in 1700, £574,000 in 1730, and £761,000 in 1760; the exports to the colonies The American in the same years were £344,000, £537,000, market. and £2,612,000. In spite of parliamentary exactions and interferences, a great and entirely new market had been opened to English trade. The difference between the year 1606, when there was not an English settler on the North-American continent, and 1760, when there were a million and a half with a great and growing commerce, is remarkable. It is still more remarkable when one considers that this population was already nearly one-fourth of that of England and Wales. Its growth, however, steadily increased the difficulties of maintaining the English system of control, which consisted mainly in the interference of the governors with legislation proposed by the assemblies. As the numbers and material interests of the subjects increased, the necessities for governmental interference increased with them, and yet the power of the subjects to coerce the governors increased as well. Only time was needed to bring the divergence to a point where change of policy must have disruption as its only alternative.

23. Merely material prosperity, the development of wealth and comfort, was very far from the whole work of the colonies. In spite of attempts in Religious almost every colony to establish some form freedom. of religious belief on a government foundation, religious

freedom had really come to prevail to an extent very
uncommon elsewhere at the time. Even in New England, where the theory of the state as an isolated opportunity for the practice of a particular form of worship
had been held most strongly, persecution was directed
chiefly against the Quakers, and that mainly on semi-
political grounds, because of their determination to annoy
congregations in their worship or to outrage some feeling
of propriety. As soon as it came to be realized that the
easiest method to deprive them of the power of annoyance was to ignore them, that method was adopted;
indeed, two of the New England colonies took hardly
any other method from the beginning.

24. In political work the colonies had been very successful. They had built up thirteen distinct political
Political
freedom. units, representative democracies so simple
and natural in their political structure that
time has hardly changed the essential nature of the
American State governments. In so doing, the Americans were really laying the foundations of the future
national structure, for there is hardly a successful feature in the present national government which was not
derived or directly copied from the original colonial
growths; while the absolutely new features, such as the
electoral system (§ 119), introduced into the national
system by way of experiment, have almost as generally
proved failures, and have been diverted from their original purposes or have become obsolete.

II.

THE STRUGGLE FOR EXPANSION.

1750-63.

25. THE English settlements along the Atlantic had covered the narrow strip of coast territory quite thoroughly before it was possible to think of expansion westward. Since about 1605 Canada had been undisputedly in the hands of the French. Their traders and missionaries had entered the present western United States; Marquette and Joliet (1673) and La Salle (1682) had explored the upper Mississippi river, and others, following their track, had explored most of the Mississippi valley and had built forts in various parts of it. About 1700 the French opened ground at the mouth of the Mississippi: D'Iberville (1702) founded Mobile and the French Mississippi Company (1718) founded the city of New Orleans. Consistent design, foiled at last only by failure of material, marks the proceedings of the French commanders in America for the next thirty years. New Orleans and Quebec were the extremities of a line of well-placed forts which were to secure the whole Mississippi valley, and to confine the English settlements forever to the strip of land along the coast bounded on the west by the Appalachian or Alleghany range of mountains, which is parallel to the coast and has but one important break in its barrier, the opening through which the Hudson river flows. The practical genius of the French plans is shown

(margin note: The French in Canada and the west.)

by the fact that so many of these old forts have since become the sites of great and flourishing western cities: Natchez, Vincennes, Peoria, Fort Wayne, Toledo, Detroit, Ogdensburgh, and Montreal either are built on or are so near to the old forts as to testify to the skill and foresight against which the English colonies had to contend.   To this whole territory, extending from the mouth of the Mississippi to that of the St. Lawrence, covering even the western part of the present State of New York, the name of New France was given. The English possessions, extending in hardly any place more than a hundred miles from the ocean, except where the Dutch had long ago planted the outpost of Fort Orange, or Albany, on the upper Hudson, were generally restricted to the immediate neighborhood of the coast, to which the early population had naturally clung as its base of supplies.

26. The French difficulties were even greater than those of the English. The French people had never had

Weakness of the French system. that love of emigration which had given the English colonies their first great impetus. Even where the French settled they showed more of a disposition to coalesce with the native population than to form a homogeneous people. The French were commonly far stronger with the Indians than were the English; but at the end of a hundred and fifty years, when the English colonists numbered a million and a quarter, all animated by the same political purposes, the population of all New France was only about 100,000, and it is doubtful whether there were 7500 in the whole Mississippi valley. The whole French system, wisely as it was designed, was subject to constant and fatal interference from a corrupt court. Its own organization was hampered by attempts to introduce the feudal features of home social life. A way was thus opened to exactions from every agent of the court, to which the people submitted with hereditary patience, but which were fatal to all healthy development. Perhaps worst of all was the natural and inevitable formation of the French line of claims. Trending westward from Quebec to meet the northward line of forts from New Orleans, it was bent at the junction of the two parts, about Detroit, and its most important part lay right athwart the path of advancing English migration. The English wave was thus to strike the weaker French line in flank and at its weakest point, so that the final issue could not in any event have been doubtful. The French and Indian war probably only hastened the result.

27. There had been wars between the French and the English colonies since the accession of William and Mary, mostly accessory to wars between the mother Inter-colonial countries. The colonies had taken part in the wars. wars ended by the peace of Ryswick (1697), the peace of Utrecht (1713), and the peace of Aix-la-Chapelle (1748). The alliance of the French and Indians made all these struggles wretched experiences for the English. The province of Canada became a prison-pen, where captives were held to ransom or adopted into savage tribes. Outlying settlements were broken up, or forced to expend a large part of their energy in watchful self-defence; and it required all the persistence of the English colonies to continue their steady forward movement. Nevertheless they even undertook offensive operations. They captured Port Royal in 1690, but it was given up to the French in 1697. They captured it again in 1710, and this time it was kept, with most of Acadia, which was now to be

known as Nova Scotia. In 1745 the colonies took the strongest French fortress, Louisburgh, on Cape Breton Island, with very little assistance from the home Government. Their land expeditions against Montreal and Quebec were unsuccessful, the reason for failure being usually defective transport.

28. In the treaties which closed these wars, the interests of the colonies met with little consideration. The The "asiento." most notable instance of this was the 12th article of the treaty of Utrecht, by which an English company was secured the exclusive right to carry African slaves into American ports. Originally meant to obtain the Spanish trade in negroes, the company had influence enough to commit the crown to a steady support of the African slave-trade in its own colonies. Again and again the English legislatures in North America attempted to stop the slave-trade, and were prevented by the royal veto. This will serve to explain a passage in Jefferson's first draft of the American Declaration of Independence, as follows : — " He [the king] has waged cruel war against human nature itself. . . . Determined to keep open a market where men should be bought and sold, he has prostituted his negative for suppressing every legislative attempt to prohibit or to restrain this execrable commerce."

29. All parties seem to have felt that the peace of Aix-la-Chapelle was but a truce at the best; and the French court seems to have come at last to some comprehension of its extensive opportunities and duties in North America. With its tardy sympathy, its agents on the new continent began the erection of barriers against the great wave of English westward migration which was just appearing over the crest of the Alleghanies. It was too

late, however, for the English colonies were really able
to sustain themselves against the French colonies and
court together. Their surveyors (1747) had crossed the
crests of the mountains, and had brought back appetiz-
ing accounts of the quality of the lands which lay beyond.
The Ohio Company (1749), formed partly of The Ohio Com-
Virginian speculators and partly of English- pany.
men, had obtained a grant of 500,000 acres of land in the
western part of Pennsylvania (then supposed to be a part
of Virginia), with a monopoly of the Indian trade. As
the grant was completely on the western side of the
Alleghanies, and was the first English intrusion into the
Ohio valley, it behooved the French to meet the step with
prompt action. Their agents traversed the Ohio country,
making treaties with the Indians and burying lead plates
inscribed with the lilies of France and a statement of the
French claims. The erection of the Ohio Company's first
fort (1752) brought on the crisis. The main line of
French forts was too far away to be any check upon it.
The French leaders therefore began to push a branch
line eastward into the disputed territory. Their first
work (1753) was put up at Presque Isle (now Erie),
about 100 miles north of the Ohio Company's fort. The
citadel of the disputed territory had been begun on the
spot where Pittsburgh now stands, where the Alleghany
and Monongahela unite to form the Ohio river. Governor Dinwiddie, of Virginia, had obtained the right to
erect the fort by treaty with the Indians. From Presque
Isle the French began running a line of forts south,
through the present "oil district" of Pennsylvania,
towards the headquarters of the English.

30. Washington was then a land-surveyor, barely of
age ; but he was the agent whom Dinwiddie selected to

carry an ultimatum to the French at Presque Isle. After a perilous winter passage through the wilderness, he found that the French had no intention of evacuating their position, and returned. Virginia at once (January, 1754) voted money and men to maintain the western claims of the colonies; and Washington was sent with 400 provincial troops to secure the half-built fort at the head of the Ohio. The French were also pushing for that place. They won in the race, drove away the English workmen, and finished Fort Du Quesne, named after their governor. Washington, compelled to stop and fortify his position, won the first skirmish of the war with the French advanced guard, but was forced to surrender on terms (July 4, 1754). The usual incidents of a general Indian warfare followed for the rest of the year.

31. Both Governments began to ship regular troops to America, though there was no formal declaration of war until 1756. The year 1755 was marked by the surprise and defeat of Braddock, a gallant and opinionated British officer who commanded an expedition against Fort Du Quesne, by the complete conquest of Nova Scotia, and by the defeat of the French, under their principal officer, Dieskau, at Lake George, in New York, by a force of provincial troops under Sir William Johnson. In 1756 the greatest of French Canadian governors, Montcalm, arrived; and the tide of war went steadily against the English. The officers sent out by the home Government were incompetent, and they generally declined to draw on the colonists for advice. Montcalm found them an easy prey; and his lines were steadily maintained at the point where they had been when Washington surrendered at Fort Necessity. Pitt's entrance to the Newcastle ministry (June,

1757) changed all this. For the first time the colonies found a man who showed a sympathy with them and a willingness to use them. Their legislatures were summoned into counsel as to the conduct of the war; and their alacrity in response was an augury of a change in its fortune. Incompetent officers were weeded out, with little regard to family or court influence. The whole force of the colonies was gathered up, and in 1758 was launched at the French. All western New York was cleared of the enemy at a blow; Fort Du Quesne was taken and renamed Fort Pitt; Louisburgh, which had been restored to France at Aix-la-Chapelle, was again taken; and the only failure of the year was the dreadful butchery of the English in assaulting the walls of Ticonderoga. Louisburgh made an excellent point of attack against Quebec, and Montcalm was forced to draw off nearly all his troops elsewhere for the defence of his principal post. The year 1759 was therefore begun by the capture of Ticonderoga and almost all the French posts within the present United States, and was crowned by Wolfe's capture of the towering walls of Quebec. In 1760, while George II. lay dying, the conquest of Canada was completed, and the dream of a great French empire in North America disappeared forever.

32. The war continued through the first three years of George III., and the colonies took part in the capture of Havana after Spain had entered the struggle as an ally of France. The peace of Paris, **Peace of Paris.** which put an end to the war, restored Havana to Spain, in exchange for Florida, which now became English. France retired from North America, giving to Spain all her claims west of the Mississippi and that small portion east of the Mississippi which surrounds New Orleans,

and to England the remainder of the continent east of
the Mississippi. Spain retained for her territory the
name of Louisiana, originally given by the French. The
rest of the continent was now "the English colonies of
North America."

33. It is evident now that the French and Indian war
was the prelude to the American revolution. It trained
the officers and men for the final struggle. It released
the colonies from the pressure of the French in Canada
so suddenly that the consciousness of their own strength
came at the same instant with the removal of the ancient
barrier to it. It united the colonies for the first time;
few things are more significant of the development of
the colonies than the outburst of plans for colonial union
between 1748 and 1755, the most promising, though it
finally failed, being that of Franklin (1754) at the
Albany conference of Indian commissioners from the
various colonies. The practical union of the colonies,
however, was so evident that it might have been foreseen
that they would now unite instinctively against any common enemy, even the mother country.

34. The war, too, while it obtained its main object in
the view of the colonies — an unlimited western expan-
The conquered sion — brought the seeds of enmity between
territory. them and the crown. The claims of the
English on the continent, as has been said, were based
on the voyages of the Cabots. Under them the crown
had granted in the charters of Massachusetts, Connecticut, Virginia, North and South Carolina, and Georgia
a western extension at first to the Pacific Ocean and
finally to the Mississippi. This was what the colonies
had fought for; and yet at the end of the war (1763)
a royal proclamation was issued forbidding present land

sales west of the Alleghanies and practically reserving the conquered territory as a crown domain. In this, if in nothing else, lay the seeds of the coming revolution, as it afterwards almost disrupted the rising Union. The war had welded the thirteen colonies into one people, though they hardly dreamed of it yet; they had an underlying consciousness that this western territory belonged to the new people, not to the crown or to the separate colonies which had charter claims to it; and they would have resisted the claims of the crown as promptly as they afterwards resisted the claims of the individual colonies.

35. Finally, the war broke the feeling of dependence on the mother country. Poorly armed, equipped, and disciplined, the colonial or "provincial" troops Effects of the had certainly shown fighting qualities of no war. mean order. Colonists would not have been disposed, under any circumstances, to underrate the military qualities of their own men, but their self-glorification found a larger material because of the frequently poor quality of the officers who were sent through family and court influence to represent Great Britain in the colonies. The bitter words in which Junius refers to British military organization in after years were certainly even more applicable in 1750; and the incompetency of many of the British officers is almost incomprehensible. Its effects were increased by an utter indifference to the advice of colonial leaders which, in a new and unknown country, was certain to place British soldiers again and again in positions where they appeared to great disadvantage alongside of their colonial allies or rivals. The provincial who had stood his ground, firing from behind trees and stumps, while the regulars ran past him in

headlong retreat, came home with a sense of his own innate superiority which was sure to bring its results. Braddock's defeat was the prologue to Bunker Hill. The results were strengthened by the fact that most of the war was fought either in New England, the most democratic of the colonies, or by New England men. Their leaders had always been sought for by annual popular elections and re-elections, the promotion of approved men, and the retention of men of poorer quality in lower grades of office. To them the aristocratic influences which gave place and power to such men as Loudoun and "Mrs. Nabbycrombie" were simply ridiculous, and marked only an essential difference between themselves and their English brethren which was to the disadvantage of the latter, even though it occasionally evolved a man like Howe or Pitt. Taking all the influences together, it is plain that the French and Indian war not only brought into being a tangible union of the colonies, but broke many of the cords which had held the colonies to the mother country.

III.

THE STRUGGLE FOR UNION.

1763–75.

36. It is generally believed that the abandonment of North America by France was the result of profound policy, — that she foresaw that her retirement would be followed by the independence of the English colonies, and that Great Britain's temporary aggrandizement would result in a more profound abasement. Vergennes and Choiseul both stated the case in just this way in 1763; and yet it may be doubted whether this was not rather an excuse for yielding to necessity than a political motive. At all events, it is certain that the peace, even with its release of the colonies from French pressure, was not enough to secure colonial union. For this it was necessary that the home Government should go on and release the colonists from their controlling feeling that they were rather Englishmen than Americans.

37. This feeling was not an easy one to eradicate, for it was based in blood, training, and sympathies of every nature. It would not have been easy to distinguish the American from the Englishman; it would, indeed, have been less easy than now, when the full effects of a great stream of immigration have begun to appear. American portraits of the time show typical English faces. Wherever life was

English sympathies of the colonists.

relieved of the privations involved in colonial struggle, the person at once reverted to the type which was then the result of corresponding conditions in England. The traditions of American officers were English; their methods were English; even the attitude which they took towards the private soldiers of their armies was that which was characteristic of the English officer of the time. In the South the men who led and formed public opinion had almost all been trained in England and were ingrained with English sympathies and even prejudices. In the North the acute general intellect had long ago settled upon the "common rights of Englishmen" as the bulwark behind which they could best resist any attempt on their liberties. The pride of the colonists in their position as Englishmen found a medium of expression in enthusiasm for "the young king"; and it would be hard to imagine a more loyal appendage of the crown than its English colonies in North America in 1760.

38. Unfortunately, the peace of Paris did not result merely in freeing the colonies from dependence on the Change of Eng- mother country; it had the more important lish policy. effect of freeing the mother country from fear of France, and of thus encouraging it to open a controversy with the colonies which had not been ventured on before. Quebec had hardly fallen and given the home Government promise of success when the work was begun (1761). The Board of Trade began to revive those regulations of colonial trade which had been practically obsolete in New England; and its customs officers applied to the Massachusetts courts for "writs of assistance" to enable them to enforce the regulations. Instant resistance was offered to the attempt to burden the colonies with these writs, which governed all men, were

returnable nowhere, gave the officers absolute power, and opened every man's house and property to their entrance. The argument of the crown advocates based the power of issuing such writs on parliament's extension of the English revenue system to the colonies, backed by a statute of Charles II. permitting writs of assistance; to refuse to grant the writs was therefore to impeach the power of parliament to legislate for the colonies. The counter-argument of James Otis was the key-note of the revolution. It declared in terms that no Act of parliament could establish such a writ, that it would be a nullity even if it were expressed in the very terms which the customs officers claimed, and that "an Act of parliament against the constitution was void."

39. Perhaps Otis meant by " the constitution " merely the fundamental relations between the mother country and the colonies, for this claim was the first The English step on the way to the final irreconcilable theory of colonial difference as to these relations. The English rights. theory of the connection had been completely put into shape by 1760, with very little objection from the colonists, whose attention had not yet been strongly drawn to the subject. It held that even the two charter colonies, and *a fortiori* still more such a royal province as New York, were merely corporations, erected by the king, but subject to all the English laws relating to such corporations. The king was their visitor, to inquire into and correct their misbehaviors; his courts, on *quo warranto*, could dissolve them; and parliament had the same omnipotent power over them which it had over any other civil corporation, — to check, amend, punish, or dissolve them. These propositions must have seemed unquestionable to the English legal mind in 1763. Their weak

point, the assumption that parliament had power to control a corporation *extra quatuor maria,* had been covered
by a new development of the English theory during the
century. Parliament, originally a merely English body,
had grown in its powers and claims until now the common
use of the phrase "imperial parliament" connoted claims
to which the "four seas" were no longer a limitation, in
law or fact. Parliament was to give the law to the whole
empire. Hitherto this had been developed as a purely
legal theory; it was now first attempted to be put into
practice when the enforcement of the Navigation Acts
was begun in 1761. The first objections offered by the
colonists were easily shown to be illogical and inconsistent with this legal theory of the relations between
the home country and the colonies, but this only drove
the colonists higher, step by step, in their objections, —
from objections to taxation by parliament into objections
to legislation by parliament, — until they had developed,
about 1775, a theory of their own, logical enough in itself,
but so inconsistent with the English theory that war was
the consequence of their collision.

40. Passing over the intermediate steps, the form
which the colonial theory finally took amounted to this.
The colonists' The introduction of the idea of an "imperial
theory. parliament" was itself a revolution, which
could not bind the colonists, or change the conditions
under which they had settled the new country. Their
relations, originally and properly, had been with the
crown alone, and they had had nothing to do with parliament. The crown had seen fit to constitute new dominions for itself beyond the seas, with forms of government
which were irrepealable compacts between it and the people whom it had thus induced to settle the new territory,

and not mere civil corporations. It would follow, then, that the king was no longer king merely of Great Britain and Ireland; he had at least thirteen kingdoms beyond seas, and a parliament in each of them. For the British parliament to interfere with the special concerns of Massachusetts was as flagrant a wrong as it would have been for the parliament of Massachusetts to interfere with the affairs of Great Britain; and Massachusetts had a right to expect her king to protect her from such a wrong. The subject of Massachusetts knew the king only as king of Massachusetts, and the parliament of Great Britain not at all. It needed many years of successful but suicidal logic on the part of their opponents to force the Americans to this point; they even continued to petition parliament until 1774; but after that time they were no further inconsistent, and held that the king was the only bond of union between the parts of the empire. When he wanted money from his American dominions, he was to get it, as he had always got it, by applying to the assembly of the colony, through the governor, for a grant. In the new seats of the race, as in the old, an Englishman was to be taxed only by his own representatives. In other words, each of the English colonies claimed, in its own field and for its own citizens, the exact principles of "English liberty" which had been established in England as the relations of the English subject to the crown. Each colony was to be governed by its own laws, just as in Jersey and Guernsey, in Scotland before the Union, or in Hanover in 1763, with appeal to the king in council, not to English courts or to the House of Lords. For the British parliament, or still more the British citizen, to talk of "our sovereignty" over the colonies was a derogation from the king's sovereignty, the only sovereignty which the colonies knew. "I am quite sick of 'our sovereignty,'" wrote Franklin in 1769. The case of the colonies was evidently that of Ireland also; and Franklin notes the fact that several members of colonial assemblies had been admitted to the privileges of the Irish parliament, on the ground that they were members of "American parliaments." To this statement of their case the Americans adhered with progressive closeness from 1763 until the end. In their final Declaration of Independence it will be found that it is a declaration of their independence of the king only; they do not then admit that the British parliament had ever had any authority over them; and that body is only mentioned in one place, in 'one of the counts of the indictment of the king, for having given his assent to certain "acts of pretended legislation," passed by "a jurisdiction foreign to our constitutions and unacknowledged by our laws," that is to say, by the British parliament.

41. Two irreconcilable theories were thus presented. Between them were two courses, either of which the Possible compromises. colonies were willing to accept. Under their theory there was no "imperial parliament." They were willing to have one constituted, even if it were only a development of the British parliament through admission of colonial representatives; but the time for this passed before the parties could debate it. On the other hand, the colonies were willing to abandon to the wealthier British parliament, which sustained so much larger a proportion of the cost of the standing army and navy, the privilege of regulating external trade for the general good. So late as 1774 the Continental Congress, while maintaining the sole right of the colonial

assemblies to levy internal taxation and make local laws, declared their willingness to yield to the British parliament the power to make such regulations of external trade as were *bona fide* meant to benefit trade, and not to raise a revenue from Americans without their own consent. This solution could have been only temporary at best, and war cut off any discussion of it.

42. The work of quiet revolution was begun in March, 1763, in the closing hours of the Bute ministry, Charles Townshend being first lord of trade and administrator of the colonies. It was decided to make a point of having all the American judges and other officials hold office during the king's pleasure, and to make their salaries independent of the colonial assemblies. The army estimates were increased by an American standing force of twenty regiments, to be paid for by Great Britain for the first year, and thereafter out of a revenue to be raised in America by Act of parliament. Bute's purposes were political,—the diminution of democracy in America. The Wilkes uproar drove him out of power before he could develop his plans; but his successor, Grenville, followed them out for financial reasons, and in February, 1765, the Stamp Act "was passed through both Houses with less opposition than a turnpike bill." *The Stamp Act.*

43. For the past two years the colonists had had other things to think of. Under Grenville the Acts in restraint of colonial trade (§§ 20, 21), which had been allowed to become practically obsolete, were *The Navigation Laws.* put into force with unsparing rigor. The numbers of the customs officers were increased; their duties were more plainly declared; naval officers were encouraged to take the oaths of customs officers and share in the plunder of the commerce which had grown up between Amer-

ica and the West Indian Islands and other parts of the world. Search was constant; confiscation usually followed search; and appeal was even more costly than confiscation. In the confusion arising from the efforts of American commerce to escape its new enemies, it was not wonderful that other questions were allowed to go by default. But the mutterings of resistance were heard. The Massachusetts assembly protested against any schemes to create a standing army in America, to make officers independent of the assemblies, or to raise a revenue without consent of the assemblies, and appointed a committee to secure the united action of all the colonies. This was the first movement in the struggle for union. Its importance was hidden from the ministry by the official class in the colonies, whose members — the governors, judges, and other crown officials — continued to urge a persistence in the new policy, and to represent the Adamses, Otis, and the other colonial leaders as animated by a perverse desire to destroy the unity of the empire.

44. The revenue to be raised by the Stamp Act was to come from the sale of stamps and stamped paper for marriage licenses, commercial transactions, suits at law, transfers of real estate, inheritances, publications, and some minor sources of revenue. With it was another startling provision, — a command to the colonial assemblies to furnish the royal troops in America with fuel, candles, vinegar, bedding, cooking utensils, and potables, and permission to billet the troops in inns, alehouses, barns, and vacant houses. The colonies were thus to be taxed without their consent; the revenue derived therefrom was to be devoted to the support of a standing army; and that army was in turn to be used for the maintenance of the scheme of taxation. Yet no one in England seems to

have dreamed of American resistance to it; and Grenville was able to say in 1770 that he "did not foresee the
opposition to the measure, and would have staked his life
for obedience."

45. The news of the passage of the Stamp Act caused
all America to hum with the signs of resistance, but
forcible resistance was at first repudiated   Resistance to
everywhere.   It took the shape, really more the Stamp Act.
significant, of declarations by the colonial assemblies,
the lower or popular houses of the legislatures.   The
Virginia assembly, under the lead of Patrick Henry and
the younger members, took the first step (May, 1765),
by a declaration of colonial rights covering the right of
each colony to make its own laws and impose and expend
its own taxation.   The Massachusetts assembly followed
with the formal proposal of an American Congress, to be
composed of representatives of all the colonies.   South
Carolina seconded the call; and the first step on the road
to union was taken.

46. Outside of these formal steps there were signs of
a less formal popular resistance.   Even peaceable resistance was *pro tanto* a suspension of royal and parliamentary authority in the colonies; and it was probably inevitable that the colonial assemblies should succeed to
the power during the interregnum before the organization
of a real national power.   But a temporary chaos was as
inevitable; and the form it took was the formation, particularly in the North, of popular organizations known
as "Sons of Liberty," the name being taken "Sons of Lib-
from a chance allusion in one of Barré's   erty."
speeches in the House of Commons.   These, backed frequently by the town organizations, forced the stamp-officers to resign, and destroyed the stamps wherever they

could be found. The Connecticut stamp-officer, as he
rode into Hartford on his white horse to deposit his resignation, with a thousand armed farmers riding after him,
said that he felt "like death on the pale horse, with all
hell following him." Newspapers and pamphlets rang
every possible change on Coke's dictum that "an Act of
parliament contrary to Magna Charta was void," and with
warnings to stamp-officers that they would be considered
enemies to the liberties of America if they attempted to
carry out their duties. When the day broke on which the
Act was to go into operation (November 1, 1765) America
had neither stamps nor stamp-officers with which to fulfil
its provisions.

47. The proposed Congress, commonly called the
"Stamp-Act Congress," met at New York (October 7,
Stamp-Act Con- 1765). —New Hampshire, Virginia, North Car-
gress.   olina, and Georgia being acquiescent but not
represented. It petitioned the king, the House of Commons, and the House of Lords to recognize fully "the
several governments formed in the said colonies, with
full powers of legislation, agreeably to the principles of
the English constitution." It also put forth a declaration of colonial rights, acknowledging allegiance to the
crown, and claiming "all the inherent rights and privileges of natural-born subjects within the kingdom of
Great Britain," including the right of petition, of trial by
jury, of taxation by representatives, and of granting supplies to the crown, and protesting against the Stamp Act
and the various Acts in restraint of trade. The action
of this congress was thus purely declaratory; there was
no attempt to legislate; and the importance of the meeting was in its demonstration of the possibility of union
and of one road to it.

48. In the meantime the Grenville ministry had fallen (July, 1765), and the Rockingham ministry (March, 1766) repealed the Stamp Act. The repeal was Repeal of the supported by Pitt, and Whigs who agreed Stamp Act. with him, on the distinction that taxation by parliament without colonial representation was in violation of the essential principles of the British constitution, but that the power of parliament to legislate in every other point for all parts of the empire must be maintained (§ 21). Nevertheless, the repeal was preceded by a declaration of the power "of the king in parliament to bind the colonies and people of America in all cases whatsoever."

49. The colonists received the repeal with an outburst of rejoicing loyalty. They cared little for Pitt's distinction of powers, or even for the declaratory Act : it seemed to them merely the honors of war with which the ministry was to be allowed to retire. It really meant much more. The ruling interest in the home Government, disordered for the moment by its sudden discovery of the strength and union of the colonies, had drawn back, but not forever. All through the year an undercurrent of irritation against the colonies is evident; and, when (June, 1767) Townshend, the chancellor of Townshend's the exchequer, had wrested the lead from the Acts. other members of the Grafton ministry, he passed through both Houses the bill for taxing imports into the colonies, to go into effect on 20th November following. It laid duties on glass, paper, painters' colors, lead and tea. As the proceeds were for the exchequer, they were to be distributed by the crown; and there was no secret that the design was to provide salaries for the crown servants in North America. About the same time other

Acts established a board of customs at Boston, legalized the "writs of assistance," and suspended the New York assembly until it should obey the Billeting Act. Townshend died soon after, leaving his system as a legacy to his successor, Lord North.

50. The New York assembly granted the necessary money, said nothing as to its use, and escaped further molestation. Beyond this the Acts accomplished nothing. Their advocates had urged that the colonies admitted the power of parliament to control external commerce, and that the new taxes were an exercise of such control. If they desired a purely technical triumph they had it, for their logic was sound, and the taxes remained on the statute-book. But, as the colonies Non-importation ceased to import the taxed articles, by popu-
agreement. lar agreement and enforcement, the taxes amounted to little. The irritations caused by the enforcement of the Navigation Act, only increased in bitterness; and the official class in the colonies, on whom must forever rest the responsibility for nine-tenths of the difficulties which followed, lost no chance of representing every pamphlet, newspaper letter, or public meeting as incipient rebellion. A popular outburst in Boston (June, 1768) following the seizure of John Hancock's sloop "Liberty," was thus used to give that town an unenviable reputation for disorder and violence. Colonial officials everywhere openly or secretly urged the strongest measures; and all the while the colonists, with the cautious tenacity of their race, were acting so guardedly that the British attorney-general was compelled to say, "Look into the papers and see how well these Americans are versed in the crown law; I doubt whether they have been guilty of an overt act of treason,

but I am sure they have come within a hair's-breadth of it."

51. The colonial officials, hoping for salaries independent of the assemblies, began to show a disposition to govern without those bodies. When the Massachusetts assembly refused by a large vote to withdraw its circular letter to the other assemblies urging united petition to the king alone, as an umpire between themselves and the British parliament, for redress of grievances, the assembly was prorogued, and did not reassemble for a year. As a gentle hint of a possible mode of re-establishing popular government, delegates from the towns met in convention at Boston (September, 1768), renewed the protests against the Acts of the ministry, and provided for the maintenance of public order. In the following December and January parliament passed a vote of censure on this proceeding, and advised that those who had taken part in it should be sent to England for trial on the charge of treason. This was a new grievance for the assemblies. They passed remonstrances against any attempt to send Americans beyond seas for trial, as a violation of the citizen's right to trial by a jury from the vicinage; and their governors at once prorogued them. Civil government in the colonies, under its original constitution, was evidently in sore straits.

52. In September, 1768, two British regiments which the colonial officials had succeeded in obtaining arrived at Boston. Instead of a rebellious population Difficulties at they found their most formidable opponents Boston. in minute law points which were made to beset them at every turn. The Billeting Act required the ordinary barracks to be filled first: the council would assign no quarters in town until the barracks outside were filled.

The assembly was not in session to authorize anything further, and the governor did not dare to summon it. The troops, who had marched into the town as into a captured place, with sixteen rounds of ammunition per man, were presently without a place in which to cook their dinners, until their commander hired houses out of the army chest. It was natural that he should denounce "this country where every man studies law." Exasperating and exasperated, the troops lived on in Boston until (March, 1770) a street brawl between soldiers and citizens resulted in the death of five of the latter and the injury of six more. Still the town kept its temper. The captain who had given the order to fire was seized by the civil authorities, subjected to the ordinary trial for murder, defended by John Adams and Quincy, two Massachusetts leaders, at the hazard of their own popularity, and acquitted for lack of evidence. But while according a fair trial to the soldiers, the colonial leaders at last represented so plainly to the crown officials the imminence of an outbreak that the troops were removed from the town to a fort in the harbor.

53. The most significant point in the history of the four years 1770–73 is the manner in which the ordi-

The colonial governments. nary colonial governments continued to go to pieces. When the assemblies met they would do nothing but denounce the Acts of the ministry; when they were prorogued the colony was left without any government for which there was popular respect. This was about the state of affairs which the crown officials had desired; but now that it had come, they were not at all prompt in their use of it. Divorced from regular government the people put out still stronger efforts to enforce the non-importation agreements which had kept down the revenues from the tax-laws of 1767. About 1773 a further development appeared. As soon as the assemblies met for their annual sessions, and before the governors conld find excuse for proroguing them, they appointed "committees of correspondence," to maintain unity of action with the other colonies. Thus, even after prorogation, there was still in existence for the rest of the year a semi-official representation of the colony. This was nearly the last step on the way to colonial union.

54. The whites had already crossed the Alleghanies. In 1768 parties from North Carolina entered Tennessee; and in 1769 Boone and a party of Virgin- Western settle-ians entered Kentucky. The settlement of ment. Tennessee was hastened by difficulties with Tryon, the governor of North Carolina. Tryon was one of the worst of the crown officials; and his government had been a scandal, even for those times. The people, denied justice and defrauded of legislative power, rose in hasty insurrection and were defeated. Tryon used his victory so savagely as to drive an increasing stream of settlers over the mountains into Tennessee. The centres of western settlement, however, were but few. There was one at Pittsburgh, another at Detroit, another near the Illinois-Indiana boundary, another in Kentucky, another near the present city of Nashville, Tennessee; but none of these, except, perhaps, Detroit, was more than a hunting or trading camp. Some efforts had been made to erect crown colonies, or to settle grants to companies, in the western territory, but they came to nothing. The settlements still clung to the coast.

55. In April, 1770, encouraged by some symptoms of a failure of the non-importation agreements, the ministry

had taken off all the taxes of 1767, retaining only that upon tea, — threepence per pound.   The general popular agreement was still strong enough to prevent the importation of this single luxury ; and it was found in 1772 that the tax produced but about £80 a year, at an expense of two or three hundred thousand for collection.   Besides, the East India Company had been accumulating a stock of teas, in anticipation of an American market, of which the tea tax had deprived it. In May, 1773, the ministry took a fresh step : the tax was to be retained, but the Company was to be allowed a drawback of the entire duty, — so that the colonists, while really paying the tax and yielding the underlying principle, would get their tea cheaper than any other people.   The first cargoes of tea under the new regulations were ordered home again by popular meetings in the American ports, and their captains generally obeyed. At Boston the governor refused to clear the vessels for Europe; and, after prolonged discussion, some fifty persons, disguised as Indians, went on board the vessels and threw the tea into the harbor in the presence of a great crowd of lookers-on (December 16, 1773).

The tea tax.

56.   It was not possible that the term American should suddenly supplant that of Englishman; but the successive steps by which the change was accomplished are easily perceptible.   Using one of the old English political phrases the supporters of colonial privileges had begun about 1768 to adopt the name of "American Whigs."   Its increasing substitution for that of Englishmen was significant.   Within a few years the terms "continental," or "the continent," began to take on a new meaning, referring to a union of the colonies at which men hardly ventured to hint clearly.   It

The new national feeling.

meant a good deal, then, when men said very truly that "the whole continent" applauded the "Boston tea-party." It was the first spoken word of the new national spirit. Nothing was less understood in England; the outbreak left America in general, and Boston in particular, hardly a friend there. The burning of the revenue schooner "Gaspee" in Narragansett Bay (June, 1772) had seemed to the ministry almost an act of overt rebellion; this was rebellion itself.

57. In March and April, 1774, on receipt of full intelligence of the proceedings at Boston, the ministry passed a series of Acts which made open struggle only ^{The "Intolerable Acts."} a question of time. The Boston Port Act shut up the town of Boston against all commerce until the destroyed tea was paid for and the town returned to loyalty. The Massachusetts Act changed the charter of that colony: the crown was now to appoint governor, council, and sheriffs; the sheriffs were to select juries; and town meetings, unless by permission of the governor, were forbidden. Gage, the British commander-in-chief in the colonies, was made governor under the Act, and four regiments were given him as a support. Any magistrates, officers, or soldiers indicted under colonial laws were to be sent for trial to Nova Scotia or Great Britain. The billeting of soldiers in the town of Boston was legalized. The Quebec Act extended the boundaries of the province of Canada over the whole territory lying north of the Ohio and east of the Mississippi. Here the ministry rested.

58. The news of these Acts of parliament crystallized every element of union in the colonies. The ^{Union.} attack on the charter of Massachusetts Bay was undoubtedly the most effective. The charters of

Connecticut and Rhode Island were the freest of the colonies; but that of Massachusetts was certainly next to them. If Massachusetts was not safe against such an attack, no colony was safe. The ministry had forced an issue on the very point on which the colonial and imperial theories were irreconcilable. The Boston Port Act furnished a grievance so concrete as to obviate the necessity of much argument on other points. The Quebec Act, with its attempt to cut off the northern colonies from the western expansion to which they all looked hopefully, was bad enough in itself, but it brought up with it the element of religious suspicion. For years the distinctively Puritan element had dreaded an attempt to establish the Church of England in the colonies; and the inclination of American Episcopalians to look to the home government for relief against unjust local restrictions had not helped to decrease the feeling. The Puritan element could see little real difference between Episcopacy and Catholicism: and, when it was found that the Quebec Act practically established the Roman Catholic system in the new territory, the old dread revived to give the agitation a hidden but strong motive.

59. The necessity of another Congress was universally felt. On the suggestion of Virginia and the call of Massachusetts, it met at Philadelphia (September First Continental Congress. 5, 1774). All the colonies but Georgia were represented; and Georgia was so certainly in sympathy with the meeting that this is commonly known as the First Continental Congress, the first really national body in American history. Its action was still mainly deliberative. It adopted addresses to the king, and to the people of the colonies, of Quebec, and of Great Britain, and passed a declaration of colonial rights, sum-

ming up the various Acts of parliament which were held to be in violation of these rights. But its tone was changed, though its language was still studiously controlled and dignified. It was significant that, for the first time, the two Houses of Parliament were ignored in the matter of petitioning: it was at last seen to be an awkward concession even to memorialize parliament. The tone of a sovereign about to take his seat is perceptible in the letter of Congress to the colonies which had not yet sent delegates. And at least two steps were taken which, if not an assumption of sovereign powers, were evidently on the road to it. The first was the preparation of Articles of Association, to be signed by the people everywhere, and to be enforced by committees of safety chosen by the people of cities and towns. These articles bound the signers to stop the importation of all goods from, and the exportation of all goods to, Great Britain and Ireland, the use of such goods, and the slave trade. The manner of the enforcement of the articles was evidently an incipient suspension of all authority proceeding from the mother country and the substitution of a general popular authority for it. The other step was a resolution, adopted October 8, as follows: — "That this Congress approve the opposition of the inhabitants of the Massachusetts Bay to the Its ultimatum. execution of the late Acts of parliament; and if the same shall be attempted to be carried into execution *by force*, in such case all America ought to support them in their opposition." This was simply an ultimatum: in the opinion of Congress, the ministry could take no further step except that of attempting to enforce its Acts, and the colonies would resist such an attempt as an act of war. Before the next Congress met the conditions had been fulfilled. The agents of the ministry had applied force; Massachusetts had resisted by force; and the new Congress found itself the representative of a nation at war, still acknowledging the king, but resisting the operations of his armies. Having summoned a new Congress to meet at Philadelphia on the 10th of May following, and having cleared the way for its action, the First Continental Congress adjourned.

60. It is an unpleasant task to record the successive steps by which two peoples, so exactly similar to one another in every characteristic, so far removed from one another, and so ignorant of one another's feelings, advanced alternately to a point where open collision was inevitable. From the standpoint of "no taxation without representation," which Pitt and his school of Whigs had approved, the colonists had now been driven by the suicidal logic of their opponents to the far more consistent position of "no legislation without representation," which the Pitt school had never been willing to grant, and which was radically inconsistent with the British "imperial" theory. Either the previous legislation of parliament was to remain a dead letter, or it must be executed by force; and that meant war. Massachusetts was already on the brink of that event. Gage, the new governor, had refused to meet the assembly; he had fortified himself in Boston, and was sending out spies as if into hostile territory. All regular government was suspended or remanded to the towns; and the people were organized into "minute men," pledged to move at a minute's notice. The first hostile movement of Gage would be the signal for the struggle. War, in fact, had come to be a possibility in the thoughts of every one. The new governor of Canada, Carleton, was sent out with in-

structions to levy the people and Indians of that province, in order that they might be marched against rebels in any province of North America. Governor Tryon's defeat of the insurgent people of North Carolina at the Alemance (§ 54) furnished a tempting precedent to Governor Gage in Massachusetts. There was strong pressure upon him to induce him to follow it. The king's speech at the opening of parliament (November 29, 1774) spoke of the prevalent "resistance and disobedience to the law" in Massachusetts; the ministry urged Gage to arrest the colonial leaders, even though hostilities should follow; the two Houses of Parliament presented a joint address to the king, declaring Massachusetts to be in rebellion, and offering all the resources of the empire to suppress the rebellion; and the king, in reply, announced his intention of acting as parliament wished.

61. The inevitable collision was narrowly escaped in February, 1775. Gage sent a water expedition to Salem to search for powder; but the day was Sunday, and a conflict was prevented by the ministers. Lexington and Concord.
Another expedition (April 19) was more momentous. It set out for Concord, a little village some twenty miles from Boston, to seize a stock of powder which was reported to be gathered there. At daybreak the troops marched into the village of Lexington, on their road. They found some minute men who had been hastily summoned, for intelligence had been sent out from Boston that the expedition was coming. There was a hurried order from an officer that the militia should disperse, then a volley from his men and a few answering shots, and the first blood of the American revolution had been shed. The troops went on to Concord and destroyed the stores there. But by this time the whole

country was up. Messengers were riding in every direction, arousing the minute men; and their mustering made
the return to Boston more dangerous than the advance
had been. When the troops began their return march
the continuous fire from fences, trees, and barns along
the route soon converted the retreat into a rout. The
opportune arrival of a rescuing party from Boston saved
the whole force from surrender, but the pursuit was kept
up until the expedition took refuge under the guns of
the war vessels at the water-side. The next morning the
isthmus which connected the town of Boston with the
mainland was blockaded; the siege of Boston was formed;
and the revolution had begun.

62. The news of Lexington and Concord fights set the
continent in a flame, but every feature of the outburst
showed the still thoroughly English characteristics of the
people. For nine long years they had been schooling
themselves to patience; and, as their impatience became
more difficult to control, it was shown most strongly in
their increasingly scrupulous care to insist upon the letter
of the law. Even in the first open conflict the colonists
were careful to base their case on their legal right to use
"the king's highway"; and Congress carefully collected
and published depositions going to show that the troops
had violated this right and had fired first. There was
everything in the affairs of Lexington and Concord to
arouse an intense popular excitement: the mustering of
undisciplined farmers against regular troops, the stern
sense of duty which moved it, the presence and encouragement of the ministers, the sudden desolation of homes
which had never known war before, were things which
stirred every pulse in the colonies when they were told.
But there was no need of waiting for such stories.

When the dam burst, the force which had been stored up for nine years took everything away before it. The news was hurried by express along the roads to the southward; men left the plough in the furrow when they heard it, and rode off to Boston; town committees of safety collected money and provisions and sent them to the same point; and before the end of the month the mainland around Boston harbor was occupied by a shifting mass of undisciplined half-armed soldiers, sufficient to keep the British troops cooped up within the peninsula on which the town was built.

63. The overturning of the royal governments in North America followed rapidly, as the news of the fights at Lexington and Concord spread abroad. In one colony after another the lower houses of the colonial legislatures, taking the name of "provincial congresses," met and assumed the reins of government; the officers of militia and subordinate magistrates accepted commissions from them; and the colonial officials, to whose advice so much of the course of events had been due, fled to England or to the nearest depot of royal troops. On the day (May 10, 1775) when the stronghold of Ticonderoga, the key of the gateway to Canada, was taken by surprise by an American force under Allen, giving the besiegers of Boston a welcome supply of weapons and ammunition, the Second Continental Congress met at Philadelphia. It came, under new circumstances, to redeem the pledge which its predecessor had given that all the colonies would support Massachusetts in resisting force by force. It was thus the representative of a united people, or of nothing. The struggle for union had been so far successful.

64. This fact of union has colored the whole subsequent history of the country. The Articles of Association had really preceded it by a substitution of general popular government, however clumsy in form, for the previously recognized governments ; in so far the authority of the various colonies was also suspended, and a general national organization took their place. It was soon found that the colonial organizations had too much innate strength to be got rid of in this summary fashion ; they held their own, and, as soon as imminent danger had disappeared, they succeeded in tearing so much power from the Continental Congress as to endanger the national existence itself. But, when the Second Continental Congress met, it met (as Von Holst maintains) as a purely revolutionary body, limited by no law, and by nothing else but by its success in war and the support which it was to receive from the people, without regard to colony governments. With the energy and recklessness of a French revolutionary body it might have blotted out the distinctions between colonies, and established a centralized government, to be modified in time by circumstances. In fact, it took no such direction. It began its course by recommendations to the new colonial governments ; it relied on them for executive acts ; and, as soon as the new colonies were fairly under way, they seized on the power of naming and recalling

Failure of the first national system.

the delegates to the Congress. From that time the decadence of the Congress was rapid ; the national idea became dimmer ; and the assertions of complete sovereignty by the political units became more pronounced. This failure of the Second Congress to appropriate the universal national powers which were within its grasp is responsible for two opposite effects. On the one hand, it built up a basis for the future assertion of the notion of State sovereignty, necessarily including the right of secession. On the other, it maintained the peculiar feature of the American Union, its large State liberty, its dislike of centralization, and its feeling that the national power is a valuable but dangerous instrument of development. The effort to find a compromise between the two forces makes up the record of subsequent national politics, ending in the present assertion of the largest possible measure of State rights, but under the guarantee of the national power, not of the State's own sovereignty.

65. The conversion of the former colonies into "States" followed hard upon the outbreak of the war (§ 72). Since that time the States have really been the peculiar feature of the American system. The circumstances just mentioned put them into a position in which they held all real powers of government; and they are still the residuary legatees of all such powers as have not been taken from them by the national power or by their State constitutions. In 1775 they differed very materially in their organization, but there has been a constant tendency to approach a general type, as States have adopted innovations which have proved successful in other States. All have now governors, legislatures of two houses, and State judiciaries. The governor, except in a few States, has a limited vote on legislation, and has a pardoning power. The State legislature is supreme in all subjects relating to the jurisdiction of the State, with two exceptions; the Constitution of the United States imposes certain limitations on them (§ 116), and there is an evident tendency in the later State constitutions to prohibit the legisla-

tures from "special legislation," and to provide that, in specified subjects, they shall pass only "general laws," applicable to the whole State and all citizens alike. With these exceptions, it is difficult to imagine a more complete autonomy than is possessed by the States of the American Union. The main restriction upon their action is in its results upon their welfare. They may even repudiate their debts, and there is no power which can make them pay; but, even in respect to this, the results upon the credit of a repudiating State have been enough to check others in any action of the kind. They control the organization of the State into counties, towns, and cities; they touch the life and interests of the citizen in a far larger degree than does the Federal Government; and, in many points, such as that of taxation, their powers are co-ordinate with those of the Federal Government, so that the two departments of the American governmental system operate on the same subjects. The admission of new States (§ 97) has raised the number of the original thirteen States to thirty-eight,[1] and the powers of the new States are exactly those of the old ones.

66. The "force resolution" of the First Congress (§ 59) shows that the national existence of the United States, in a purely political sense, dates from the fulfilment of the conditions of the force resolution — that is, from the first shot fired at Lexington. From that instant the fact of union was consummated in the support given to Massachusetts by the other commonwealths; and George III. was king no longer of thirteen

---

[1] The preliminary steps for the admission of four new States, however, were taken by Congress in February, 1889.

separate kingdoms, but of one. The fact that he did not recognize the union did not alter the fact of union ; that was to be decided by events. The success of the struggle for union gave the United States a date for the political, as distinguished from the legal, existence of the nation (April 19, 1775).

IV

THE STRUGGLE FOR INDEPENDENCE.

1775–83.

67. THE Second Congress adopted the "army" around Boston as "the American continental army"; rules and articles of war were formulated for it; and Ward, Charles Lee (a British soldier of fortune), Schuyler and Putnam were named as major-generals, with eight brigadiers, and Gates as adjutant-general. Union, though accomplished, was still weak. Sectional interests, feelings, and prejudices were strong; and the efforts of the delegates to accommodate them had, as one result, the appearance of Washington on the historical stage which he was to fill so completely. He had been of special service on the military committee of Congress; and the Massachusetts members — the Adamses and others — saw in him the man whose appointment as commander-in-chief would be most acceptable to all the sections, and would "cement and secure the union of these colonies," as John Adams wrote in a private letter. He was chosen unanimously, and commissioned, and set out for Boston. But another collision, the battle of Bunker Hill, had taken place on the date of his commission (June 17).

Washington.

68. In one of the irregular surgings of the colonial force around Boston, it took possession of Breed's (now known as Bunker) Hill, some 75 feet high, commanding

Boston, and separated from it by a sheet of water. The British officers might have landed men so as to take the line of entrenchments in the rear, or might have raked it from end to end from the water. They chose to send 2500 men over in boats, and charge straight up the hill. The all-important question was whether the "embattled farmers" within the works would stand fire.

Bunker Hill.

Not a shot from the line of entrenchments returned the scattering fire of the advancing column until the latter was within a hundred feet; then a sheet of flame ran along the line, and, when the smoke cleared away, the charging troops were retreating down the hill. The officers moved the men again to the assault, with exactly the same result. At the third assault the ammunition of the farmers was exhausted; but they retreated fighting stubbornly with gun-stocks, and even with stones. "The success," wrote Gage to the ministry, "has cost us dear; the trials we have had show the rebels are not the despicable rabble too many have supposed them to be." He had lost 1100 out of 2500 men. A serious American loss was that of Warren, a Boston leader of high promise.

69. While Washington was endeavoring to form an army out of the heterogeneous material around Boston, another American force was attempting to drive the British out of Canada. On the last

Canada.

day of the year 1775, in an assault on Quebec, one of the leaders, Montgomery, was killed, and another, Benedict Arnold, was wounded. Shortly afterwards the American force was driven back into the northern part of New York, near the Canada line, where it held its ground. Congress began in June the issue of bills of credit, or "continental currency," as a substitute for taxation — a most unhappy step. The bills soon began to depreciate. Congress insisted on holding them to be legal tender; but it had not seized, as it might have done, the power of taxation, in order to provide for the redemption of the bills; and its recommendation to committees of safety to treat as enemies of their country those who should refuse to receive the bills at their face value, never accomplished its object. Successive emissions of paper enabled Congress to support the army for a few years, and even to begin the organization of a navy. Privateers and public armed vessels had been sent out by the several colonies; the first American fleet, of eight vessels, sailed in February, 1776, but its cruise accomplished little.

70. All this time, Congress had been protesting its horror of the idea of independence; and the colonial

Drift towards independence. congresses had instructed their delegates not to countenance any such project. The last petition to the king was adopted by Congress in July, 1775, and sent to London by the hands of Richard Penn. It besought the king to consider the complaints of the colonists, and to obtain the repeal of the Acts which they had found intolerable. The news of the battle of Bunker Hill had preceded Penn; the king refused to answer the petition; but by a proclamation (August 23, 1775) he announced the existence of open rebellion in the colonies, and called on all good subjects to give any information of those persons in Great Britain who were aiding and abetting the rebellion. This was but the first of a series of attacks on that strong sentiment in Great Britain which felt the cause of the colonies to be the old cause of English liberty. At the opening of the struggle, this sentiment was intense : officers resigned their commissions rather than serve in America; the great cities took open ground in favor of the colonies; and some of the English middle classes wore mourning for the dead at Lexington. As the war increased in its intensity, this sentiment necessarily decreased; but, even while parliament was supporting the war by votes of more than two to one, the ministry was constantly hampered by the notorious consciousness that the real heart of England was not in it. Even when 25,000 men were voted at the king's wish, provision had to be made to obtain them from Germany. Privilege and officialism were against the colonies; the popular heart and conscience were either ignorant or in favor of them.

71. But in America everything spoke of war. Howe, who had succeeded Gage, passed a very bad winter. His men were often short of supplies; their quarters were uncomfortable; and their efforts to better their position were a severe infliction on the inhabitants. Along the coast the commanders of British ships acted everywhere as if on the borders of an enemy's country; Gloucester, Bristol, Falmouth, and other defenceless towns were cannonaded; and the flag of the king tended more and more to appear that of an enemy. On the first day of the new year the distinctive standard of the thirteen united colonies was raised at Washington's headquarters. It introduced the stripes of the present flag, but retained the crosses of St. George and St. Andrew on a blue ground in the corner, the whole implying the surviving acknowledgment of the royal power, with the appearance of a new nation. When independence had eliminated the royal element, the crosses were replaced (1777) by stars, as at present. Congress had been compelled to go so far in national action as to threaten reprisals for the threats of

special punishment by the ministry. The first step towards the ultimate application for admission to the family of nations was really taken in November, 1775, when Franklin, Jay, and three other delegates, were appointed a committee to maintain intercourse with friends of the colonies " in Great Britain, Ireland, and elsewhere "; the main importance of the appointment was in the last two words. The end of the year left independence in the air, though hardly spoken of.

72. Thomas Paine turned the scale (January 9, 1776) by the publication of his pamphlet *Common Sense.* His argument was that independence was the only consistent line to pursue; that " it must come to that some time or other "; that it would only be more difficult the more it was delayed; and that independence was the surest road to union. Written in simple language, it was read everywhere; and the open movement to independence dates from its publication. In the meantime events were urging Congress on. Washington in March seized and fortified Dorchester Heights, to the south of Boston and commanding it. Before the British could move upon the works, they had been made so strong that the garrison evacuated the place (March 17, 1776), sailing away to Halifax on the fleet. For the moment the British had hardly an organized force within the thirteen colonies; Charles Lee had just seized New York city and harbor: and the ministry seemed not only hostile, but impotent. The spirit of Congress rose with success. It had already ordered (November 25, 1775), on receipt of news of instructions to British war-vessels to attack American seaport towns "as in the case of actual rebellion," that British war-vessels or transports should be open to capture; now (March 23, 1776) it

Paine.

Evacuation of Boston.

declared all British vessels lawful prize. It then went on (April 6) to open all American ports to the vessels of all other nations than Great Britain, still forbidding the slave trade. It had even opened communication with the French court, which, using the name of a fictitious firm in Paris, was shipping money, arms, and supplies to the colonies. All these were acts of an independent power; and colony after colony, changing the colonial into State forms of government, was instructing its delegates to vote for independence. In May some of the colonies had become too impatient to wait longer, for it was evident that the king had finally ranged himself against the new American nation. Virginia spoke in most emphatic tones; and one of her delegates, Richard Henry Lee, moved a resolution in Congress for independence, seconded by John Adams (June 7, 1776). A committee to draw up a declaration in conformity with the resolution was chosen, consisting of Thomas Jefferson of Virginia, John Adams, Franklin, Roger Sherman of Connecticut, and Robert R. Livingston of New York; but the resolution was not adopted until July 2, as follows: — " Resolved that these united colonies are and of right ought to be free and independent States; that they are absolved from all allegiance to the British crown; and that all political connection between them and the state of Great Britain is and ought to be totally dissolved."

73. Jefferson had come from Virginia with the reputation of a very ready and able writer; and the committee, by common consent, left the preparation Declaration of of the first draft of the Declaration of Inde- Independence. pendence to him. He wrote it almost at one heat; and, though parts of it were rejected or modified by Congress, the whole instrument, as it was adopted by that body

(July 4, 1776), must stand as Jefferson's own work. John Adams was its champion on the floor of Congress, for Jefferson was not a public speaker, — and the coincidence of the deaths of these two men, just fifty years afterwards (July 4, 1826), was a remarkable one. The language of the Declaration, like that of all the American state-papers of the time, was strong and direct. Ignoring parliament, it took every act of oppression which had been aimed at the colonies as the act and deed of the king; it concluded that "a prince whose character is thus marked by every act which may define a tyrant, is unfit to be the ruler of a free people"; and it announced the independence of the United States in the terms of the resolution already stated. The date of its adoption is, by the decision of the Supreme Court, the date of the legal existence of the United States in matters of municipal law.

74. Meanwhile clouds were gathering about the young republic. A British expedition was beaten off from Charleston (June 28); but two days afterwards a stronger force, under Howe, landed on Staten Island, just below New York city. The ministry, abandoning New England, had decided to transfer the war to the middle colonies. Here was the originally alien element among the colonies (§ 7), though the ministry was disappointed in it; here was the commercial element, which had sometimes been willing to prefer profit to patriotism; above all, the Hudson gave a safe path for British frigates, so that the British forces might control at the same time the road into Canada and the moat which should cut off New England from the other colonies. Most of the reasons which made the opening of the Mississippi a severe blow to the Confed-

<small>Attack on the middle colonies.</small>

eracy in 1863, applied to the capture of New York city and the operations in the Hudson river in 1776.

75. Washington had hurried to New York city as soon as Boston had surrendered, but his preparations were not far advanced when Howe appeared (June 30). He and his brother, Admiral Lord Howe, the commander of the fleet, had high hopes of receiving the confidence of both parties to the struggle, by reason of their hereditary connection with the crown and the liking of the colonies for their elder brother, killed at Ticonderoga ; and they brought conciliatory proposals and the consent of the ministry to an unofficial exchange of prisoners. The country was now committed to independence, and in August, Howe began offensive operations. Washington's force numbered 27,000, about four-fifths of them having never seen action; and about one-third of his army had been placed on Long Island. Howe had 31,000 trained soldiers, largely Hessians ; and he debarked 20,000 of them on Long Island, beating Putnam, the American commander there, and driving him into Brooklyn (August 27). The British hesitated Battle of Long to attack the American works there, so that Island. Washington was able to draw off the defeated force, and the British followed slowly to the New York side of the river. Through September and October, Washington retreated northwards, fighting stubbornly, until he reached the strong defensive positions where the mountains begin to make a figure in the landscape north of New York city. Here he faced about, and prepared to give battle from behind fortifications. Again Howe hesitated, and then turned back to occupy New York.

76. Howe was cut off from the water-way to Canada by Washington's fortification of the highlands, but his

lieutenant, Cornwallis, secured a lodgement by surprise on the other side of the Hudson, and thus drew Washington across the river to oppose him. Forced to retreat through Washington's New Jersey, pursued by the British, Washington at least used up the month of December in the retreat. But affairs were in a desperate plight. His army had been driven across the Delaware; the British held all New Jersey, and were only waiting for the river to freeze over to "catch Washington and end the war"; Philadelphia was in a panic, and Congress had taken refuge in Baltimore, leaving Washington with almost dictatorial powers; hosts of half-hearted people were taking British protections and returning to their allegiance; and the time was one which "tried men's souls." Washington's soul was proof against all tests; and in the midst of his discouragements he had already planned that which was to be the turning-point of the war. The advance post of the British was one of Hessians, under Rahl, at Trenton, on the Delaware. Battles of Trenton Seizing all the boats on the river, and choosing the night of Christmas, on the probability that the Hessians would be drunk, he crossed the river, assaulted the town with the bayonet, and captured the garrison. Taking his prisoners to Philadelphia, he recrossed the river on the last day of the year, and reoccupied Trenton. Cornwallis brought almost all his available forces towards that place; and Washington's diminishing army was in greater danger than before. and Princeton. Leaving his camp-fires burning, he abandoned his position by night, swept around the sleeping British forces, met, fought, and captured at Princeton (January 3, 1777) a detachment on its march to Trenton, and threatened the British base of supplies at

New Brunswick. It was only a threat; but it served its purpose of drawing Cornwallis off from Philadelphia.

77. New Jersey is crossed from south-west to north-east by a spur of the Alleghanies. Thus far operations had been confined to the flat country to the south; Washington now swept on to the northern or mountainous part, and the day after Princeton fixed his headquarters at Morristown, where they really remained almost all through the rest of the war. He was aided by the unwillingness of the British to attack entrenchments. His long line across New Jersey was everywhere strong; the British could now reach Philadelphia only by passing in front of his line and risking a flank attack; and they at once drew in their outposts to New Brunswick. With the exception of the occupation of Newport by the British, and attacks on minor outlying places, as Danbury, there was a short breathing space.

78. Kalb, Kosciusko, Conway, and other foreign officers were already serving in the American army; Pulaski, Steuben, and others were soon to come. Some of the minor foreign acquisitions of this sort were selfish, conceited, and troublesome; the most unselfish and devoted was the young Marquis de la Fayette, who came this year with a shipload of supplies as his gift to the republic. Franklin made his appearance at the French court (December 7, 1776) as Franklin. one of the American envoys, and soon took the lead in negotiations. Shrewd, sensible, far-sighted, and prompt, never missing or misusing an opportunity, he soon succeeded in committing the French Government, in all but the name, as an ally of the United States; and, though his success with other European courts was small, he opened the way for the general commercial treaties which

followed the war. His unofficial influence was a more important factor in his work. Carefully maintaining the character of a plain American burgher, he seemed to the French the veritable man of nature for whom they had been longing. The pithy sense and homely wit which had given force to his *Poor Richard's Almanac* had impressed even his unemotional countrymen strongly; his new audience took them as almost inspired. He, and his country with him, became the fashion; and it became easier for the Government to cover its own supplies to the insurgents by an appearance of embarrassment in dealing with the enthusiasm of its subjects. The foreign aid, however, did the Americans a real harm. Congress, relying upon it, grew more and more into the character of a mere agent of the States for issuing paper and borrowing money; and the taxing function, which should have been forced upon it from the beginning, fell more positively into the hands of the States. As the national character of Congress dwindled, the State jealousies and ambitions of its delegates increased; little cliques had their favorite officers — Gates, Charles Lee, Conway, or some other soldier of fortune; and Washington, neglected and harassed by turns, must have found it difficult to face Howe with half his number of men, foil the various competitors for his own position, and maintain his invariably respectful tone towards Congress.

79. In July, 1777, Burgoyne, with an army of British, Germans, and Indians, attempted the Hudson river route

Burgoyne's ex- from the north, and forced his way nearly to
pedition. Albany. The utter defeat of a detachment at Bennington (August 16) by the farmers of Vermont and New Hampshire under Stark, the atrocities of the Indians before they deserted Burgoyne's standard, and

the end of the harvest brought abundant reinforcements
to Gates, whom Congress had put in command.   He
gained the battle of Bemis Heights (October 7), and ten
days afterwards forced Burgoyne to surrender near Saratoga.   The news of this success brought to   Saratoga.
Franklin (February 6, 1778) the desire of his   Treaty with
heart in a treaty of alliance, offensive and de-   France.
fensive, between the United States and France, and this
was followed in the next month by war between Great
Britain and France and an ineffectual proposal for reconciliation from Great Britain to the United States, covering colonial representation in parliament and everything
short of independence.

80. Meantime Howe had taken the water-route to
Philadelphia, by way of the ocean and Chesapeake Bay,
and had captured the city (September 25,   Capture of Phil-
1777) ; but Washington had at least made his   adelphia.
army capable of fighting two battles, those of Chad's
Ford on the Brandywine (September 11) and German-
town in the outskirts of Philadelphia (October 4), both
stubbornly contested. Taking up winter-quarters at Valley
Forge, about twenty miles from Philadelphia,
he watched Howe vigilantly, and struggled   Valley Forge.
manfully with the responsibilities of supreme command,
which the fugitive Congress had again left to him, with
the misery and almost despair of his own men, and with
the final intrigues of those who now wished to supersede
him by the appointment of Gates.   In June, 1778, the
news of the treaty with France, and of the departure of
a French fleet and army for America, compelled Clinton,
who had succeeded Howe, to set out for New York, in
order to reunite his two main armies. Washington broke
camp at once, followed him across New Jersey, and over-

took the rear at Monmouth, or Freehold (June 29). An indecisive battle enabled the British to gain New York

Battle of Monmouth.

city; Washington formed his line from Morristown around the north of the city, so as to be able to interpose between Clinton and Philadelphia or New England; and these positions were maintained until the Yorktown campaign began in 1781. Beyond skirmishes, there were no more important events in the north, except some unsuccessful attempts to recover Newport with French assistance, the capture of Stony Point by Wayne (July 15, 1779), and the treason of the American commander of West Point, Benedict Arnold, with the execution of the British adjutant-general, Major John André, whom the Americans had captured within their lines while he was carrying on the negotiations (September, 1780).

81. Midsummer, 1778, marks the beginning of the end. 33,000 men, the high-water mark of the British army in the United States, had maintained a footing at but two places, New York city and Newport; the ministry, in a war which had no real popular momentum, found German mercenaries an expensive resource; and the Germans were very apt to desert in America. An extraordinary number of leading men in England, while they would not hamper the nation in its struggle, made no scruple of expressing their practical neutrality or their high regard for various American leaders. France was now in the war, and Spain and Holland were soon to be the allies of France. The difficulties of supplying the British army were now aggravated by the presence of French fleets in American waters. English commerce had been decimated by American privateers; and Franklin was gathering vessels in France, in one of which (the "Richard")

Paul Jones was to fight with the "Serapis" one of the most desperate naval battles on record (September 23, 1779). Perhaps hopeless of success in the Northern and Middle States, the ministry decided to begin operations in the south, where it was believed that the slave population would be a fatal source of weakness to the Americans.

Attack on
the southern
colonies.

82. Late in 1778 a British expedition from New York captured Savannah, and rapidly took possession of the thinly populated State of Georgia. An attempt to retake Savannah in the following year cost the Americans the life of Pulaski. Evacuating Newport, and leaving only troops enough to hold New York city, Clinton sailed southward and captured Charleston (May 12, 1780). Thence his forces swept over South Carolina until they had reduced it to a submission broken by continual outbursts of partisan warfare under Sumter, Marion, and other leaders. This work finished, Clinton returned to New York, leaving Conwallis in command in the south. As soon as the summer heats had passed away Gates entered the State from the north with a militia army, and was badly beaten at Camden (August 16) by an inferior British force. Even North Carolina now needed defence, and the work was assigned to Greene, one of the best of the American officers developed by the war. The commander of his light troops, Morgan, met his British rival, Tarleton, at the Cowpens (January 17), and inflicted upon the latter the first defeat he had met in the south. This event brought Cornwallis up to the pursuit of the victor. Morgan and Greene retreated all the way across North Carolina, followed by Cornwallis, and then, having raised fresh troops in Vir-

Capture of
Charleston.

Battle
of Camden.

Cowpens.

ginia, they turned and gave battle at Guilford Court House (March 15, 1781). Greene was beaten, as was Guilford Court House. usually the case with him, but he inflicted so heavy a loss in return that Cornwallis retired to the coast at Wilmington to repair damages. Greene, energetic as well as cautious, passed on to the south, and gave battle to Rawdon, whom Cornwallis had left in com- Hobkirk's Hill. mand in South Carolina, at Hobkirk's Hill (April 25), and was beaten again. But Raw- don's loss was so severe that he drew in his lines toward Charleston. Greene followed, and at Eutaw Springs Eutaw Springs. (September 8) fought the last pitched battle in the south. He was beaten again, but Raw- don again fell back, and thereafter did all that man could do in holding the two cities of Charleston and Savannah. Greene had won no battle, but he had saved the south.

83. Arnold, now a general in the British service (§ 80), had been sent, early in the year, to make a lodge- ment in Virginia. It seems to have been believed by the British authorities that the three southernmost States were then secure, and that Virginia could be carved out next. La Fayette was sent to oppose Arnold, but the Cornwallis in Virginia. latter was soon relieved, and in June, Corn- wallis himself entered the State. He had not been willing to serve with Arnold. Directed to select a suitable position for a permanent post on the Chesa- peake, he had chosen Yorktown, where, with the troops already in Virginia, he fortified his army. The general ground was that of McClellan's campaign of 1862 (§ 285), and Grant's of 1864–65 (§ 296).

84. Washington, reinforced by a lately arrived force of 6000 excellent French troops (July, 1780), under Ro-

chambeau, was still watching Clinton at New York. The news that De Grasse's French fleet, on its way to the American coast, would enter the Chesapeake, where Cornwallis had left himself open to the chances of such an event, led Washington to conceive the campaign which captured Cornwallis and ended the war. He began elaborate preparations for an attack on New York, so that Clinton actually called upon Cornwallis for aid. Moving down the Hudson, he kept Clinton in ignorance of any movement to the south as long as possible, and then changed the line of march to one through New Jersey. The allied armies passed through Philadelphia, were hurried down the Chesapeake, and drove Cornwallis within his entrenchments at Yorktown. De Grasse had arrived August 30, had defeated the British fleet, and was master of the Chesapeake waters. After three weeks' siege, Cornwallis, having exhausted a soldier's resources, surrendered his army of 8000 men (October 19, 1781).

85. The country at large had really been at peace for a long time. Everywhere, except in the immediate neighborhood of the British forces, the people were working almost with forgetfulness that they had ever been English colonists; and, where the enemy had to be reckoned with, they were looked upon much as the early settlers looked on bears or Indians, as an unpleasant but inevitable item in the debit side of their accounts. Their legislatures were making their laws; their governors, or "presidents," were the representatives whom their States acknowledged; nothing but an American court had the power to touch a particle of the judicial interests of the American people; the American flag was recognized on the ocean; independence was a fact,

and the ministry received from the English people so
emphatic a call to acknowledge it that it yielded so far
as to propose a defensive war. The House of Commons
(March 4, 1782) voted to regard as enemies to the king
and country all who should advise the further prosecu-
tion of the war; the Rockingham ministry succeeded to
power, to be followed shortly by the Shelburne ministry; and Rodney's victory over De Grasse gave the new
ministries very much the same cover for an unsuccessful
peace as Jackson's victory at New Orleans afforded the
United States in 1815 (§ 181). Franklin, John Adams,
and Jay, the American negotiators, concluded the preliminary treaty of peace, by which Great Britain acknowledged the independence of the United States (November
30, 1782); hostilities ceased; and the definite
treaty of peace was concluded (September 3,
1783). A number of American loyalists (usually called
Tories) accompanied the departing armies.

Treaty of peace.

86. In the winter of 1778–79 George Rogers Clark, a
Kentucky leader, acting under the authority of the State
of Virginia, had led a force of backwoodsmen
into the country north of the Ohio river,
captured the British posts in it, and made the soil American up to the latitude of Detroit. The treaty of peace
acknowledged the conquest, and even more than this.
It settled the northern boundary of the United States,
so far as the longitude of the Mississippi river, nearly as
it now runs; the Mississippi as the western boundary
down to 31° N. lat., thence east on that line to the
present northern boundary of Florida, and east on that
to the Atlantic. Great Britain restored the Floridas to
Spain, so that the new nation had Great Britain as a
neighbor on the north, and Spain on the south and west.

The north-west.

Some disposition had been shown to exclude the Americans from the fishing ground off Newfoundland, but it was abandoned. The United States by the treaty entered the family of nations with recognized boundaries, and all the territory within these boundaries could be recognized by other nations only as the property of the United States. But, so far as internal arrangements were concerned, a great question remained to be settled. There were thirteen organized States, covering but a part of this territory; a part of them claimed to be sole proprietors of the western territory outside of the present State limits; and it remained to be seen whether they would make good their claim, or the other States would compel them to divide, or the new national power would compel as clear an internal as an international recognition of its claim (§ 89).

87. The American army was now disbanded, its officers receiving a grudging recognition of their claims and the privates hardly anything. Poverty was to blame for much of this, and the popular suspicion of military power for the rest. Washington's influence was strong enough to keep the dissatisfied army from any open revolt, though that step was seriously proposed. The organization of the hereditary order of the Cincinnati by the officers brought about a more emphatic expression of public dislike, and the hered-   The Cincinnati. itary feature was abandoned. But, wherever the officers and men went, they carried a personal disgust with the existing frame of government which could not but produce its effect in time. Their miseries had been largely due to it. The politicians who controlled the State legislatures had managed to seize the reins of government and reduce Congress, the only body with pretensions to a

national character, to the position of a purely advisory body. The soldiery knew instinctively that the lack of power to feed them and clothe them, the payment of their scanty wages in paper worth two per cent. of its face value, were due to the impotence of Congress and the too great power of the States, that the nation presented the "awful spectacle," as Hamilton called it, of "a nation without a national government"; and the commonest toast in the army was "Here's a hoop to the barrel" — a stronger national government to bind the States together.

The struggle for the establishment of this national government is the next step in the development of the United States, but to reach it naturally it will be necessary to go back into the midst of the struggle for independence.

V.

THE STRUGGLE FOR NATIONAL GOVERNMENT.

1777–89.

88. THE fact that the Continental Congress was really a revolutionary body, not limited in its powers by any fundamental law imposed by the underlying popular sovereignty, but answering most closely to the British parliament, has already been noted (§ 64). This state of affairs was repugnant to all the instincts and prejudices of the American people, and of the delegates who represented them. Just at the time of the Declaration of Independence Congress set about preparing a Articles of "form of confederation," which should ex- Confederation. press exactly the relative powers of the State and national governments. Its work was finished November 15, 1777, and recommended to the States for adoption. Unluckily, before the work had been finished, the State legislatures had succeeded in establishing their power to appoint and recall at pleasure the delegates to Congress, so that Congress had come to be the mere creature of the State legislatures. The "Articles of Confederation," adopted in 1777, were thus calculated for the meridian of the State legislatures which were to pass upon them. The new government was to be merely "a firm league of friendship" between sovereign States, which were to retain every power not "expressly" delegated to Congress; there was to be but one house of Congress, in which each

State was to have an equal vote, with no national executive or judiciary; and Congress, while keeping the power
to borrow money, was to have no power to levy taxes, or
to provide in any way for payment of the money bor-
rowed — only to make recommendations to the States or
requisitions on the States, which they pledged their public faith to obey. The States were forbidden to make
treaties, war, or peace, to grant titles of nobility, to
keep vessels of war or soldiers, or to lay imposts which
should conflict with treaties already proposed to France
or Spain. Important measures required the votes of
nine of the thirteen States, and amendments the votes of
all. Congress had hardly more than an advisory power
at the best. It had no power to prevent or punish
offences against its own laws, or even to perform effec-
tively the duties enjoined upon it by the Articles of
Confederation. It alone could declare war, but it had no
power to compel the enlistment, arming, or support of
an army. It alone could fix the needed amount of
revenue, but the taxes could only be collected by the
States at their own pleasure. It alone could decide disputes between the States, but it had no power to compel
either disputant to respect or obey its decisions. It
alone could make treaties with foreign nations, but it
had no power to prevent individual States from violating
them. Even commerce, foreign and domestic, was to be
regulated entirely by the States, and it was not long
before State selfishness began to show itself in the regulation of duties on imports. In everything the States
were to be sovereign, and their creature, the Federal
Government, was to have only strength enough to bind
the States into nominal unity, and only life enough to
assure it of its own practical impotence.

89. Most of the States signed the Articles at once; New Jersey, Delaware, and Maryland held out against ratifying them for from two to four years. The secret of their resistance was in the claims to the western territory already mentioned (§§ 34, 86). The three recalcitrant States had always had fixed western boundaries, and had no legal claim to a share in the western territory; the Articles, while providing for the decision of disputes between individual States, were careful to provide also that "no State shall be deprived of territory for the benefit of the United States"; and this meant that those States whose charters carried them to the Pacific Ocean, while admitting the national authority to limit their claims by the Mississippi river, were to divide up the western territory among them. New Jersey and Delaware gave up the struggle in 1778 and 1779; but Maryland would not and did not yield, until her claims were satisfied.

90. Dr. H. B. Adams has shown that the whole question of real nationality for the United States was bound up in this western territory; that even a "league government" could not continue long to govern a great and growing territory like this without developing into a real national government, even without a change of strict law; and that the Maryland leaders were working under a complete consciousness of these facts. It is creditable, however, to the change which the struggle for union had wrought in the people, that it was not until very late in this struggle that Virginia, the most omnivorous western claimant, proposed to have the Articles go into effect without Maryland, and still more creditable that her proposal hardly received notice from the other States. They

were already conscious that the thirteen were really one.

91. The solution of the difficulty was found in 1780. The western boundary of the State of New York had

New York's claim. always been very much in the air. Her main claim to her present extensive territory lay in the assertions that the western part had once belonged to the Six Nations of Indians, and that the Dutch conquering the Six Nations, the English conquering the Dutch, and New York conquering the English, had succeeded to these rights. But the Six Nations had exercised an undefined suzerainty over all the Indian tribes from Tennessee to Michilimackinac, covering all the territory in dispute. New York proposed, if Congress would confirm her present western boundary, to transfer to Congress her western claims by conquest, superior to any mere charter claims; and Congress approved the offer as "expressly calculated to accelerate the federal alliance." On March 1, 1781, the New York delegates formally completed the deed of transfer to the United States; on the same day the Maryland delegates signed the Articles; and by this action of the last State the Articles of Confederation came into force as the first attempt to frame a national government.

92. The long struggle had given time for careful consideration of the Articles. Maryland's persistent criticism had prepared men to find defects in them. Conventions of New England States, pamphlets, and private correspondence had found flaws in the new plan of government; but a public trial of it was a necessary preliminary to getting rid of it. The efforts of the individual States to maintain the war, the disposition of each State to magnify its own share in the result,

the popular jealousy of a superior power, transferred now from parliament to the central government, and inflamed by the politicians who saw their quickest road to dignity in the State governments, were enough to ensure the Articles some lease of life. A real national government had to be extorted through the "grinding necessities of a reluctant people."

93. Congress and its committees had already begun to declare that it was impossible to carry on a government efficiently under the Articles. Its expostula- Territorial cestions were to be continued for several years sions. before they were heard. In the meantime it did not neglect the great subject which concerned the essence of nationality — the western territory. Virginia had made a first offer to cede her claims, but it was not accepted. A committee of Congress now made a report (1782) maintaining the validity of the rights which New York had transferred to Congress; and in the next year Virginia made an acceptable offer. Her deed was accepted (March 1, 1784) ; the other claimant States followed; and Congress, which was not authorized by the Articles to hold or govern territory, became the sovereign of a tract of some 430,000 square miles, nearly equal to the areas of France, Spain, and Portugal, combined, covering all the country between the Atlantic tier of States and the Mississippi river, from the British possessions nearly to the Gulf of Mexico.

94. In this territory Congress had now on its hands the same question of colonial government in which the British parliament had so signally failed. Territorial The manner in which Congress dealt with it government. has made the United States the country that it is. The leading feature of this plan was the erection, as rapidly

as possible, of States, similar in powers to the original States. The power of Congress over the territories was to be theoretically absolute, but it was to be exerted in encouraging the development of thorough self-government, and in granting it as fast as the settlers should become capable of exercising it. Copied in succeeding Acts for the organization of Territories, and still con-
The Ordinance of 1787. trolling the spirit of such Acts, the Ordinance of 1787 (July 13, 1787) is the foundation of almost everything which makes the modern American system peculiar.

95. The preliminary plan of Congress was reported by a committee (April 23, 1784) of which Jefferson was chairman. It provided for the erection of seventeen States, north and south of the Ohio, with some odd names, such as Sylvania, Assenisipia, Metropotamia, Polypotamia, and Pelisipia. These States were forever to be a part of the United States, and to have republican governments, and the Ordinance creating them was to be a compact between the Federal Government and each State, unalterable unless by mutual consent. "After the year 1800 there shall be neither slavery nor involuntary servitude in any of the said States, other than in the punishment of crimes whereof the party shall have been duly convicted." This provision, which represented Jefferson's feeling on the subject, was lost for want of seven States in its favor.

96. The final plan of 1787 was reported by a committee of which Nathan Dane, of Massachusetts, was chairman. The prohibition of slavery was made perpetual, and a fugitive slave clause was added (§ 124). The Ordinance covered only the territory north of the Ohio, and provided for not less than three nor more than five States. Ohio,

Indiana, Illinois, Michigan, and Wisconsin have been the resultant States. The inhabitants were to be secured in the equal division of real and personal property of intestates to the next of kin in equal degree. At first Congress was to appoint the governor, secretary, judges, and militia generals, and the governor and judges were to make laws subject to the veto of Congress. When the population reached 5000 the inhabitants were to have an assembly of their own, to consist of the governor, a legislative council of five, selected by Congress from ten nominations by the lower house, and a lower house of representatives of one delegate for every 500 inhabitants. This assembly was to choose a delegate to sit, but not to vote, in Congress, and was to make laws not repugnant to "the articles of fundamental compact," which were as follows: the new States or Territories were to maintain freedom of worship, the benefits of the writ of *habeas corpus*, trial by jury, proportionate representation, bail, moderate fines and punishments, and the preservation of liberty, property, and private contracts; they were to encourage public education and keep faith with the Indians; they were to remain forever a part of the United States; and they were not to interfere with the disposal of the soil by the United States, or to tax the lands of the United States, or to tax any citizen of the United States for the use of the Mississippi or St. Lawrence rivers. These articles were to be unalterable unless by mutual consent of a State and the United States. The transformation of the Territory, with its quite limited government, into a State, with all the powers of an original State, was promised by Congress as soon as the population should reach 60,000.

97. The Constitution, which was adopted almost imme-

diately afterwards, provided merely that "Congress shall
have power to dispose of, and make all needful rules and
regulations respecting, the territory or other property
belonging to the United States," and that "new States
may be admitted by the Congress into the Union."
Opinions have varied as to the force of the Ordinance of
1787.   The southern school of writers have naturally
been inclined to consider it *ultra vires* and void; and they
adduce the fact that the new Congress under the Constitution thought it necessary to re-enact the Ordinance.
The opposite school have inclined to hold the Ordinance
as still in force.   Even as to the territorial provision of
the Constitution, opinions have varied.   The Dred Scott
decision held that it applied only to the territory then in
possession of the United States, and that territory subse-
quently acquired, by conquest or purchase, was not to be
governed by Congress with absolute power, but subject
to constitutional limitations.

98. In the interval of the settlement of the territorial
question, the affairs of the "league of friendship" known
as the United States had been going from bad to worse,
culminating in 1786.   The public debt amounted in 1783
to about $42,000,000, of which $8,000,000 was owed
abroad — in Holland, France, and Spain.   Congress had
no power to levy taxes for the payment of interest or
principal; it could only make requisitions on the States.
In the four years ending in 1786 requisitions had been
made for $10,000,000, and the receipts from
them had amounted to but one-fourth of what
had been called for.   Even the interest on
the debt was falling into arrears, and the first instalment
of the principal fell due in 1787.   To pay this, and
subsequent annual instalments of $1,000,000, was quite

Difficulties
of the confeder-
ation.

impossible. Robert Morris, the financier of the revolution, resigned in 1783, "rather than be the minister of injustice," hoping thus to force upon the States the necessity of granting taxing powers to Congress. Washington, on retiring from the command-in-chief, wrote a circular letter to the governors of all the States, urging the necessity of granting to Congress some power to provide a national revenue. Congress (April 18, 1783) appealed to the States for power to levy specific duties on certain enumerated articles, and five per cent. on others. It was believed that with these duties and the requisitions, which were now to be met by internal taxation, $2,500,000 per annum could be raised. Some of the States ratified the proposal; others ratified it with modifications; others rejected it, or changed their votes; and it never received the necessary ratification of all the States. The obedience to the requisitions grew more lax. Some of the States paid them; others pleaded poverty, and allowed more or less of them to run into arrears; others offered to pay in their own depreciated paper currency; and others indignantly refused to pay in any currency until the delinquent States should pay all their obligations. In 1786 a committee of Congress reported that any further reliance on requisitions would be "dishonorable to the understandings of those who entertain such confidence."

99. In the States the case was even worse. Some of them had been seduced into issuing paper currency in such profusion that they were almost bank- Difficulties rupt. Great Britain, in the treaty of peace, of the States. had recognized the independence of the individual States, naming them in order; and her Government followed the same system in all its intercourse with its late col-

onies.   Its restrictive system was maintained, and the
States, vying with each other for commerce, could adopt
no system of counteracting measures.   Every possible
burden was thus shifted to American commerce; and
Congress could do nothing, for, though it asked for the
power to regulate commerce for fifteen years, the States
refused it.   The decisions of the various State courts began to conflict, and there was no power to reconcile them
or to prevent the consequences of the divergence.   Several States, towards the end of this period, began to
prepare or adopt systems of protection of domestic productions or manufactures, aimed at preventing competition by neighboring States.   The Tennessee settlers were
in insurrection against the authority of North Carolina;
and the Kentucky settlers were apparently disposed to
cut loose from Virginia if not from the United States.
Poverty, with the rigid execution of process for debt, drove
the farmers of western Massachusetts into an insurrection which the State had much difficulty in suppressing;
and Congress was so incompetent to aid Massachusetts
that it was driven to the expedient of imagining an Indian war in that direction, in order to transfer troops
Difficulties thither.   Congress itself was in danger of dis-
of Congress. appearance from the scene.   The necessity
for the votes of nine of the thirteen States for the passage of important measures made the absence of a State's
delegation quite as effective as a negative vote.   In order
to save the expense of a delegation, the States began to
neglect the election of them, unless they had some object
to obtain by their attendance.   It was necessary for Congress to make repeated and urgent appeals in order to obtain a quorum for the ratification of the treaty of peace
with Great Britain.   In 1784 Congress even broke up in

disgust, and the French minister reported to his Government, "There is now in America no general government — neither Congress nor President, nor head of any one administrative department." Everywhere there were symptoms of a dissolution of the Union.

100. Congress was evidently incompetent to frame a new plan of national government; its members were too dependent on their States, and would be recalled if they took part in framing anything stronger than the Articles. The idea of a convention of the States, Proposals for a independent of Congress, was in the minds convention. and mouths of many; Thomas Paine had suggested it as long ago as his *Common Sense* pamphlet : "Let a continental conference be held, to frame a continental charter, drawing the line of business and jurisdiction between members of Congress and members of assembly." To a people as fond of law and the forms of law as the Americans, there was a difficulty in the way. The Articles had provided that no change should be made in them but by the assent of every State legislature. If the work of such a convention was to be subject to this rule, its success would be no greater than that of Congress ; if its plan was to be put into force on the ratification of less than the whole number of States, the step would be more or less revolutionary. In the end, the latter course was taken, though not until every other expedient had failed; but the act of taking it showed the underlying consciousness that union, independence, and nationality were now inextricably complicated, and that the thirteen had become one in some senses.

101. The country drifted into a convention by a roundabout way. The navigation of Chesapeake Bay needed regulation ; and the States of Maryland and Vir-

ginia, having plenary power in the matter, appointed delegates to arrange such rules. The delegates met (1785) at Washington's house, Mount Vernon; and Maryland, in adopting their report, proposed a meeting of commissioners from all the States to frame commercial regulations for the whole. Virginia acceded at once, and named Annapolis, in Maryland, as the place. The convention met (1786), but only five States were represented, and their delegates adjourned, after recommending another convention at Philadelphia, in May, 1787.

Convention of 1786.

102. Congress had failed in its last resort — a proposal that the States should grant it the impost power alone; New York's veto had put an end to this last hope. Confessing its helplessness, Congress approved the call for a second convention; twelve of the States (all but Rhode Island) chose delegates; and the convention met at Philadelphia (May 14, 1787), with an abler body of men than had been seen in Congress since the first two Continental Congresses. Among others, Virginia sent Washington, Madison, Edmund Randolph, George Mason, and George Wythe; Pennsylvania, Franklin, Robert and Gouverneur Morris, and James Wilson; Massachusetts, Rufus King, Gerry, and Strong; Connecticut, William S. Johnson, Sherman, and Ellsworth; New York, Hamilton; New Jersey, Paterson; and South Carolina, the two Pinckneys and Rutledge. With hardly an exception the fifty-five delegates were clear-headed, moderate men, with positive views of their own, and firm purpose, but with a willingness to compromise.

Convention of 1787.

103. Washington was chosen to preside, and the convention began the formation of a new Constitution, instead

of proposing changes in the old one. Two parties were
formed at once. The Virginia delegates offered The Virginia plan.
a plan, proposing a Congress of two houses,
having power to legislate on national subjects, and to
compel the States to fulfil their obligations. This is
often spoken of as a "national plan," but very improp-
erly. It was a "large-State" plan, proposed by those
States which had or hoped for a large population. It
meant to base representation in both houses on population, so that the large States could control both of them,
and it left the appointment of the President or other
executive and the Federal judges to Congress, — so that
the whole administration of the new government would
fall under large-State control. On behalf of The New Jersey plan.
the "small States" Paterson of New Jersey
brought in another plan. It continued the old Confederation, with its single house and equal State vote, but
added the power to regulate commerce and raise a revenue, and to compel the States to obey requisitions. The
State representation was fortunate. New Hampshire's
delegates did not attend until after those of New York
(then classed as a small State) had retired from the convention in anger at its evident drift toward the "large-
State" plan. The large States had a general majority of
six to five, but the constant dropping off of one or more
votes, on minor features, from their side to that of the
small States prevented the hasty adoption of any radical
measures. Nevertheless, the final collision could not be
evaded; the basis of the two plans was in the question of
one or two houses, of equal or proportionate State votes,
of large-State supremacy or of State equality. In July
the large States began to show a disposition to force their

plan through, and the small States began to threaten a concerted withdrawal from the convention.

104. The Connecticut delegates, from their first appearance in the convention, had favored a compromise. They had been trained under the New England system, in which the assemblies were made up of two houses, one representing the people of the whole State, according to population, and the other giving an equal representation to the towns. They proposed that the new Congress should be made up of two houses, one representing the States in proportion to their population, the other giving an equal vote to each State. At a deadlock, the convention referred the proposition to a committee, and it reported in favor of the Connecticut compromise. Connecticut had been voting in the large-State list, and the votes of her delegates could not be spared from their slender majority; now another of the large States, North Carolina, came over to Connecticut's proposal, and it was adopted. Thus the first great struggle of the convention resulted in a compromise, which took shape in the peculiar feature of the Constitution, the senate.

The compromise.

105. The little States were still anxious, in every new question, to throw as much power as possible into the hands of their special representative, the senate; and that body thus obtained its power to act as an executive council as a restraint on the President in appointments and treaties. This was the only survival of the first alignment of parties; but new divisions arose on almost every proposal introduced. The election of the President was given at various times to Congress and to electors chosen by the State legislatures; and the final mode of choice, by electors chosen by the

The work of the convention.

States, was settled only two weeks before the end of the
convention, the office of Vice-President coming in with
it. The opponents and supporters of the slave trade
compromised by agreeing not to prohibit it for twenty
years. Another compromise included three-fifths of the
slaves in enumerating population for representation.
This was the provision which gave the slave-holders
abnormal power as the number of slaves increased; for
a district in the "black belt" of the south, while three-
fifths of its slaves were enumerated, really gave representation to its few whites only.

106. Any explanation of the system introduced by the
Constitution must start with the historical fact that while
the national Government was practically suspended, from
1776 until 1789, the only power to which political privileges had been given by the people was the States, and
that the State legislatures were, when the convention
met, politically omnipotent, with the exception of the
few limitations imposed on them by the early State constitutions, which were not at all so searching or severe
as those of more recent years. The general rule, then,
is that the Federal Government has only the powers
granted to it by the Federal Constitution, while the State
has all governmental powers not forbidden to it by the
State or the Federal Constitution. But the phrase defin-
ing the Federal Government's powers is no longer "expressly granted," as in the Articles of Confederation, but
merely "granted," so that powers necessary to the execution of granted powers belong to the Federal Government, even though not directly named in the Constitution.
This question of the interpretation, or "construction," of
the Constitution is at the bottom of real national politics
in the United States: the minimizing parties have sought

to hold the Federal Government to a strict construction of granted powers, while their opponents have sought to widen those powers by a broad construction of them. The strict-construction parties, when they have come into power, have regularly adopted the practice of their opponents, so that construction has pretty steadily broadened; the power to "regulate commerce between the States" is now interpreted so as to include the power of Congress to regulate the fares and contracts of railways engaged in inter-State commerce (§ 327), which would have been deemed preposterous in 1787.

107. Popular sovereignty, then, is the oasis of the American system. But it does not, as does the English system, choose its legislative body and leave unlimited powers to it. It makes its "Constitution" the permanent

The Constitu- medium of its orders or prohibitions to all
tion.   branches of the Federal Government and to
many branches of the State Governments : they must do what the Constitution directs and leave undone what it forbids. The people, therefore, are continually laying their commands on their Governments; and they have instituted a system of Federal courts to ensure obedience to their commands. An English court must obey the Act of parliament; the American court is bound and sworn to obey the Constitution first and the Act of Congress or of the State legislature only so far as it is warranted by the Constitution. But the American court does not deal directly with the Act in question; it deals with individuals who have a suit before it. One of these individuals relies on an Act of Congress or of a State legislature; the Act thus comes before the court for examination; and it supports the Act or disregards it as "unconstitutional," or in violation of the Constitution.

If the court is one of high rank or reputation, or one to which a decision may be appealed, as the United States Supreme Court, other courts follow the precedent, and the law falls to the ground. The court does not come into direct conflict with the legislative body ; and, where a decision woul1 be apt to produce such a conflict, the practice has been for the court to regard the matter as a "political question" and refuse to consider it.

108. The preamble states that "we, the people of the United States," establish and ordain the Constitution. Events have shown that it was the people of the whole United States that established The preamble. the Constitution, but the people of 1787 seem to have inclined to the belief that it was the people of each State for itself. This belief was never changed in the south ; and in 1861 the people of that section believed that the ordinances of secession were merely a repeal of the enacting clause by the power which had passed it, the people of the State.

109. The original Constitution was in seven articles. The first related to the organization and powers of Congress, which consists of a senate and The house of house of representatives. Representatives representatives. are to be inhabitants of the State for which they are chosen, to be twenty-five years old at least, and are to serve two years. Each house of representatives thus lasts for two years, and this period is usually known as "a Congress"; the fiftieth Congress expired March 4, 1889, having completed the first century of the Constitution. Representatives are assigned to the States in proportion to population, and this fact forced the provision for a decennial census, the first appearance of such a provision in modern national history. The first

census was taken in 1790. Apportionment of representatives from 1883 to 1893 is governed by the census
of 1880; by Act of Congress the number 154,325 is the
divisor into a State's population which fixes the number
of the State's representatives, the whole number of
representatives being 325,[1] with eight delegates from the
Territories, having seats and the right to debate, but not
to vote. The house elects its speaker and other officers,
and has the power of impeachment.

110. The legislature of each State elects two senators,
to serve for six years; and no State can ever be
deprived of its equal share of representation
except by its own consent. The senators are
divided into three classes, the term of one class expiring
every two years. Six years are therefore necessary to
completely change the composition of the senate, and it
is considered a continuous body. Senators are to be at
least thirty years old, and must be inhabitants of the
States from which they are chosen and citizens of the
United States for at least nine years previous to their
election. The Vice-President presides over the senate,
having no vote unless in case of an equal division. But
the legislative provision (continuing until 1887) that the
death or disability of the President and Vice-President
devolved the office of President on the presiding officer
pro tempore of the senate made that officer one of great
possible importance, and the Vice-President regularly
retired just before the end of a session, so that a *pro
tempore* officer might be selected (§ 117).

The senate.

---

[1] The admission of North Dakota, South Dakota, Montana, and
Washington (see note, page 58), will increase the number of representatives to 330, with one delegate from each of the four remaining Territories, New Mexico, Arizona, Utah, and Idaho.

111. All officers of the United States are open to impeachment by the house of representatives, the impeachment to be tried by the senate, and the penalty to be no more than removal and disqualification to serve further under the United States. When the President is tried, the chief-justice of the Supreme Court presides.

Impeachment.

112. The members of both houses are privileged from arrest and from being questioned elsewhere for words spoken in debate. Each house passes on the election of its own members; but an Act of Congress may control the Acts of the State legislature as to time, place, and manner of elections, except as to the place of choosing senators, in which the legislature remains supreme. Congress has exercised the power by passing a general election law. The two houses cannot adjourn to another place or for more than three days, unless by common consent. Their members are paid by the United States, and must not be office-holders or receive any office created or increased in pay during their term of service in Congress.

Both houses.

113. When a bill passes both houses it goes to the President. If he signs, it becomes a law. If he holds it without signing for ten days (Sundays excepted) it becomes law, unless the final adjournment of Congress comes in the ten days. All bills passed in the last ten days of a Congress are therefore at the mercy of the President; he can prevent them from becoming laws by simply retaining them. If the President decides to veto a bill he returns it, with a statement of his objections, to the house in which it originated. It can then only become law by the vote of two-thirds of both houses.

Veto power.

114. The powers of Congress are fully stated. The first is to "lay and collect taxes, duties, imposts, and Powers of Con- excises, [in order] to pay the debts and pro- gress. vide for the common defence and general welfare of the United States." The words in brackets are not in the original, but they are included in construction by all respectable authorities, as essential to its meaning; any other construction would give Congress absolute power over whatever it thought to be for "the common defence or general welfare." Duties, etc., are to be uniform throughout the United States. Other powers are: to borrow money; to regulate foreign and domestic commerce; to make rules for naturalization, and bankruptcy laws; to coin money, regulate the value of foreign coins, and fix the standard of weights and measures; to punish the counterfeiting of Federal securities and current coin; to establish post-offices and post-roads; to establish patent and copyright systems; to establish courts inferior to the Supreme Court; to punish offences on the high seas or against international law; to declare war, grant letters of marque and reprisal, and make rules for captures; to raise and support armies, no appropriation to be for more than two years; to provide and maintain a navy; to make articles of war; to use the militia of the States in executing Federal laws, suppressing insurrections, and repelling invasions; to provide for organizing, arming, and disciplining this militia, leaving the States to appoint the officers, and carry out the system; to establish a national capital or Federal district (the District of Columbia, containing the city of Washington), and to exercise exclusive powers of legislation over it, and over sites for forts, dockyards, etc., bought by permission of

the States; and, finally, "to make all laws which shall be necessary and proper for carrying into execution the foregoing powers, and all other powers vested by this Constitution in the Government of the United States, or in any department or office thereof." This last power has been the subject of most debate. It was urged that, unless an Act of Congress was strictly "necessary" for the execution of one of the granted powers, it was invalid. The Supreme Court has held that the Act need not be "absolutely necessary," or even "very necessary," — that it is enough if it is "necessary." As the decision of the necessity is with the legislative body, the word opens a wide sweep for construction; but it has always furnished a barricade which the opponents of a bill have often found very strong.

115. The real sovereignty which made the Constitution shows itself in a double series of prohibitions — on the Federal Government and on the States. Powers forbidden The Federal Government shall not suspend to the Federal the privilege of the writ of *habeas corpus* ex- Government. cept in case of rebellion or invasion, when the public safety requires it. Since the Civil War the Supreme Court has decided that the writ itself can never be suspended while the courts are open, that the Federal Government may suspend the *privilege* of the writ as to classes of persons directly interested in the war, but that the writ is still to issue and the court to decide whether the applicant comes within the excepted classes or not. Congress must not pass any bill of attainder or *ex post facto* law, tax exports, give commercial preference to the ports of one State over those of another, lay direct taxes except in proportion to census population, or grant any title of nobility. Money is to be taken from the treasury only

in consequence of appropriations made by law. And no person in the service of the United States may accept any gift or title from a foreign power without consent of Congress.

116. The States are absolutely forbidden to make treaties of any kind, to grant letters of marque and reprisal, Powers forbidden to coin money, to emit bills of credit, to make to the States. anything but silver a legal tender, to grant any title of nobility, to pass any bill of attainder, *ex post facto* law, or law impairing the obligation of contracts. It follows from the last clause that States cannot pass bankruptcy laws. The States are forbidden, except by consent of Congress, to lay any duties on imports or exports, except inspection charges, to be paid into the Federal treasury; to lay any tonnage duties; to keep troops (a word which does not cover militia) or ships in peace; to make any agreement with another State or with a foreign power; or to engage in war unless actually invaded.

117. The President is to be a native citizen, at least thirty-five years old, and at least fourteen years a resi- The President dent within the United States. He is paid by and his powers. the United States; and his salary is not to be increased or diminished by Congress during his term: the Act must apply to the successors of the President who signs the Act. He is sworn to execute his office faithfully, and to "preserve, protect, and defend the Constitution of the United States." In case of his death, resignation, or inability (by impeachment or otherwise) the Vice-President succeeds him; and, in case of the inability of both, the members of the cabinet succeed in a prescribed order, according to the Presidential Succession Act of 1886. The President has the veto power already described, sends messages to Congress on the state of the

Union or on special subjects, convenes either house or both on extraordinary occasions, receives foreign envoys, commissions officers of the United States, and oversees the execution of the laws passed by Congress. He makes treaties; but no treaty is valid unless passed by the senate by a two-thirds vote of those present. He appoints ministers and consuls, judges, and all other officers whose appointment Congress had not vested in other officers; but presidential appointments must be confirmed by the senate, though the President may make temporary appointments during the recess of the senate, to hold until the end of their next session. He is commander-in-chief of the army and navy, and has power of pardon or reprieve for offences against Federal laws, except in case of impeachment. And he may call upon heads of departments for an opinion in writing on any subject relating to his department.

118. The last clause has evolved the "cabinet," a term not known in the Constitution. When Congress has by law organized a department, its leading officer is called its secretary. There are The cabinet. now (1887) seven departments — those of state, of the treasury, of war, of the navy, of the post-office, of the interior, and of justice; and departments of agriculture and of labor have been proposed.[1] The secretaries are selected by the President and are confirmed by the senate, but are not responsible to any one but the President. Nor is he bound by their individual opinions, or even by a unanimous opinion from one of their periodical meetings. They are his advisers only.

119. The people have no direct voice in the choice of President and Vice-President: they choose electors, each

---

[1] A department of agriculture was organized in February, 1889.

State having as many electors as it has senators and
representatives together; and the electors choose the
President and Vice-President, meeting at their State capi-
The electoral tals for that purpose, and sending separate
system. certificates of their choice of President and of
Vice-President to the presiding officer of the senate at
Washington. The electors are to be chosen in such
manner as the legislature of each State shall direct; and
this plenary power of the legislatures was the source of
the unhappy disputed election of 1876–77. By Acts of
Congress, the electors are to be chosen on the Tuesday
after the first Monday of November; they meet in their
States and vote on the first Wednesday of December;
and Congress meets on the second Wednesday of February to witness the counting of the electoral votes. The
electors are legally State officers; and the action of their
States in regard to them was evidently intended to be
final. Until 1887 Congress refused to provide for necessary proof of the State's action, and claimed the power
to provide from time to time for emergencies. Such
emergencies were constantly occurring; and Congress,
which was meant to be merely a witness of the count by
the presiding officer of the senate, had seized, before 1876,
a general supervisory power over the electors and their
votes. This illegitimate function of Congress broke down
in 1876–77, for several Southern States sent different sets
of certificates; the two houses of Congress were controlled by opposite parties, and could agree on nothing;
and an extra-constitutional machine, the "electoral commission," was improvised to tide over the difficulty.
Now provision is made by the Electoral Count Act of
1887, for the State's certification of its votes; and the
certificate which comes in legal form is not to be rejected

but by a vote of both houses. If there is no majority
of electoral votes for any person for Vice-President, the
senate, by a majority of its members, chooses from the
two names highest on the list. If there is no majority
for President, the house of representatives chooses one
from the three names highest on the list, each State
having one vote.

120. The electors were meant to exercise a perfect
freedom of choice, and there are instances in early years
of electors voting for personal friends of the Powers of the
opposite party. It was originally provided electors.
that each elector was to name two persons, without
specifying which was to be President or Vice-President.
When the votes were counted, the highest name on the
list, if it had a majority of all the votes, obtained the
presidency, and the next highest became Vice-President.
It has been said that the convention cut out the office of
President according to the measure of George Washington, and there was no difficulty while he served: each
elector cast one of his votes for Washington, and he was
chosen unanimously; the struggle was for the second
office. When he went out of office in 1796 the parties
began to name candidates in advance for the two offices;
the electors began to feel bound to vote for their party
candidates; and the individuality of the electors disappeared at once. In the election of 1800 the electors
of the successful party voted together like a well-drilled
army, and the result was that the two candidates of the
successful party had an equal vote. The defeated party
controlled the house of representatives, and their efforts to
choose Burr President instead of Jefferson ex- The 12th
asperated the Democrats and sealed the fate amendment.
of the old system. An amendment to the Constitution

was adopted in 1804, changing the method of the electors in voting, so that each should vote separately for the two offices and thus prevent any tie vote from this cause.

121. The Constitution provides for one Supreme Court, having original jurisdiction in cases affecting foreign The Federal ministers and consuls, and those to which a courts. State shall be a party, and appellate jurisdiction from such subordinate courts as Congress should from time to time establish. All judges were to hold office during good behavior (§ 237), and their salaries were not to be diminished during their continuance in office. Criminal trials were to be by jury, except in impeachments, and were to be held within the State in which the offence had been committed, or in places assigned by law for the trial of offences committed outside the jurisdiction of any State. The whole jurisdiction of Federal courts, covering both the original and the appellate jurisdiction of the Supreme Court, was clearly stated. Federal courts were to deal with all cases in law or equity arising under the Constitution or the laws or treaties made under it; with all cases affecting public ministers and consuls, or admiralty or maritime law; with suits by or against the United States; and with suits by one State against another, by a State against citizens of another State, by a citizen of one State against a citizen of another, by a citizen of a State against citizens of his own State when the question was one of a grant of land from different States, by a State or its citizens against foreigners, or by a foreigner against an American. As the section first stood, it was open to the construction of giving the power to the citizen of one State to sue another State, and the Supreme Court so construed it in 1793–94. The States at once took the

alarm; and the 11th amendment, forbidding suit against a State under this section except by another State, was ratified in 1798.

122. As soon as the new Government was organized in 1789, a Judiciary Act was passed, organizing the whole system of inferior Federal courts. Subse- Organization of quent development has not changed the essen- the judiciary. tial nature of this first Act. The Supreme Court now consists of a chief-justice and eight associate justices; there are nine circuit courts, each consisting of a Supreme Court justice and a circuit judge; and fifty-six district courts, each with a district judge. Each circuit comprises several States; and the Supreme Court justices, in addition to their circuit work, meet in bank annually at Washington. The districts cover each a State or a part of a State. Appeal lies from the district to the circuit court when the matter involved is of a value greater than $500, and from the circuit to the Supreme Court when $5000 or more is involved. There are also Territorial courts; but these are under the absolute power of Congress over the Territories, and are not covered by the constitutional provisions as to courts. Consular courts, held abroad, fall under the treaty power.

123. The Constitution's leading difference from the Confederation is that it gives the national Government power over individuals. The Federal courts Its power over are the principal agent in securing this essen- individuals. tial power; without them, the Constitution might easily have been as dismal a failure as the Confederation. It has also been a most important agent in securing to the national Government its supremacy over the States. From this point of view the most important provision of the Constitution is the grant of jurisdiction to Federal

courts in cases involving the construction of the Constitution or of laws or treaties made under it.   The 25th
section of the Judiciary Act permitted any Supreme
Court justice to grant a writ of error to a State court in
a case in which the constitutionality of a Federal law or
treaty had been denied, or in which a State law objected
to as in violation of the Federal Constitution had been
maintained.   In such cases, the defeated party had the
right to carry the "Federal question" to the Federal
courts.   It was not until 1816 that the Federal courts
undertook to exercise this power; it raised a storm of
opposition, but it was maintained, and has made the Constitution what it professed to be — "the supreme law of
the land."   As a subsidiary feature in the
judiciary system, treason was restricted to the
Treason.
act of levying war against the United States, or of adher-
ing to their enemies, giving them aid and comfort; the
evidence of it to confession in open court, or to the testimony of two witnesses to an overt act; and any forfeiture
in the punishment to a life effect only.   The States,
however, have always asserted their power to punish for
treason against them individually.   It has never been
fully maintained in practice; but the theory had its
effect in the secession period.

124. The States were bound to give credit to the public records of other States, to accord citizenship to the
Fugitive crimi- citizens of other States, to return criminals
nals and slaves. fleeing from other States, and to return "persons held to service or labor" under the laws of another
State.   This last was the "fugitive slave" provision
of the Constitution, which became so important after
1850 (§ 228).

125. The Federal Government was to guarantee a

republican form of government to each of the States, and
to protect each of them against invasion, or, Guarantee
on application of the legislature or governor, clause.
against domestic violence. The "guarantee clause" really
substituted State rights under the guarantee of the Federal Government for the notion of State sovereignty
under the guarantee of the State itself. A still stronger
case of this was in the 5th article of the Constitution,
stating the manner of amendment. The convention of
1787, it must be borne in mind, was working under a system of government which provided expressly that it was
not to be altered in the least unless by consent of all the
States. The Constitution provided that it was to go into
force, so far as the ratifying States were concerned, as
soon as nine of the thirteen States should ratify it, and
that any future amendment, when passed by two-thirds
of both houses and ratified by the legislatures or conventions of three-fourths of the States, should become a part
of the Constitution. By application of the legislatures
of two-thirds of the States, a new convention, like that
which framed the Constitution, might take the place of
the two houses of Congress in proposing amendments. A
system under which a State submits its whole future
destiny to an unlimited power of decision in three-
fourths of its associate States can hardly be called one
of State sovereignty.

126. The debts of the Confederation, and its engage-
ments, were made binding on the new Government;
the Constitution, and laws and treaties to be Supreme law of
made under it, were declared to be "the su- the land.
preme law of the land"; judges of State courts were to
be bound thereby, "anything in the Constitution or laws
of any State to the contrary notwithstanding"; all the

legislative, executive, and judicial officers of the United States and of each and every State were to be bound by oath or affirmation to support the Constitution of the United States; but religious tests were forbidden.

127. Ten amendments were adopted so soon after the ratification of the Constitution that they may fairly be considered a part of the original instrument.

The first ten amendments. They were due to a general desire that a "bill of rights" of some kind should be added to it; but they did not alter any of the articles of the Constitution. They forbade any establishment of religion by Congress, or any abridgment of freedom of worship, of the press, or of speech, or of the popular right to assemble and petition the Government for redress of grievances; the billeting of soldiers; unreasonable searches or seizures, or general warrants; trials for infamous crimes except through a grand jury's action; subjecting a person for the same offence to be twice put in jeopardy of life or limb; compelling him to witness against himself in criminal cases; the taking of life, liberty, or property without due process of law or without compensation for property; and the demand of excessive bail, or the imposition of excessive fines or of cruel or unusual punishments. They asserted the right of the people to keep and bear arms, to a jury trial from the vicinage in criminal cases or in cases involving more than twenty dollars, to a copy of the indictment, to the testimony against the prisoner, to compulsory process on his behalf, and to counsel for him. And they stated expressly the general principle already given, that the Federal Government is restricted to granted powers, while those not mentioned are reserved "to the States respectively or to the people."

128. The omission of the word "thereof" after the

clause last mentioned seems significant. The system of
the United States is almost the only national
system, in active and successful operation, as
to which the exact location of the sovereignty is still a
mooted question. The contention of the Calhoun school
— that the separate States were sovereign before and
after the adoption of the Constitution, that each State
adopted it by its own power, maintained it by its own
power, and could put an end to it by its own power, that
the Union was purely voluntary, and that the whole people, or the people of all the other States, had no right to
maintain or enforce the Union against any State — has
been ended by the Civil War. But that did not decide
the location of the sovereignty. The prevalent opinion
is still that first formulated by Madison : that the States
were sovereign before 1789; that they then gave up a
part of their sovereignty to the Federal Government;
that the Union and the Constitution were the work of the
States, not of the whole people; and that reserved powers
are reserved to the people of the States, not to the whole
people. The use of this bald phrase "reserved to the
people," not to the people of the several States, in the
10th amendment, seems to argue an underlying consciousness, even in 1789, that the whole people of the United
States was already a political power quite distinct from
the States, or the people of the States ; and the tendency
of later opinion is in this direction. It must be admitted
that the whole people has never acted in a single capacity ; but the restriction to State lines seems to be a self-
imposed limitation by the national people, which it might
remove, as in 1789, if an emergency should make it necessary. The Civil War amendments are considered below
(§§ 305–309).

The sovereignty.

129. By whatever sovereignty the Constitution was framed and imposed, it was meant only as a scheme in Details of the outline, to be filled up afterwards, and from system. time to time, by legislation. The idea is most plainly carried out in the Federal justiciary: the Constitution only directs that there shall be a Supreme Court, and marks out the general jurisdiction of all the courts, leaving Congress, under the restriction of the President's veto power, to build up the system of courts which shall best carry out the design of the Constitution. But the same idea is visible in every department, and it has carried the Constitution safely through a century which has radically altered every other civilized government. It has combined elasticity with the limitations necessary to make democratic government successful over a vast territory, having infinitely diverse interests, and needing, more than almost anything else, positive opportunities for sober second thought by the people. A sudden revolution of popular thought or feeling is enough to change the house of representatives from top to bottom; it must continue for several years before it can make a radical change in the senate, and for years longer before it can carry this change through the judiciary, which holds for life; and all these changes must take place before the full effects upon the laws or Constitution are accomplished. But the minor changes which are essential to an accommodation with the growth and development of a great nation are reached in the meantime easily and naturally in the course of legislation, to which the skeleton outline of the Constitution lends itself kindly. The members of the convention of 1787 showed their wisdom most plainly in not trying to do too much; if they had done more they would have done far less.

130. The convention adjourned 17th September, 1787, having adopted the Constitution. Its last step was a resolution that the Constitution be sent to the Submission to Congress of the Confederation, with the rec- Congress. ommendation that it be submitted to conventions elected by the people of each State for ratification or rejection; that, if nine States should ratify it, Congress should appoint days for the popular election of electors, for the choice of President and Vice-President by the electors, and for the meeting of senators and representatives to be chosen under the new plan of government; and that then the new Congress and President should, "without delay, proceed to execute this Constitution." Congress, having received the report of the convention, resolved that it be sent to the several legislatures, to be submitted to conventions; and this was all the approval the Constitution ever received from Congress. Both Congress and the convention were careful not to open the dangerous question, How was a government which was not to be changed but by the legislatures of all the States to be entirely supplanted by a different system through the approval of conventions in three-fourths of them? They left such questions to be opened, if at all, in the less public forum of the legislatures.

131. Before the end of the year Delaware, Pennsylvania, and New Jersey had ratified; and Georgia, Connecticut, and Massachusetts followed during the first two months of 1788. Thus far the Federalists and Antifeder- only strong opposition had been in Massachu- alists. setts, a "large State." In it the struggle began between Federalists and Antifederalists, between the friends and the opponents of the Constitution, with its introduction of a strong Federal power; and it raged in the conventions,

legislatures, newspapers, and pamphlets. The best of the last was *The Federalist*, written mainly by Hamilton, with the assistance of Madison and Jay, explaining the new Constitution and defending it. As it was written before the Constitution went into force, it speaks much for the ability of its writers that it has passed into a standard text-book of American constitutional law.

132. The seventh and eighth States — Maryland and South Carolina — ratified in April and May, 1788; and, while the conventions of Virginia and New York were still wrangling over the great question, the ninth State, New Hampshire, ratified, and the Constitution passed out of theory into fact. This left the other States in an unpleasant position. The Antifederalists of the Virginia and New York conventions offered conditional ratifications of all sorts; but the Federalists stubbornly refused to consider them, and at last, by very slender majorities, these two States ratified. North Carolina refused to ratify the Constitution, and Rhode Island refused even to consider it (§ 145). Congress named the first Wednesday of January, 1789, as the day for the choice of electors, the first Wednesday in February for the choice of President and Vice-President, and the first Wednesday in March for the inauguration of the new Government at New York city. The last date fell on the 4th of March, which has been the limit of each President's term since that time.

Ratification.

Inauguration.

133. When the votes of the electors were counted before Congress, it was found that Washington had been unanimously elected President, and that John Adams, standing next on the list, was Vice-President. Long before the inauguration the Congress

Fall of the Confederation.

of the Confederation had expired of mere inanition; its attendance simply ran down until (October 21, 1788) its record ceased, and the United States got on without any national Government for nearly six months. The struggle for nationality had been successful, and the old order faded out of existence.

134. The first census (1790) followed so closely upon the inauguration of the Constitution that the country may fairly be said to have had a population of nearly four millions in 1789. Something over half a million of these were slaves of African birth or blood. Slavery of this sort had taken root in all the colonies, its Slavery in the original establishment being everywhere by United States. custom, not by law. When the custom had been sufficiently established statutes came in to regulate a relation already existing. Indented servants came only for a term of years, and then were free. Slaves were not voluntary immigrants: they had come as chattels, not as persons, and had no standing in law, and the law fastened their condition on their children. But it is not true, as the Dred Scott decision held long afterwards (§ 249), that the belief that slaves were chattels simply, things not persons, held good at the time of the adoption of the Constitution. Times had changed somewhat. The peculiar language of the Constitution itself, describing slaves as " persons held to service or labor, under the laws of any State," puts the general feeling exactly : they were persons from whom the laws of some of the States withheld personal rights for the time. In accordance with this feeling most of the Northern States were on the high road towards abolition of slavery. Vermont Abolition in the had never allowed it. In Massachusetts it north. was swept out by a summary court decision that it was

irreconcilable with the new State constitution. Other States soon began systems of gradual abolition, which finally extinguished slavery north of Virginia, but so gradually that there were still eighteen apprentices for life in New Jersey in 1860, the last remnants of the former slave system. In the new States north of the Ohio slavery was prohibited by the Ordinance of 1787 (§ 96), and the prohibition was maintained in spite of many attempts to get rid of it and introduce slavery.

135. The sentiment of thinking men in the south was Feeling in the exactly the same, or in some cases more bitter south. from their personal entanglement with the system. Jefferson's language as to slavery is irreconcilable with the chattel notion ; no abolitionist agitator ever used warmer language than he as to the evils of slavery, and the expression, "our brethren," used by him of the slaves, is conclusive. Washington, Mason, and other Southern men were as warm against slavery as Jefferson, and societies for the abolition of slavery were very common in the south. No thinking man could face with equanimity the future problem of holding a separate race of millions in slavery. Like most slave laws, the laws of the Southern States were harsh: rights were almost absolutely withheld from the slave, and punishments of the severest kind were legal ; but the execution of the system was milder than its legal possibilities might lead one to imagine. The country was as yet so completely agricultural, and agriculture felt so few of the effects of large production and foreign commerce, that southern slavery kept all the patriarchal features possible to such a system.

136. Indeed, the whole country was almost exclusively agricultural, and, in spite of every effort to encourage

manufactures by State bounties and colonial protection, they formed the meagrest element in the national production. Connecticut, which now teems with manufactures, was just beginning the production of tinware and clocks; Rhode Island and Massachusetts were just beginning to work in cotton from models of jennies and Arkwright machinery surreptitiously obtained from England after several failures and in evasion of penal Acts of parliament; and other States, beyond local manufactures of paper, glass, and iron, were almost entirely agricultural, or were engaged in industries directly dependent on agriculture. Commerce was dependent on agriculture for exports; and manufactured imports were enough to drown out every other form of industry.

Agriculture, commerce, and manufactures.

137. There were but four cities in the United States having a population of more than 10,000 — Philadelphia (42,000), New York (33,000), Boston (18,000), and Baltimore (13,000). The population of the city of New York and its dependencies is now more than half as large as that of the whole United States in 1789; the State of New York or of Pennsylvania has now more inhabitants than the United States in 1790; and the new States of Ohio and Illinois, which had hardly any white inhabitants in 1789, do not fall far behind. Imports have swollen from $23,000,000 to $650,000,000, exports from $20,000,000 to $700,000,000, since 1790. The revenues of the new Government in 1790 were $4,000,000; they have now grown to $300,000,000 or more. The expenditures of the Government, excluding interest on the public debt, were but $1,000,000 in 1790, where now they are $200,000,000 or upwards per annum. It is not easy for the modern American to realize

Changes since 1790.

the poverty and weakness of his country at the inauguration of the new system of government, however he may realize the simplicity of the daily life of its people. Even the few large cities were but larger collections of the wooden houses, with few comforts, which composed the villages; the only advantage of their inhabitants over those of the villages was in the closer proximity to their neighbors; and but a little over three per cent. of the population had this advantage, against about twenty-five per cent. in 1880.

138. Outside the cities communication was slow. One stage a week was enough for the connection between the great cities; and communication elsewhere depended on private conveyance. The great rivers by which the continent is penetrated in every direction were with difficulty ascended by sailing vessels or boats; and the real measure of communication was thus the daily speed of a man or a horse on roads bad beyond present conception. The western settlements were just beginning to make the question more serious. Enterprising land companies were the moving force which had impelled the passage of the Ordinance of 1787; and the first column of their settlers was pouring into Ohio and forming connection with their predecessors in Kentucky and Tennessee. Marietta and Cincinnati (at first a Government fort, and named after the society of the Cincinnati) had been founded. But the intending settlers were obliged to make the journey down the Ohio river from Pittsburgh in bullet-proof flat-boats, for protection against the Indians, and the return trip depended on the use of oars. For more than twenty years these flat-boats were the chief means of river commerce in the west; and, in the longer

trips, as to New Orleans, the boats were generally broken up at the end and sold for lumber, the crew making the trip home on foot or on horseback. John Fitch and others were already experimenting on what was soon to be the steamboat (§ 167); but the statesman of 1789, looking at the task of keeping under one Government a country of such distances, with such difficulties of communication, may be pardoned for having felt anxiety as to the future. To almost all thinking men of the time the Constitution was an experiment, and the unity of the new nation a subject for very serious doubt.

139. The comparative isolation of the people everywhere, the lack of books, the poverty of the schools and newspapers, were all influences which worked strongly against any pronounced literary de- Literature. velopment. Poems, essays, and paintings were feeble imitations of European models; history was annalistic, if anything; and the drama hardly existed. In two points the Americans were strong, and had done good work. Such men as Jonathan Edwards had excelled in various departments of theology, and American preaching had reached a high degree of quality and influence; and, in the line of politics, the American state-papers rank among the very best of their kind. Having a very clear perception of their political purposes, and having been restricted in study and reading to the great masters of pure and vigorous English, and particularly to the English translators of the Bible, the American leaders came to their work with an English style which could hardly have been improved. The writings of Franklin, Washington, the Adamses, Hamilton, Jefferson, Madison, Jay, and others show the secret of their strength in every page. Much the same reasons, with the influences of

democracy, brought oratory, as represented by Patrick
Henry, Fisher Ames, John Randolph, and others, to a
point not very far below the mark afterwards reached by
Daniel Webster.   The effect of these facts on the subsequent development of the country is not often estimated
at its full value.   All through an immigration of every
language and dialect under heaven the English language
has been protected in its supremacy by the necessity of
going back to the "fathers of the republic" for the first,
and often the complete, statement of principles in every
great political struggle, social problem, or lawsuit.

140. The cession of the "north-west territory" by
Virginia and New York had been followed up by similar
Limits of set- cessions by Massachusetts (1785), Connecticut
tlement.   (1786), and South Carolina (1787).   North
Carolina did not cede Tennessee until late in 1789, nor
Georgia her western claims until 1802.   Settlement in
all these regions was hardly advanced beyond what it
had been at the outbreak of the revolution.   The centres
of western settlement, in Tennessee and Kentucky, had
merely become more firmly established, and a new one,
in Ohio, had just been begun.   The whole western limits
of settlement of the old thirteen States had moved much
nearer their present boundaries ; and the acquisition of
the western title, with the liberal policy of organization
and government which had been begun, was to have its
first clear effects during the first decade of the new Government.   Almost the only obstacle to its earlier success
had been the doubts as to the attitude which the Spanish
authorities, at New Orleans and Madrid, would take
The Mississippi towards the new settlements.   They had
river.   already asserted a claim that the Mississippi
was an exclusively Spanish stream from its mouth up to

the Yazoo, and that no American boat should be allowed to sail on it. To the western settler the Alleghanies and bad roads were enough to cut him off from any other way to a market than down the Mississippi; and it was not easy to restrain him from a forcible defiance of the Spanish claim. The Northern States were willing to allow the Spanish claim in return for a commercial treaty; the Southern States and the western settlers protested angrily; and once more the spectre of dissolution appeared, not to be laid again until the new Government had made a treaty with Spain in 1795, securing common navigation of the Mississippi.

141. All contemporary authorities agree that a marked change had come over the people since 1775, and few of them seem to think the change one for the Social condi- better. Many attribute it to the looseness of tions. manners and morals introduced by the French and British soldiers; others to the general effects of war; a few, Tories all, to the demoralizing effects of rebellion. The successful establishment of nationality would be enough to explain most of it; and if we remember that the new nation had secured its title to a vast western territory, of unknown but rich capacities, which it was now moving to reduce to possession by emigration, it would seem far more strange if the social conditions had not been somewhat disturbed.

VI.

THE DEVELOPMENT OF DEMOCRACY.

1789–1801.

142. ALL the tendencies of political institutions in the United States had certainly been towards democracy;
Democracy in the United States; but it cannot be said that the leading men were hearty or unanimous in their agreement with this tendency. Not a few of them were pronounced republicans even before 1775, but the mass of them had no great objection to a monarchical form of government until the war-spirit had converted them. The Declaration of Independence had been directed rather against *the* king than against *a* king. Even after popular sovereignty had pronounced against a king, class spirit was for some time a fair substitute for aristocracy. The obstacles to communication, which compelled the mass of the people to live a very isolated existence, gave abnormal prominence and influence to those who, by ability or wealth, could overcome these obstacles; and common feeling made these a class, with many symptoms of strong class feelings. As often happens, democracy at least thought of a Cæsar when it apprehended class control. The discontented officers of the revolutionary armies offered to make Washington king, though he put the offer by without even considering it. The suggestion of a return to monarchy in some form, as a possible road out of the confusion of the

Confederation, occurs in the correspondence of some of the leading men. And while the convention of 1787 was holding its secret sessions a rumor went out that it had decided to offer a crown to an English prince.

143. The State constitutions were democratic, except for property or other restrictions on the right of suffrage, or provisions carefully designed to keep the control of at least one house of the State legislature "in the hands of property." The Federal Constitution was so drawn that it would have lent itself kindly either to class control or to democracy. The electoral system of choosing the President and Vice-President was altogether anti-democratic, though democracy has conquered it: not an elector, since 1796, has disobeyed the purely moral claim of his party to control his choice (§§ 119, 120). Since the senate was to be chosen by the State legislatures, "property," if it could retain its influence in those bodies, could control at least one house of Congress. The question whether the Constitution was to have a democratic or an anti-democratic interpretation was to be settled in the next twelve years.

Democracy in the States; in the Constitution.

144. The States were a strong factor in the final settlement, from the fact that the Constitution had left to them the control of the elective franchise: they were to make its conditions what each of them saw fit. Religious tests for the right of suffrage had been quite common in the colonies; property tests were almost universal. The former disappeared shortly after the revolution; the latter survived in some of the States far into the constitutional period. But the desire to attract immigration was always a strong impelling force to induce States, especially frontier States,

Influence of immigration.

to make the acquisition of full citizenship and political rights as easy and rapid as possible. This force was not so strong at first as it was after the great stream of immigration began about 1848 (§ 236), but it was enough to tend constantly to the development of democracy; and it could not but react on the national development. In later times, when State laws allow the immigrant to vote even before the period assigned by Federal laws allows him to become a naturalized citizen, there have been demands for the modification of the ultra State democracy; but no such danger was apprehended in the first decade.

145. The Antifederalists had been a political party, but a party with but one principle. The absolute failure of that principle deprived the party of all cohesion;

Organization of the new Government.

and the Federalists controlled the first two Congresses almost entirely. Their pronounced ability was shown in their organizing measures, which still govern the American system very largely. The departments of state, of the treasury, of war, of justice, and of the post-office were rapidly and successfully organized; Acts were passed for the regulation of seamen, commerce, tonnage duties, lighthouses, intercourse with the Indians, Territories, and the militia; a national capital was selected; a national bank was chartered; the national debt was funded, and the State debts were assumed as part of it. The first four years of the new system showed that the States had now to deal with a very different power from the impotent Congress of the Confederation. The new power was even able to exert a pressure upon the two States which had not yet ratified the Constitution, though, in accordance with the universal American prejudice, the pressure was made as gentle as possible. As a first step, the higher duties imposed on imports from foreign countries were expressly directed to apply to imports from North Carolina and Rhode Island. North Carolina having called a second convention, her case was left to the course of nature; and the second convention ratified the Constitution (November 21, 1789). The Rhode Island legislature wrote to ask that their State might not be considered altogether foreigners, made their duties agree with those of the new Government, and reserved the proceeds for "continental" purposes. Still no further steps were taken. A bill was therefore introduced directing the President to suspend commercial intercourse with Rhode Island, and to demand from her her share of the continental debt. This was passed by the senate, and waited but two steps further to become law. Unofficial newspaper proposals to divide up the little State between her two nearest neighbors were stopped by her ratification (May 29, 1790). All the "old thirteen" were thus united under the Constitution; and yet, so Completion of strong is the American prejudice for the au- the Union. tonomy of the States that these last two were allowed to enter in the full conviction that they did so in the exercise of sovereign freedom of choice. Their entrance, however, was no more involuntary than that of others. If there had been real freedom of choice, nine States would never have ratified: the votes of Pennsylvania, Massachusetts, New Hampshire, Virginia, and New York were only secured by the pressure of powerful minorities in their own States, backed by the almost unanimous votes of the others.

146. Protection was begun in the first Tariff Act, whose object, said its preamble, was the protection of

domestic manufactures. The duties, however, ranged only from $7\frac{1}{2}$ to 10 per cent. averaging about $8\frac{1}{2}$ per

Hamiltonian protection.

cent. The system, too, had rather a political than an economic basis. Until 1789 the States had controlled the imposition of duties. The separate State feeling was a factor so strong that secession was a possibility which every statesman had to take into account. Hamilton's object, in introducing the system, seems to have been to create a class of manufacturers, running through all the States, but dependent for prosperity on the new Federal Government and its tariff. This would be a force which would make strongly for national Government, and against any attempt at secession, or against the tendency to revert in practice to the old system of control by State legislatures, even though it based the national idea on a conscious tendency towards the development of classes. The same feeling seems to have been at the bottom of his establishment of a national bank, his assumption of State debts, and most of the general scheme which his influence forced upon the Federal party.

147. In forming his cabinet, Washington had paid attention to the opposing elements which had united

The first cabinet.

for the temporary purpose of ratifying the Constitution. The national element was represented by Hamilton, secretary of the treasury, and Knox, secretary of war; the particularist element (using the term to indicate support of the States, not of a State) by Jefferson, secretary of state, and Edmund Randolph, attorney-general. It was not long before the drift of opinion in cabinet meetings showed an irreconcilable divergence, on almost every subject, between these two elements, and Hamilton and Jefferson became the representatives of the two opposite tendencies which have together made up the sum of public American history. At the end of 1792 matters were in train for the general recognition of the existence of two parties, whose struggles were to decide the course of the Constitution's development. The occasion came in the opening of the following year, when the new nation was first brought into contact with the French Revolution.

148. The controlling tendency of Jefferson and his school was to the maintenance of individual rights at the highest possible point, as the Hamilton *The Jefferson school of politics.* school was always ready to assert the national power to restrict individual rights for the general good. Other points of difference are rather symptomatic than essential. The Jefferson school supported the States, not out of love for the States, but out of a belief that the States were the best bulwarks for individual rights. When the French Revolution began its usual course in America by agitating for the "rights of man," it met a sympathetic audience in the Jefferson party and a cold and unsympathetic hearing from the Hamilton school of Federalists. The latter were far more interested in securing the full recognition of the power and rights of the nation than in securing the individual against imaginary dangers, as they thought them. For ten years, therefore, the surface marks of distinction between the two parties were to be connected with the course of events in Europe; but the essence of distinction was not in the surface marks.

149. The new Government was not yet four years old; it was not familiar, nor of assured *The Hamilton school.* permanency. The only national Governments of which Americans had had previous experience were

the British Government and the Confederation; in the former they had had no share, and the latter had had no power. The only places in which they had had long-continued, full, and familiar experience of self-government were their State Governments; these were the only governmental forms which were then distinctly associated in their minds with the general notion of republican government. The governing principle of the Hamilton school, that the construction or interpretation of the terms of the Constitution was to be such as to broaden the powers of the Federal Government, necessarily involved a corresponding trenching on the powers of the States (§ 106). It was natural, then, that the Jefferson school should look on every feature of the Hamilton programme as "anti-republican," meaning, probably, at first no more than opposed to the State system as, hitherto known, though, with the growth of political bitterness, the term soon came to imply something of monarchical, and, more particularly, of English tendencies. The disposition of the Jefferson school to claim for themselves a certain peculiar title to the position of "republicans" soon developed into the appearance of the first Republican party, about 1793.

150. Many of the Federalists were shrewd and active business men, who naturally took prompt advantage of the opportunities which the new system offered. The Republicans therefore believed and asserted that the whole Hamilton programme was dictated by selfish or class interest; and they added this to the accusation of monarchical tendencies. These charges, with the fundamental differences of mental constitution, exasperated by the passion which differences as to the French Revolution seemed to carry with

them everywhere, made the political history of this decade a very unpleasant record. The provision for establishing the national capital on the Potomac (1790) was declared to have been carried by a corrupt bargain; and accusations of corruption were renewed at every opportunity. In 1793 a French agent, Genet, appeared to claim the assistance of the United States for the French republic. Washington decided to issue a proclamation of neutrality, the first act of the kind in American history. It was the first indication, also, of the policy which has made the course of every President, with the exception of Polk (§ 223), a determined leaning to peace, even when the other branches of the Government have been intent on war. The proclamation of 1793 brought about the first distinctly party feeling; and it was intensified by Washington's charge that popular opposition in western Pennsylvania (1794) to the new excise law had been fomented by the extreme French party. Their name, Democrat, was applied by the Federalists to the whole Republican party as a term of contempt, but it was not accepted by the party for some twenty years; then the compound title of "Democratic-Republican" became, as it still is, the official title of the party. There was no party opposition, however, to the re-election of Washington in 1792, or to the admission of Vermont (1791), Kentucky (1792), and Tennessee (1796) as new States.

The national capital.

Genet's mission.

The Whiskey Insurrection.

Admission of Vermont, Kentucky, and Tennessee.

151. The British Government had accredited no minister to the United States, and it refused to make any commercial treaty or to give up the forts in the western territory of the United States, through which its agents still exercised a commanding influence over the Indians.

In the course of its war with France, the neutral American vessels, without the protection of a national navy, fared

Jay's treaty.
badly. A treaty negotiated by Chief-Justice Jay (1794) settled these difficulties for the following ten years. But, as it engaged the United States against any intervention in the war on behalf of France, and as it granted some unfamiliar privileges to Great Britain, particularly that of extradition, the Republicans made it very unpopular, and the first personal attacks on Washington's popularity grew out of it. In spite of occasional Republican successes, the Federalists retained a general control of national affairs ; they elected

Election of 1796.
John Adams President in 1796, though Jefferson was chosen Vice-President with him ; and the national policy of the Federalists kept the country out of entangling alliances with any of the European belligerents. To the Republicans, and to the French republic, this last point of policy was only a practical intervention against France and against the rights of man.

152. At the end of Washington's administration the French Directory, following up its successes in Germany and Italy and its exactions from conquered powers, broke off relations with the United States, demanding the abrogation of Jay's treaty and a more pronounced sympathy

The "X.Y.Z." mission.
with France. Adams sent three envoys to endeavor to re-establish the former relations ; they were met by official or unofficial demands for "money, a great deal of money," as a prerequisite to peace. They refused; their letters home were published; and the Federalists at last had the opportnnity of riding the whirlwind of an intense popular desire for war with France. Intercourse with France was suspended by Con-

gress (1798) ; the treaties with France were declared at an end : American frigates were authorized to capture French vessels guilty of depredations on American commerce, and the President was authorized to issue letters of marque and reprisal; and an American army was formed, Washington being called from his retirement at Mount Vernon to command it. The war never went beyond a few sea-fights, in which the little American navy did itself credit, and Napoleon, seizing power the next year, renewed the peace which should never have been broken. But the quasi-war had internal consequences to the young republic which surpassed in interest all its foreign difficulties : it brought on the crisis which settled the development of the United States towards democracy.

Quasi-war with France.

153. The reaction in Great Britain against the indefinite "rights of man" had led parliament to pass an alien law, a sedition law suspending the writ of *habeas corpus,* and an Act giving wide and scarcely defined powers to magistrates for the dispersion of meetings to petition for redress of grievances. The Federalists were in control of a Congress of limited powers; but they were strongly tempted by sympathies and antipathies of every sort to form their programme on the model furnished from England. The measures which they actually passed were based only on that construction of the Constitution which is at the bottom of all American politics; they only tended to force the Constitution into an anti-democratic direction. But it was the fixed belief of their opponents that they meant to go farther, — to forget the limitations imposed by the ten years' old Constitution, and to secure their own control by some wholesale measure of political persecution.

Error of the Federalists.

154. Three alien laws were passed. The first raised
the number of years necessary for naturalization from
five to fourteen. The third permitted the
arrest of subjects of any foreign power with
which the United States should be at war.
The second, which is usually known as the Alien Law,
was limited to a term of two years; it permitted the
President to arrest or order out of the country any alien
whom he should consider dangerous to the country. As
many of the Republican editors and local leaders were
aliens, this law really put the whole Republican organization in the power of the President elected by their opponents. The Sedition Law made it a crime, punishable
by fine and imprisonment, to publish or print any false,
scandalous, and malicious writings against the Government of the United States, either house of Congress, or
the President, with intent to defame them, or to bring
them into contempt or disrepute, or to excite against
them the hatred of the good people of the United States,
or to stir up sedition or opposition to any lawful Act of
Congress or of the President, or to aid the designs of any
foreign power against the United States. In its first
form the bill was even more loose and sweeping than
this, and alarmed the opposition thoroughly.

155. Almost all the ability of the country was in the
Federalist ranks; the Republicans had but two first-rate
men — Jefferson and Madison. In the sudden
issue thus forced between individual rights
and national power, Jefferson and Madison
could find but one bulwark for the individual — the
power of the States; and their use of it gave their
party a permanent list to State sovereignty from which it
did not recover for years. They objected to the Alien

Law on the grounds that aliens were under the jurisdiction of the State, not of the Federal Government; that the jurisdiction over them had not been transferred to the Federal Government by the Constitution, and that the assumption of it by Congress was a violation of the Constitution's reservation of powers to the States; and, further, because the Constitution reserved to every " person," not to every citizen, the right to a jury trial (§ 127). They objected to the Sedition Law on the grounds that the Constitution had specified exactly the four crimes for whose punishment Congress was to provide; that criminal libel was not one of them; and that Amendment I. forbade Congress to pass any law restricting freedom of speech or of the press. The Federalists asserted a common-law power in Federal judges to punish for libel, and pointed to a provision in the Sedition Law permitting the truth to be given in evidence, as an improvement on . the common law, instead of a restriction on individual liberty.

156. The Republican objections might have been made in court, on the first trial. But the Republican leaders had strong doubts of the impartiality of the Federal judges, who were Federalists. They resolved to intrench the party in the State legislatures. The Virginia legislature in 1789 passed a series of resolutions prepared by Madison, and the Kentucky legislature in the same year passed a series prepared by Jefferson. Neglected or rejected by the other States, they were passed again by their legislatures in 1799, and were for a long time the documentary basis of the Democratic party (§ 320). The leading idea expressed in both was that the Constitution was a "compact" between the States, and that the powers (the

States) which had made the compact had reserved the power to restrain the creature of the compact, the Federal Government, whenever it undertook to assume powers not granted to it. Madison's idea seems to have been that the restraint was to be imposed by a second convention of the States. Jefferson's idea is more doubtful; if it meant that the restraint should be imposed by any State which should feel aggrieved, his scheme was merely Calhoun's idea of nullification (§ 206); but there are some indications that he agreed with Madison.

157. The first Congress of Adams's term of office ended in 1799. Its successor, elected in the heat of the war excitement, kept the Federalist policy up to its first

Effects of the laws.

pitch. Out of Congress the execution of the objectionable laws had taken the shape of political persecution. Men were arrested, tried, and punished for writings which the people had been accustomed to consider quite within legitimate political methods. Some of the charges were petty, and some ridiculous. The Republican leaders made every trial as public as possible, and gained votes constantly, so that the Federalists began to be shy of the very powers which they had sought. Every new election was a storm-signal for the Federal party; and the danger was increased by the appearance of schism in their own ranks.

158. Hamilton was now a private citizen of New York; but he had the confidence of his party more largely than

Federalist schism.

its nominal head, the President, and he maintained close and confidential relations with the cabinet which Adams had taken unchanged from Washington. The Hamilton faction saw no way of preserving and consolidating the newly acquired powers of the Federal Government but by keeping up and increasing the war feeling against France; Adams had the instinctive leaning of an American President towards peace. Amid cries of wrath and despair from his party he accepted the first overtures of the new Napoleonic Government, sent envoys to negotiate a peace, and ordered them to depart for France when they delayed too long. Then, discovering flat treachery in his cabinet, he dismissed it and blurted out a public expression of his feeling that Hamilton and his adherents were "a British faction." Hamilton retorted with a circular letter to his party friends, denouncing the President; the Republicans intercepted it and gave it a wider circulation than its author had intended; and the Hamilton faction tried so to arrange the electoral vote that Pinckney should be chosen President in 1800 and Adams should be shelved into the vice-presidency. Even so, Election of 1800. the Federal party barely missed success. As things turned out, the result depended on the electoral vote of New York; and Aaron Burr, who had introduced the drill and machinery of a modern American political party there, had made the State Republican and secured a majority for the Republican candidates. There was an effort by the Federalists to disappoint the Republicans by making Burr President; but Jefferson obtained that office, Burr becoming Vice-President for four years (§ 120).

159. The "revolution of 1800" decided the future development of the United States. The new dominant party entered upon its career weighted with "Revolution of the theory of State sovereignty; and a civil 1800." war was necessary before this dogma, put to use again in the service of slavery, could be banished from the American system. But the democratic development never was checked. From that time the interpretation

of the Federal Constitution has generally favored individual rights at the expense of governmental power. As
the Republicans obtained control of the States they
altered the State constitutions so as to cut out all the
arrangements that favored property or class interests,
and reduced political power to the dead level of manhood
suffrage. In most of the States outside of New England
this process was completed before 1815; but New England tenacity was proof against the advancing revolution
until about 1820. For twenty years after its downfall of
1800 the Federal party maintained its hopeless struggle, and then it faded away into nothing, leaving as its
permanent memorial the excellent organization of the
Federal Government, which its successful rival hardly
changed. Its two successors — the Whig and the second
Republican party — have been broad-constructionist parties, like the Federal party, but they have admitted
democracy as well; the Whig party adopted popular
methods at least, and the Republican party grew into a
theory of individual rights even higher than Jefferson's
— the emancipation of enslaved labor.

160. The disputed election of 1800 was decided in the
new capital city of Washington, to which the Government
had just been removed. Its streets and
parks existed only on paper. The capitol
had been begun ; the White House was unfinished, and
its audience room was used by Mrs. Adams as a drying
room for clothes ; and the Congressmen could hardly find
lodgings. The inconveniences were only an exaggeration
of the condition of other American cities. Their sanitary conditions were so bad that yellow fever from time
to time reduced them almost to depopulation. Again
and again, during this decade, the fever visited Phila-

The new capitol.

delphia and New York, drove out the people, and left the
grass growing in the streets. The communication between the cities was still as bad as could be. The traveller
was subject to every danger or annoyance
that bad roads, bad carriages, bad horses, bad   Communication.
inns, and bad police protection could combine to inflict
upon him. But the rising spirit of migration seemed to
urge the people to conquer these difficulties. The first
attempts were made to introduce turnpike roads and
canals ; and proposals were advanced for greater improvements. The war with natural obstacles had fairly begun,
though it had little prospect of success until steam was
brought into use as the ally of man.

161. About this time the term "the West" appears.
It meant then the western part of New York State, the
new territory north of the Ohio, and Kentucky
and Tennessee. In settling land boundaries   The West.
New York had transferred to Massachusetts, whose claims
crossed her territory, the right to a large tract of land in
central New York. The sale of this had carried population considerably west of the Hudson. After several
American expeditions against the Ohio Indians had been
defeated, another under General Anthony Wayne (1794)
had compelled them to give up all the territory now in
the State of Ohio. Settlement received a new impetus
with increased security, and the new state of affairs
added to the population of Kentucky, whose growth had
been seriously checked by periodical attacks from the
Indians across the Ohio. Between 1790 and 1800 the
population of Ohio had risen from almost nothing to
45,000, that of Tennessee from 36,000 to 106,000, and that
of Kentucky from 74,000 to 221,000—the last-named
State now exceeding five of the "old thirteen" in popu-

lation. The difficulties of the western emigrant, however, were still enormous. He obtained land of his own,
fertile land and plenty of it, but little else. The produce
of the soil had to be consumed at home, or near it; ready
money was scarce and distant products scarcer; and
comforts, except the very rudest substitutes of home
manufacture, were unobtainable. The new life bore
most hardly upon women; and, if the record of woman's
share in the work of American colonization could be fully
made up, the price paid for the final success would seem
very great.

162. The number of post-offices rose during these ten
years from 75 to 903, the miles of post-routes from 1900
to 21,000, and the revenue from $38,000 to
$231,000. These figures seem small in com-
parison with the 25,000 post-offices, 375,000 miles of
post-routes, and $45,000,000 of revenue of 1887, but the
comparison with the figures of 1790 shows a development
in which the new Constitution, with its increased security,
must have been a factor.

Post-office.

163. The power of Congress to regulate patents was
already bearing fruit. Until 1789 this power was in the
hands of the States, and the privileges of the
inventor were restricted to the territory of the
patenting State. Now he had a vast and growing territory within which all the profits of the invention were
his own, and that development began by which human
invention has been urged to its highest point, as a factor
in the struggle against natural forces. Twenty patents
were issued in 1793, and 22,000 ninety years afterwards;
but one of the inventions of 1793, Whitney's cotton
gin, has affected the history of the United States more
than most of its wars or treaties.

Patents.

164. When the Constitution was adopted it was not known that the cultivation of cotton could be made profitable in the Southern States. The "roller gin" could clean only a half dozen pounds a day by slave labor. In 1784 eight bags of cotton landed in Liverpool from an American ship, were seized on the ground that so much cotton could not be the produce of the United States. Eli Whitney, a Connecticut school-teacher residing in Georgia, invented the saw-gin, by which the cotton was dragged through parallel wires with openings too narrow to allow the seeds to pass; and one slave could now clean a thousand pounds a day. The exports of cotton leaped from 189,000 pounds in 1791 to 21,000,000 pounds in 1801, and doubled in three years more. The influence of this one invention, combined with the wonderful series of British inventions which had paved the way for it, can hardly be estimated in its commercial aspects. Its political influences were even wider, but more unhappy. The introduction of the commercial element into the slave system of the south robbed it at once of the partriarchal features which had made it tolerable ; but, at the same time, it developed in slave-holders a new disposition to uphold and defend a system of slave labor as a "positive good." The abolition societies of the south began to dwindle as soon as the results of Whitney's invention began to be manifest.

165. The development of a class whose profits were merely the extorted natural wages of the black laborer was certain; and its political power was as certain, though it never showed itself clearly until after 1830. And this class was to have a peculiarly distorting effect on the political history of the United States. Aristocratic in every sense but one, it was

ultra-Democratic (in a purely party sense) in its devotion
to State sovereignty, for the legal basis of the slave system was in the laws of the several States.   In time, the
aristocratic element got control of the party which had
originally looked to State rights as a bulwark of individual rights ; and the party was finally committed to
the employment of its original doctrine for an entirely
different purpose — the suppression of the black laborer's
wages.

VII.

DEMOCRACY AND NATIONALITY.

1801-29.

166. WHEN Jefferson took office in 1801 he succeeded to a task larger than he imagined. His party, ignoring the natural forces which tied the States Democracy and together even against their wills, insisted that nationality. the legal basis of the bond was in the power of any State to withdraw at will. This was no nationality; and foreign nations naturally refused to take the American national coin at any higher valuation than that at which it was current in its own country. The urgent necessity was for a reconciliation between democracy and nationality; and this was the work of this period. An underlying sense of all this has led Democratic leaders to call the war of 1812-15 the "second war for independence"; but the result was as much independence of past ideas as of Great Britain.

167. The first force in the new direction was the acquisition of Louisiana (§ 32) in 1803. Napoleon had acquired it from Spain, and, fearing an attack upon it by Great Britain, offered it to the Louisiana. United States for $15,000,000. Jefferson and his party were eager to accept the offer; but the Constitution gave the Federal Government no power to buy and hold territory, and the party was based on a strict construction of the Constitution. Possession of power forced the strict-

construction party to broaden its ideas, and Louisiana was bought, though Jefferson quieted his conscience by talking for a time of a futile proposal to amend the Constitution so as to grant the necessary power. The acquisition of the western Mississippi basin more than doubled the area of the United States, and gave them control of all the great river-systems of central North America.

The steamboat. The difficulties of using these rivers were removed almost immediately by Fulton's utilization of steam in navigation (1807). Within four years steamboats were at work on western waters; and thereafter the increase of steam navigation and that of population stimulated one another. Population crossed the Mississippi; constantly increasing eddies filled up the vacant places to the east of the great river; and all sections of the country advanced as they had never

Centre of population. advanced before. The "centre of population" has been carefully ascertained by the census authorities for each decade, and it represents the westward movement of population very closely. During this period it advanced from about the middle of the State of Maryland to its extreme western limit; that is, the centre of population was in 1830 nearly at the place which had been the western limit of population in 1770.

168. Jefferson also laid the basis for a further acquisition in the future by sending an expedition under Lewis

The Oregon country. and Clarke to explore the territory north of the then Spanish territory of California and west of the Rocky Mountains — the "Oregon country" as it was afterwards called (§§ 221, 224). The explorations of this party (1804), with Captain Gray's discovery of the Columbia river (1792), made the best part of the claims of the United States to the country forty years later.

169. Jefferson was re-elected in 1804, serving until 1809; his party now controlled almost all the States outside of New England, and could elect almost any one whom it chose to the presidency. Election of 1804. Imitating Washington in refusing a third term of office, Jefferson established the precedent, which has not since been violated, restricting a President to two terms, though the Constitution contains no such restriction. The great success of his presidency had been the acquisition of Louisiana, which was a violation of his party principles; but all his minor successes were, like this, recognitions of the national sovereignty which he disliked so much. After a short and brilliant naval war the Barbary pirates were reduced to submission (1805). And the authority of the nation was asserted for the first time in internal affairs. The long-continued control of New Orleans by Spain, and the persistent intrigues of the Spanish authorities, looking towards a separation of the whole western country from the United States, had been ended by the annexation of Louisiana, and they will probably remain forever hidden in the secret history of the early west. They had left behind a dangerous ignorance of Federal power and control, of which Burr took advantage (1807). Organizing an expedition in Kentucky and Tennessee, probably for the conquest of the Spanish colony of Mexico, he was arrested on the lower Mississippi and brought back to Virginia. He was acquitted; but the incident opened up a vaster view of the national authority than democracy had yet been able to take. It had been said, forty years before, that Great Britain had long arms, but that 3000 miles was too far to extend them; it was something to know now that the arms of the Federal Government were long enough to reach from Washington city to the Mississippi.

170. All the success of Jefferson was confined to his first four years ; all his heavy failures were in his second Difficulties with term, in which he and his party as persist-
Great Britain. ently refused to recognize or assert the inherent power of the nation in international affairs. The Jay treaty expired in 1804 by limitation, and American commerce was thereafter left to the course of events, without any restriction of treaty obligations, since Jefferson refused to accept the only treaty which the British Government was willing to make. All the difficulties which followed may be summed up in a few words: the British Government was then the representative of the ancient system of restriction of commerce, and had a powerful navy to enforce its ideas; the American Government was endeavoring to force into international recognition the present system of neutral rights and unrestricted commerce, but its suspicious democracy refused to give it a navy sufficient to command respect for its ideas. Indeed, the American Government did not want the navy ; it apparently expected to gain its objects without the exhibition of anything but moral force.

171. Great Britain was now at war, from time to time, with almost every other nation of Europe. In Neutral com- time of peace, European nations followed gen-
merce. erally the old restrictive principle of allowing another nation, like the United States, no commercial access to their colonies ; but, when they were at war with Great Britain, whose navy controlled the ocean, they were very willing to allow the neutral American merchantmen to carry away their surplus colonial produce. Great Britain had insisted for fifty years that the neutral nation, in such cases, was really intervening in the war as an ally of her enemy ; but she had so far

modified her claim as to admit that "transshipment," or breaking bulk, in the United States was enough to qualify the commerce for recognition, no matter whither it was directed after transshipment. The neutral nation thus gained a double freight, and grew rich in the traffic; the belligerent nations no longer had commerce afloat for British vessels to capture; and the "frauds of the neutral flags" became a standing subject of complaint among British merchants and naval officers. About 1805, British prize courts began to disregard transshipment, and to condemn American vessels which had made the voyage from a European colony to the mother country by way of the United States. This was really a restriction of American commerce to purely American productions, or to commerce with Great Britain direct, with the payment of duties in British ports.

172. The question of expatriation, too, furnished a good many burning grievances. Great Britain maintained the old German rule of perpetual allegiance, though she had modified it by allowing the right of emigration. The United States, founded by immigration, was anxious to establish what Great Britain was not disposed to grant, the right of the subject to divest himself of allegiance by naturalization under a foreign jurisdiction. Four facts thus tended to break off friendly relations: (1) Great Britain's claim to allegiance over American naturalized subjects; (2) her claim to the belligerent right of search of neutral vessels; (3) her claim or right to impress for her vessels of war her subjects who were seamen wherever found; and (4) the difficulty of distinguishing native-born Americans from British subjects, even if the right to impress naturalized American subjects were granted.

Expatriation.

Impressment.

British naval officers even undertook to throw the *onus probandi* upon Americans — to consider all who spoke the English language as British subjects, unless they could produce proof that they were native-born Americans. The American sailor who lost his papers was thus open to impressment. The American Government in 1810 published the cases of such impressments since 1803, as numbering over 4000, about one-third of the cases resulting in the discharge of the impressed man; but no one could say how many cases had never been brought to the attention of a Government which never did anything more than remonstrate about them.

173. In May, 1806, the British Government, by orders in council, declared a blockade of the whole continent of

Orders in council.

Europe from Brest to the Elbe, about 800 miles. In November, after the battle of Jena, Napo-

Berlin and Milan decrees.

leon answered by the "Berlin decree," in which he assumed to blockade the British Isles, thus beginning his "continental system." A year later the British Government answered by further orders in council, forbidding American trade with any country from which the British flag was excluded, allowing direct trade from the United States to Sweden only, in American products, and permitting American trade with other parts of Europe only on condition of touching in England and paying duties. Napoleon retorted with the "Milan decree," declaring· good prize any vessel which should submit to search by a British ship; but this was evidently a vain fulmination.

174. The Democratic party of the United States was

The Navy.

almost exclusively agricultural, and had little knowledge of or sympathy with commercial interests; it had little confidence in the American navy;

it was pledged to the reduction of national expenses and the debt, and did not wish to take on its shoulders the responsibility for a navy; and, as the section of country most affected by the orders in council, New England, was Federalist, and made up the active and irreconcilable opposition, a tinge of political feeling could not but color the decisions of the dominant party. Various ridiculous proposals were considered as substitutes for a necessarily naval war; and perhaps the most ridiculous was adopted. Since the use of non-intercourse agreements as revolutionary weapons against Great Britain (§ 50), an overweening confidence in such measures had sprung up, and one of them was now resorted to — the embargo (1807), forbidding foreign commerce altogether. It was expected to starve Great The embargo. Britain into a change of policy; and its effects may be seen by comparing the $20,000,000 exports of 1790, $49,000,000 of 1807, and $9,000,000 of 1808. It does not seem to have struck those who passed the measure that the agricultural districts also might find the change unpleasant; but that was the result, and their complaints reinforced those of New England, and closed Jefferson's second term in a cloud of recognized misfortune. The pressure had been slightly relieved by the substitution of the Non-intercourse Law (1809) for the Non-intercourse law. embargo; it prohibited intercourse with Great Britain and France and their dependencies, leaving other foreign commerce open; but Madison, Jefferson's successor in 1808–9, assumed in the presidency a burden which was not enviable. New Eng- Election of 1808. land was in a ferment, and was even suspected of designs to resist the restrictive system by force (§ 180); and the administration did not feel secure enough in its position to face the future with confidence.

175. The Non-intercourse Law was to be abandoned as to either belligerent which should abandon its attacks on neutral commerce, and maintained against the other. In 1810 Napoleon officially informed the American Government that he had abandoned his system. He continued to enforce it in fact; but his official fiction served its purpose of limiting the non-intercourse for the future to Great Britain, and thus straining relations between that country and the United States still further. The elections of 1811–12 resulted everywhere in the defeat of "submission men" and in the choice of new members who were determined to resort to war against Great Britain; France had not been able to offer such concrete cases of injury as her enemy, and there was no general disposition to include her in the war. Clay, Calhoun, Crawford, and other new men seized the lead in the two houses of Congress, and forced Madison to agree to a declaration of war as a condition of his re-election in Election of 1812. 1812. War was begun by the declaration of War with Eng- June 18, 1812. The New England Federalists land. always called it "Mr. Madison's war," but the President was about the most unwilling participant in it.

176. The national democracy meant to attack Great Britain in Canada, partly to gratify its western constituency, who had been harassed by Indian attacks, asserted to have been instigated from Canada. Premonitions of Tippecanoe. success were drawn from the battle of Tippecanoe, in which Harrison had defeated the north-western league of Indians formed by Tecumseh (1811). Between the solidly settled Atlantic States and Theatre of the the Canadian frontier was a wide stretch of war. unsettled or thinly settled country, which

was itself a formidable obstacle to war. Ohio had been admitted as a State in 1802, and Louisiana was admitted in 1812; but their admission had been due to the desire to grant them self-government rather than to their full development in population and resources. Cincinnati was a little settlement of 2500 inhabitants; the fringe of settled country ran not very far north of it; and all beyond was a wilderness of which little was known to the authorities. The case was much the same with western New York; the army which was to cross the Niagara river must journey almost all the way from Albany through a country far more thinly peopled than the far western territories are now. The difficulties of transport gave opportunities for peculation; and a barrel of flour sometimes reached the frontier army with its cost multiplied seven or eight fold. When a navy was to be built on the lakes, the ropes, anchors, guns, and all material had to be carried overland for a distance about equal to the length of England; and even then sailors had to be brought to man the navy, and the vessels were built of green timber; one vessel was launched nine weeks after her timber was cut. It would have been far less costly, as events proved, to have entered at once upon a naval war; but the crusade against Canada had been proclaimed all through Kentucky and the west, and their people were determined to wipe out their old scores before the conclusion of the war.

177. The war opened with disaster — Hull's surrender of Detroit; and disaster attended it for two years. Political appointments to positions in the regular army were numerous, and such officers were worse than useless. The men were not fitly trained or supplied. The war department showed no great knowl-

Disasters by land.

edge, and poverty put its little knowledge out of service.
Several futile attempts at invasion were followed by defeat or abortion, until the political officers were weeded
out at the end of the year 1813, and Brown, Scott, Rip-
ley, and others who had fought their way up were put in
command. Then for the first time the men were drilled
and brought into effective condition; and two successful
Chippewa and Lundy's Lane. battles in 1814 — Chippewa and Lundy's Lane
— threw some glory on the end of the war.
So weak were the preparations even for defence that a
British expedition in 1814 met no effective resistance
when it landed and burned Washington. It
Washington burnt. was defeated, however, in an attempt to take
Baltimore.

178. The American navy at the outbreak of the war
numbered half a dozen frigates and about the same
State of the navy. number of smaller vessels. This was but a
puny adversary for the thousand sail of the
British navy, which had captured or shut up in port all
the other navies of Europe. But the small number of
American vessels, with the superabundance of trained
officers, gave them one great advantage; the training
and discipline of the men, and the equipment of the
vessels, had been brought to the very highest point.
Captains who could command a vessel but for a short
time, yielding her then to another officer, who was to
take his sea service in rotation, were all ambitious to
make their mark during their term. "The art of
handling and fighting the old broadside sailing frigate"
had been carried in the little American navy to a
point which unvarying success and a tendency to fleet-
combats had now made far less common among British
captains.

179. The first year of the war saw five ship-duels, in all of which the American frigates either captured or sunk their adversaries. Four others followed in 1813, in two of which the British vessels came off victorious. The attention of the British Government had by that time been fully diverted to the North-American coast; its blockading fleets made it very difficult for the larger American vessels to get to sea; and there were but seven other ship-combats, in only one of which the American vessel was taken. Most of the work was done by three frigates, the " Constitution," the " Essex," and the " United States." There was fighting also on the Great Lakes between improvised fleets of small vessels. Perry captured the British fleet on Lake Erie (1813) and Macdonough the British fleet on Lake Champlain (1814). The former victory led to the end of the war in the west. Harrison, the American commander in that section, shipped his army across the lake in Perry's fleet, and routed the British and Canadian army at the Thames.

Naval successes.

Victories on the Lakes.

180. The home dislike to the war had increased steadily with the evidence of incompetent management by the administration. The Federalists, who had always desired a navy, pointed to the naval successes as the best proof of the folly with which the war had been undertaken and managed. New England Federalists complained that the Federal Government utterly neglected the defence of their coast, and that southern influence was far too strong in national affairs. They showed at every opportunity a disposition to adopt the furthest stretch of State sovereignty, as stated in the Kentucky resolutions; and every such development urged the national democracy unconsciously

Feeling in New England.

further on the road to nationality.   When the New Eng-
Hartford con- land States sent delegates to meet at Hartford
vention. and consider their grievances and the best
remedies — a step perfectly proper on the Democratic
theory of a "voluntary Union" — treason was suspected,
and a readiness to suppress it by force was plainly shown.
The recommendations of the convention came to nothing;
but the attitude of the dominant party towards it is one
of the symptoms of the manner in which the trials of
actual war were steadily reconciling democracy and nationality.   The object which Hamilton had sought by
high tariffs and the development of national classes had
been attained by more natural and healthy means.

181.   In April, 1814, the first abdication of Napoleon
took place, and Great Britain was able to give more
attention to her American antagonist.   The main attack
was to be made on Louisiana, the weakest and most distant portion of the Union.   A fleet and army were sent
thither, and, after much delay, landed below the city.
The nearest settled country was Tennessee; and between
it and New Orleans was a wilderness four
New Orleans. hundred miles long.   Andrew Jackson had
become the most prominent citizen of Tennessee, and he
was ordered to the defence of New Orleans.   His popularity and energy brought riflemen down the river and
put them into position.   The British assault was marred
by hopeless blunders, and the gallantry of the men only
made their slaughter and repulse more complete (January 8, 1815).   Peace had been made at Ghent
Peace. fifteen days before the battle was fought, but
the news of the battle and the peace reached Washington
almost together, the former going far to make the latter
tolerable.

182. Though the land war had gone almost uniformly against the United States, and the American naval successes had been just enough to irritate the English mind, and though the British negotiators *Its terms.* had nothing to dread and everything to demand, the treaty was quite satisfactory to the United States. It is true that it said not a word about the questions of impressment, search, and neutral rights, the grounds of the war; Great Britain did not abandon her position on any of them. But everybody knew that circumstances had changed. The new naval power whose frigates alone in the past twenty years had shown their ability to fight English frigates on equal terms was not likely to be troubled in future with the question of impressment; and in fact, while not renouncing the right, the British Government no longer attempted to enforce it. The navy, it must be confessed, was the force which had at last given the United States a recognized and cordial acceptance in the family of nations; it had solved the problem of the reconciliation of democracy and nationality. From this time the dominant party shows an increasing disposition to exalt and maintain the national element of the American system.

183. The remainder of this period is one of the barrenest in American history. The opposition of the Federal party to the war completed the measure of its unpopularity, and it had only a perfunctory *Extinction of the Federal party.* existence for a few years longer. There was but one real party, and the political struggles within it tended to take the shape of purely personal politics. Scandal, intrigue, and personal criticism became the most marked characteristics of American politics until the dominant party broke at the end of the period, and

real party conflict was renewed. But the seeds of the final disruption are visible from the peace of 1814. The old-fashioned Republicans looked with intense suspicion on the new form of republicanism generated by the war, a type which instinctively bent its energies toward the further development of national power. Clay was the natural leader of the new democracy; but John Quincy Adams and others of Federalist antecedents or leanings took to the new doctrines kindly; and even Calhoun, Crawford, and others of the southern interest, were at first strongly inclined to support them. One of the first effects was the revival of protection and of a national bank.

184. The charter of the national bank (§ 146) had expired in 1811, and the dominant party had refused to recharter it. The attempt to carry on the war by loans resulted in almost a bankruptcy and in a complete inability to act efficiently. As soon as peace gave time for consideration, a second bank was chartered for twenty years, with a capital of $35,000,000, four-fifths of which might be in Government stock. It was to have the custody of the Government revenues, but the secretary of the treasury could divert the revenues to other custodians, giving his reasons for such action to Congress. This clause, meant to cover cases in which the Bank of the United States had no branch at a place where money was needed, was afterwards put to use for a very different purpose (§ 204).

185. Protection was advocated again on national grounds, but not quite on those which had moved Hamilton (§ 146). The additional receipts were now to be expended for fortifications and other national defences, and for national roads and canals,

the latter to be considered solely as military measures, with an incidental benefit to the people. Business distress among the people gave additional force to the proposal. The war and blockade had been an active form of protection, under which American manufactures had sprung up in great abundance. As soon as peace was made English manufacturers poured their products into the United States, and drove their American rivals out of business or reduced them to desperate straits. Their cries to Congress for relief had a double effect. They gave the spur to the nationalizing advocates of protection, and, as most of the manufacturers were in New England or New York, they developed in the citadel of Federalism a class which looked for help to a Republican Congress, and was therefore bound to oppose the Federal party. This was the main force which brought New England into the Republican fold before 1825. An increase in the number of spindles from Manufactures. 80,000 in 1811 to 500,000 in 1815, and in cotton consumption from 500 bales in 1800 to 90,000 in 1815, the rise of manufacturing towns, and the rapid development of the mechanical tendencies of a people who had been hitherto almost exclusively agricultural, were influences which were to be reckoned with in the politics of a democratic country.

186. The tariff of 1816 imposed a duty of about twenty-five per cent. on imports of cotton and woollen goods, and specific duties on iron imports. The *ad valorem* duties carried most of the manufac- Tariff of 1816. turers through the financial crisis of 1818–19, but the iron duties were less satisfactory. In English manufacture the substitution of coke for charcoal in iron production led to continual decrease in price. As the price went

down the specific duties were continually increasing the absolute amount of protection. Thus spared the necessity for improvements in production, the American manufacturers felt English competition more keenly as the years went by, and called for more protection.

187. Monroe succeeded Madison as President in 1817, and, re-elected with hardly any opposition in 1820, he served until 1825. So complete was the supremacy of the Republican party that this is often called "the era of good feeling." It came to an end when a successor to

"Era of good feeling." Monroe was to be elected; the two sections of the dominant party then had their first opportunity for open struggle. During Monroe's two terms of office the nationalizing party developed the policy on which it proposed to manage national affairs. This was largely the product of the continually swelling western movement of population. The influence of the steamboat was felt more and more every year, and the want of a similar improvement in land transport was correspondingly evident. The attention drawn to western New York by the war had filled that part of the State with a new population. The Southern Indians had been completely overthrown by Jackson during the war of 1812, and forced to cede their lands; all the territory west of Georgia was thus opened up to settlement. The

Admission of Indiana, Mississippi, Illinois, Alabama, Maine, and Missouri. admission of the new States of Indiana (1816), Mississippi (1817), Illinois (1818), Alabama (1819), Maine (1820), and Missouri (1821)— all but Maine the product and evidence of western growth—were the immediate results of the development consequent upon the war. All the territory east of the Mississippi, except the northern part of the north-west territory, was now formed into self-governing States; the State system had already crossed the Mississippi; and all that was needed for further development was the locomotive engine. The four millions of 1790 had grown into thirteen millions in 1830; and there was a steady increase of one-third in each decade.

188. The urgent demand of western settlers for some road to a market led to a variety of schemes to facilitate intercourse between the east and the west, — the most successful being that completed in New York in 1825, the Erie Canal. The Hudson river forms the great natural breach in the barrier range   Erie Canal. which runs parallel to the Atlantic coast. When the traveller has passed up the Hudson through that range he sees before him a vast champaign country extending westward to the Great Lakes, and perfectly adapted by nature for a canal. Such a canal, to turn western traffic into the lake rivers and through the lakes, the canal, and the Hudson to New York city, was begun by the State through the influence of De Witt Clinton, was derisively called "Clinton's big ditch" until its completion, and laid the foundations for the great commercial prosperity of New York State and city. Long before it was finished the evident certainty of its success had seduced other States into far less successful enterprises of the kind and had established as a nationalizing policy the combination of high tariffs and expenditures for internal improvements which was long known as the "American system." The tariffs of duties on imports The "American were to be carried as high as revenue results   system." would approve; within this limit the duties were to be defined for purposes of protection; and the superabundant revenues were to be expended for the improvement of roads, rivers, and harbors, and for every enterprise

which would tend to aid the people in their efforts to subdue the continent. Protection was now to be for national benefit, not for the benefit of classes. Western farmers were to have manufacturing towns at their doors, as markets for the surplus which had hitherto been rotting on their farms; competition among manufacturers was to keep down prices; migration to all the new advantages of the west was to be made easy at national expense; and Henry Clay's eloquence was to commend the whole policy to the people. The old democracy, particularly in the south, insisted that the whole scheme really had its basis in benefits to classes, that its communistic features were not such as the Constitution meant to cover by its grant of power to Congress to levy taxation for the general welfare, and that any such legislation would be unconstitutional. The Tariffs of 1824 and 1828. dissatisfaction in the south rose higher when the tariffs were increased in 1824 and 1828. The proportion of customs revenue to dutiable imports rose to 37 per cent. in 1825 and to 44 per cent. in 1829; and the ratio to aggregate imports to 33 per cent. in 1825 and 37 per cent. in 1829. As yet, however, the southern dissatisfaction showed itself only in resolutions of State legislatures.

189. In the sudden development of the new nation circumstances had conspired to give social forces an abnormally materialistic cast, and this had strongly influenced the expression of the national life. Its literature and its art had amounted to little, for the American people were still engaged in the fiercest of warfare against natural difficulties, which absorbed all their energies.

190. In international relations the action of the Government was strong, quiet, and self-respecting. Its first

weighty action took place in 1823. It had become pretty evident that the Holy Alliance, in addition to its interventions in Europe to suppress popular risings, meant to aid Spain in bringing her revolted South American colonies to obedience. Great Britain had been drifting steadily away from the Alliance, and Canning, the new secretary, determined to call in the weight of the trans-Atlantic power as a check upon it. A hint to the American minister was followed by a few pregnant passages in President Monroe's annual message in De- The Monroe cember. Stating the friendly relations of the doctrine. United States with the new South American republics, he went on to say, "We could not view an interposition for oppressing them (the South American states), or controlling in any other manner their destiny by any European power, in any other light than as a manifestation of an unfriendly disposition towards the United States." If both the United States and Great Britain were to take this ground the fate of a fleet sent by the Alliance across the Atlantic was not in much doubt, and the project was at once given up. The "Monroe doctrine," however, has remained the rule of foreign intercourse for all American parties. Added to the already established refusal of the United States to become entangled in any European wars or alliances, it has separated the two continents, to their common advantage.

191. It was supposed at the time that Spain might transfer her colonial claims to some stronger power ; and Mr. Monroe therefore went on to say that "the The colonial American continents should no longer be sub- clause. jects for any new European colonial settlement." The meaning of this was well understood at the time ; and, when its condition failed, the statement lost its force. It has

been supposed that it bound the United States to resist any further establishment of European colonies in the Americas. Such a role of universal arbiter has always been repudiated by the United States, — though its sympathies, more or less active, must always go with any American republic which falls into collision with any such colonizing scheme.

192. By a treaty with Russia (1825) that power gave up all claims on the Pacific coast south of the present *The north-west* limits of Alaska. The northern boundary of *boundary.* the United States had been settled by the treaty of 1783; and, after the acquisition of Louisiana, a convention with Great Britain settled the boundary on the line of 49° N. lat. as far west as the Rocky Mountains (1818). West of these mountains the so-called Oregon country (§ 168), on whose limits the two powers could not agree, was to be held in common possession for ten years. This common possession was prolonged by another convention (1827) indefinitely, with the privilege to either power to terminate it on giving twelve months' notice. This arrangement lasted until 1846 (§ 224).

193. Monroe's terms of office came to an end in 1825. He had originally been an extreme Democrat, who could hardly speak of Washington with patience; he had slowly changed into a very moderate Republican, whose tendencies were eagerly claimed by the few remaining Federalists as identical with their own. The nationalizing faction of the dominant party had scored almost all the successes of the administration, and the divergence between it and the opposing faction was steadily becoming more apparent. All the candidates for the presidency in 1824 — Andrew Jackson, a private citizen of Tennessee;

William H. Crawford, Monroe's secretary of the treasury; John Quincy Adams, his secretary of state; and Henry Clay, the speaker of the house of representatives — claimed to be Republicans alike; but the personal nature of the struggle was shown by the tendency of their supporters to call themselves "Adams men" or "Jackson men," rather than by any real party title. Calhoun was supported by all parties for the vice-presidency, and was elected without difficulty. The choice of a President was more doubtful.

Election of 1824.

194. None of the four candidates had anything like a party organization behind him. Adams and Clay represented the nationalizing element, as Crawford and Jackson did not; but there the likeness among them stopped. The strongest forces behind Adams were the new manufacturing and commercial interests of the east; behind Clay were the desires of the west for internal improvements at public expense as a set-off to the benefits which the seaboard States had already received from the Government; and the two elements were soon to be united into the National Republican or Whig party. Crawford was the representative of the old Democratic party, with all its southern influences and leanings. Jackson was the personification of the new democracy — not very cultured, perhaps, but honest, and hating every shade of class control instinctively. As he became better known the whole force of the new drift of things turned in his direction; "hurrah for Jackson" undoubtedly often represented tendencies which the speaker would have found it hard to express otherwise. Crawford was taken out of the race, just after this election, by physical failure, and Adams by the revival of ancient quarrels with the Federalists of New England;

Party divergence.

and the future was to be with Clay or with Jackson. But in 1824 the question of success among the four was not an easy one to decide. The electors gave no one a majority; and the house of representatives gave the presidency to Adams (§§ 119, 120).

195. Adams's election in 1824 was due to the fact that Clay's friends in the house — unable to vote for him, as he was the lowest in the electoral vote, and only three names were open to choice in the house — very naturally gave their votes to Adams. As Adams appointed Clay The Adams ad- to the leading position in his cabinet, the ministration. defeated party at once raised the cry of "bargain and intrigue," one of the most effective in a democracy, and it was kept up throughout Adams's four years of office. Jackson had received the largest number of electoral votes, though not a majority; and the hazy notion that he had been injured because of his devotion to the people increased his popularity. Though demagogues made use of it for selfish purposes, this feeling was an honest one, and Adams had nothing to oppose to it. He tried vigorously to uphold the "American system," and succeeded in passing the tariff of 1828; he tried to maintain the influence of the United States on both the American continents; but he remained as unpopular as Election of 1828. his rival grew popular. In 1828 Adams was easily displaced by Jackson. Calhoun was re-elected Vice-President.

196. Jackson's inauguration in 1829 closes this period, as it ends the time during which a disruption of the Democracy and Union by the peaceable withdrawal of any nationality. State was even possible. The party which had made State sovereignty its bulwark in 1798 was now in control of the Government again; but Jackson's

proclamation in his first term, in which he warned South Carolina that "disunion by armed force is treason," and that blood must flow if the laws were resisted, speaks a very different tone from the speculations of Jefferson on possible future divisions of the United States. And even the sudden attempt of South Carolina to exercise independent action (§ 206), which would have been looked upon as almost a right forty years before, shows that some interest dependent upon State sovereignty had taken alarm at the evident drift of events, and was anxious to lodge a claim to the right before it should slip from its fingers forever. Nullification was but the first skirmish between the two hostile forces of slavery and democracy.

197. When the vast territory of Louisiana was acquired in 1803 the new owner found slavery already established there by custom recognized by French and Spanish law. Congress tacitly **Slavery.** ratified existing law by taking no action; slavery continued legal, and spread further through the territory; and the State of Louisiana entered as a slave State in 1812. The next State to be carved out of the territory was Missouri, admitted in 1821. A Territory, on applying for admission as a State, brings a constitution for inspection by Congress; and when it was found that the new State of Missouri proposed to recognize and continue slavery, a vigorous opposition spread through the north and west, and carried most of the senators and representatives from those sections with it. In the house of representatives these two sections had a greatly superior number of members; but, as the number of Northern and Southern States had been kept about equal, the compact southern vote, with one or two

northern allies, generally retained control of the senate. Admitted by the senate and rejected by the house, Missouri's application hung suspended for several years, until it was successful by the admission of Maine, a balancing Northern State, and by the following arrange-
The Missouri ment, known as the Missouri compromise of
compromise. 1820: Missouri was to enter as a slave State; slavery was forever prohibited throughout the rest of the Louisiana purchase north of lat. 36° 30', the main southern boundary of Missouri; and, though nothing was said of the territory south of the com-promise line, it was understood that any State formed out of it was to be a slave State, if it so wished (§ 249). Arkansas entered under this provision in 1836.

198. The question of slavery was thus set at rest for the present, though a few agitators were roused to more
Sectional diver- zealous opposition to the essence of slavery
gence.   itself. In the next decade these agitators succeeded only in the conversion of a few recruits, but these recruits were the ones who took up the work at the opening of the next period and never gave it up until slavery was ended. It is plain now, however, that north and south had already drifted so far apart as to form two sections, and that, as things stood, their drift for the future could only be further apart, in spite of the feeble tie furnished by the Missouri compromise. It became evident, during the next forty years, that the wants and desires of these two sections were so diver-gent that it was impossible for one Government to make satisfactory laws for both. The moving cause was not removed in 1820; one of its effects was got out of the way for the time, but others were soon to take its place.

199. The vast flood of human beings which had been pour-

ing westward for years had now pretty well occupied the territory east of the Mississippi, while, on the west side of that stream, it still showed a dis- **The settled area.** position to hold to the river valleys. The settled area had increased from 240,000 square miles in 1790 to 633,-000 square miles in 1830, with an average of 20.3 persons to the square mile. There was still a great deal of Indian territory in the Southern States of Georgia, Alabama, and Mississippi, and in Florida, for the southern Indians were among the finest of their race; they had become semi-civilized, and were formidable antagonists to the encroaching white race. The States interested had begun preparations for their forcible removal, in public defiance of the attempts of the Federal Government to protect the Indians (1827); but the removal was not completed until 1835. In the north, Wisconsin and Michigan, with the northern halves of Illinois and Indiana, were still very thinly settled, but everything indicated early increase of population. The first lake steamboat, the "Walk-in-the-Water," had ap- **The steamboat.** peared at Detroit in 1818, and the opening of the Erie Canal added to the number of such vessels. Lake Erie had seven in 1826; and in 1830, while the only important lake town, Detroit, was hardly yet more than a frontier fort, a daily line of steamers was running to it from Buffalo, carrying the increasing stream of emigrants to the western territory.

200. The land system of the United States had much to do with the early development of the west. From the first settlement, the universally recog- **The land system.** nized rule had been that of absolute individual property in land, with its corollary of unrestricted competitive or "rack" rents: and this rule was accepted fully

in the national land system, whose basis was reported by Jefferson, as chairman of a committee of the Confederation Congress (1785). The public lands were to be divided into hundreds of ten miles square, each containing one hundred mile-square plots. The hundred was called a "township," and was afterwards reduced to six miles square, of thirty-six mile-square plots of 640 acres each. From time to time principal meridians and east and west base lines have been run, and townships have been determined by their relations to these lines. The sections (plots) have been subdivided, but the transfer describes each parcel from the survey map, as in the case of "the southwest quarter of section 20, township 30, north, range 1 east of the third principal meridian." The price fixed in 1790 as a minimum was two dollars per acre; it has tended to decrease, and no effort has ever been made to gain a revenue from it. When the nation acquired its western territory it secured its title to the soil, and always made it a fundamental condition of the admission of a new State that it should not tax United States lands. To compensate the new States for the freedom of unsold public lands from taxation, one township in each thirty-six was reserved to them for educational purposes; and the excellent public school systems of the Western States have been founded on this provision. The cost of obtaining a quarter section (160 acres), under the still later homestead system of granting lands to actual settlers, has come to be only about twenty-six dollars; the interest on this, at six per cent., represents an annual rent of one cent per acre — making this, says F. A. Walker, as nearly as possible the "no-rent land" of the economists.

201. The bulk of the early westward migration was of

home production ; the great immigration from Europe did
not begin until about 1847 (§ 236). The
west as well as the east thus had its institu-   Immigration.
tions fixed before being called upon to absorb an enormous foreign element.

VIII.

INDUSTRIAL DEVELOPMENT AND SECTIONAL
DIVERGENCE.

1829-50.

202. THE eight years after 1829 have been called "the reign of Andrew Jackson"; his popularity, his long
New political struggle for the presidency, and his feeling of
methods. his official ownership of the subordinate offices gave to his administration at least an appearance of Cæsarism. But it was strictly constitutional Cæsarism; the restraints of written law were never violated, though the methods adopted within the law were new to national politics. Since about 1800 State politics in New York and Pennsylvania had been noted for the systematic use of the offices and for the merciless manner in which the office-holder was compelled to work for the party which kept him in place. The presence of New York and Pennsylvania politicians in Jackson's cabinet taught him to use the same system. Removals, except for cause, had been almost unknown before; but under Jackson men were removed almost exclusively for the purpose of installing some more serviceable party tool; and a clean sweep was made in the civil service. Other parties adopted the system, and it has remained the rule at a change of administration until comparatively recent years (§ 323).

203. The system brought with it a semi-military reorganization of parties.   Hitherto nominations for the more important offices had been made mainly   The new by legislative caucuses; candidates for Presi- organization of dent and Vice-President were nominated by   parties. caucuses of Congressmen, and candidates for the higher State offices by caucuses of the State legislatures.   Late in the preceding period "conventions" of delegates from the members of the party in the State occur in New York and Pennsylvania; and in 1831–32 this became the rule for presidential nominations.   It rapidly developed into systematic State, county, and city "conventions"; and the result was the appearance of that complete political machinery, the American political party, with its local organizations, and its delegates to county, State, and national conventions.   The Democratic machinery was the first to appear, in Jackson's second term (1833–37). Its workers were paid in offices, or hopes of office, so that it was said to be built on the "cohesive power of public plunder"; but its success was immediate and brilliant. The opposing party, the Whig party, had no chance of victory in 1836; and its complete overthrow drove its leaders into the organization of a similar machinery of their own, which scored its first success in 1840.   Since that time these strange bodies, unknown to the law, have governed the country by turns; and their enormous growth has steadily made the organization of a third piece of such machinery more difficult or hopeless.

204. The Bank of the United States had hardly been heard of in politics until the new Democratic organization came into hostile contact with it.   A semi-   Bank of the official demand upon it for a political appoint- United States. ment was met by a refusal; and the party managers

called Jackson's attention to an institution which he could not but dislike the more he considered it. His first message spoke of it in unfriendly terms, and every succeeding message brought a more open attack. The old party of Adams and Clay had by this time taken the name of Whigs, probably from the notion that they were struggling against "the reign of Andrew Jackson," and they adopted the cause of the bank with eagerness. The bank charter did not expire until 1836, but in 1832 Clay brought up a bill for a new charter. It was passed and vetoed (§ 113); and the Whigs went into the presidential election of that year on the veto. They were beaten; Jackson was re-elected; and the bank party could never again get a majority in the house of representatives for the charter. The insistence of the President on the point that the charter was a "monopoly" bore weight with the people. But the President could not obtain a majority in the senate. He determined to take a step which would give him an initiative, and which his opponents could not induce both houses to unite in overriding or punishing. Taking advantage of the provision that the secretary of the treasury might order the public funds to be deposited elsewhere than in the bank or its branches (§ 184), he directed the secretary to deposit *all* the public funds elsewhere. Thus deprived of its great source of dividends, the bank fell into difficulties, became a State bank after 1836, and then went into bankruptcy.

205. All the political conflicts of Jackson's terms of office were close and bitter. Loose in his ideas before 1829, Jackson shows a steady tendency to adopt the strictest construction of the powers of the Federal Government, except in such official perquisites as the offices.

He grew into strong opposition to all traces of the "American system," and vetoed bills for in- Opposition to the "American system." ternal improvements unsparingly; and his feeling of dislike to all terms of protection is as evident, though he took more care not to make it too public. There are many reasons for believing that his drift was the work of a strong school of leaders —Van Buren, Benton, Livingston, Taney, Woodbury, Cass, Marcy, and others —who developed the policy of the party, and controlled it until the great changes of parties about 1850 took their power from them. At all events, some persistent influence made the Democratic party of 1830–50 the most consistent and successful party which had thus far appeared in the United States.

206. Calhoun and Jackson were of the same stock — Scottish-Irish — much alike in appearance and characteristics, the former representing the trained Calhoun and Jackson. and educated logic of the race, the latter its instincts and passions. Jackson was led to break off his friendly relations with Calhoun in 1830, and he had been led to do so more easily because of the appearance of the doctrine of nullification, which was generally attributed, correctly enough, to the authorship of Calhoun. Asserting, as the Republican party of 1798 had done, the sovereign powers of each State, Calhoun held that, as a means of avoiding secession and violent struggle upon every occasion of the passage of an Act of Congress which should seem unconstitutional to any State, the State might properly suspend or "nullify" the operation of the law within its jurisdiction, in order Nullification. to protect its citizens against oppression. Webster, of Massachusetts, and Hayne, of South Caro-.

lina, debated the question in the senate in 1830, and the supporters of each claimed a virtual victory for their leader. The passage of the Tariff Act of 1832, which organized and systematized the protective system, forced the Calhoun party into action. A State convention in South Carolina declared the Tariff Act null and not law or binding on the people of the State, and made ready to enforce the declaration.

207. But the time was past when the power of a single State could withdraw it from the Union. The President issued a proclamation, warning the people of South Carolina against any attempt to carry out the ordinance of nullification ; he ordered a naval force to take possession of Charleston harbor to collect the duties under the Act; he called upon Congress for additional executive powers, and Congress passed what nullifiers called the "bloody bill," putting the land naval forces at the disposal of the President for the collection of duties against "unlawful combinations " ; and he is said to have announced, privately and profanely, his intention of making Calhoun the first victim of any open conflict. Affairs looked so threatening that an unofficial meeting of "leading nullifiers " agreed to suspend the operation of the ordinance until Congress should adjourn; whence it derived the right to suspend has never been stated.

208. The President had already asked Congress to reduce the duties ; and many Democratic members of Congress, who had yielded to the popular clamor for Protection, were very glad to use the "crisis " as an excuse for now voting against it. A compromise Tariff

Tariff of 1833.

Act, scaling down all duties over twenty per cent. by one-tenth of the surplus each year, so as to bring duties to a uniform rate of twenty per cent. in **1843,** was introduced by Clay and became law. Calhoun and his followers claimed this as all that the nullification ordinance had aimed at; and the ordinance was formally repealed. But nullification had received its death-blow; even those southern leaders who maintained the right of secession refused to recognize the right of a State to remain in the Union while nullifying its laws; and, when protection was reintroduced by the tariff of 1842, nullification was hardly thought of.

209. All the internal conditions of the United States were completely altered by the introduction of railways. For twenty years past the Americans had been pushing in every direction which offered *The locomotive engine.* a hope of the means of reconciling vast territory with enormous population. Stephenson's invention of the locomotive came just in time, and Jackson's two terms of office marked the outburst of modern American life. English engines were brought over in 1829, and served as models for a year or two; and then the lighter forms of locomotives, better suited to American conditions, were introduced. The miles of railroad were 23 in 1830, 1098 in 1835, nearly 2000 in 1840, and thereafter they about doubled every five years until 1860.

210. A railway map of 1840 shows a fragmentary system, designed mainly to fill the gaps left by the means of communication in use in 1830. One or two short lines run back into the country from *Railways of 1840.* Savannah and Charleston; another runs north along the coast from Wilmington to Baltimore; several lines connect New York with Washington and other points; and short lines elsewhere mark the openings which needed to be filled at once — a number in New England and the middle States, three in Ohio and Michigan, and three in

Louisiana.   Year after year new inventions came in to
increase and aid this development.   The an-
Anthracite. thracite coal of the middle States had been
known since 1790 (§ 19), but no means had been de-
vised to put the refractory agent to work.   It was now
successfully applied to railroads (1836), and
Iron. to the manufacture of iron (1837).   Hitherto
wood had been the best fuel for iron making; now the
States which relied on wood were driven out of competition, and production was restricted to the States in
which nature had placed coal alongside of iron.   Steam
Ocean naviga- navigation across the Atlantic was established
tion. in 1838.   The telegraph came next, Morse's
The telegraph. line being erected in 1844.   The spread of the
railway system brought with it, as a natural development, the rise of the American system of express companies, whose first phases of individual enterprise
appeared in 1839.   No similar period in American history is so extraordinary for material development as the
decade 1830–40.   At its beginning the country was an
overgrown type of colonial life; at its end American life
had been shifted to entirely new lines, which it has since
followed.   Modern American history had burst in with
the explosiveness of an Arctic summer.

211.   If the steamboat had aided western development,
the railway made it a freshet.   Cities and States grew
Western settle- as if the oxygen of their surroundings had
ment. been suddenly increased.   The steamboat influenced the railway, and the railway gave the steamboat new powers.   Vacant places in the States east of
the Mississippi were filling up; the long lines of emigrant wagons gave way to the new and better methods
of transport; and new grades of land were made ac-

cessible. Chicago was but a frontier fort in 1832; within a half-dozen years it was a flourishing town, with eight steamers connecting it with Buffalo, and dawning ideas of its future development of railway connections. The maps change from decade to decade, as mapmakers hasten to insert new cities which have sprung up. Two new States, Arkansas and Michigan, were admitted (1836 and 1837). The population of Ohio leaps from 900,000 to 1,500,000, that of Michigan from 30,000 to 212,000, and that of the country from 13,000,000 to 17,000,000, between 1830 and 1840.

Admission of Arkansas and Michigan.

212. With the change of material surroundings and possibilities came a steady amelioration of social conditions and a development of social ideals. Such features of the past as imprisonment for debt and the cruel indifference of old methods of dealing with crime began to disappear; the time was past when a State could use an abandoned copper-mine as its State prison. The domestic use of gas and anthracite coal, the introduction of expensive aqueducts for pure water, and the changing life of the people forced changes in the interior and exterior of American dwellings. Wood was still the common building material; imitations of Greek architecture still retained their vogue; but the interiors were models of comfort in comparison with the houses even of 1810. In the "new" regions this was not yet the case, and here social restraints were still so few that society seemed to be reduced almost to its primitive elements. Western steamers reeked with gambling, swindling, duelling, and every variety of vice. Public law was almost suspended in some regions; and organized associations of counterfeiters and horse-thieves terrorized whole sections of country. But this state of

Social conditions.

affairs was altogether temporary, as well as limited in its area; the older and more densely settled States had been well prepared for the change and had never lost command of the social forces, and the process of settling down went on, even in the newer States, with far more rapidity than could reasonably have been expected. Those who took part in the movements of population in 1830–40 had been trained under the rigid forms of the previous American life; and these soon reasserted themselves. The rebound was over before 1847, and the Western States were then as well prepared to receive and digest the great immigration which followed as the older States would have been in 1830.

213. A distinct American literature dates from this period. Most of the publications in the United States were still cheap reprints of foreign works; but native productions no longer followed Literature. foreign models with servility. Between 1830 and 1840 Whittier, Longfellow, Holmes, Poe, Hawthorne, Emerson, Bancroft, and Prescott joined the advance-guard of American writers — Bryant, Dana, Halleck, Drake, Irving, and Cooper; and even those writers who had already made their place in literature showed the influence of new conditions by their growing tendency to look less to foreign models and methods than before 1830. Popular education was improved. The new States had from the first endeavored to secure the best possible system of common schools. The attempt came naturally from the political instincts of the class from which the migration came; but the system which resulted was to be of incalculable service during the years to come. Common school Their absolute democracy and their universal system. use of the English language have made the common

schools most successful machines for converting the raw material of immigration into American citizens. This supreme benefit is the basis of the system and the reason for its existence and development, but its incidental benefit of educating the people has been beyond calculation. It was an odd symptom of the general change that American newspapers Newspapers. took a new form during these ten years. The old "blanket-sheet" newspaper, cumbrous to handle and slow in all its ways, met its first rival in the type of newspaper which appeared first in New York city, in the *Sun*, the *Herald*, and the *Tribune* (1833, 1835, and 1841). Swift and energetic in gathering news, and fearless, sometimes reckless, in stating it, they brought into American life, with very much that is evil, a great preponderance of good.

214. The chaos into which a part of American society had been thrown had a marked effect on the financial institutions of the country, which went to pieces before it for a time. It had not been Land sales. meant to make the public lands of the United States a source of revenue so much as a source of development. The sales had touched their high-water mark during the speculative year 1819, when receipts from them had amounted to $3,274,000; in other years they seldom went above $2,000,000. When the railroad set the stream of migration moving faster than ever, and cities began to grow like mushrooms, it was natual that speculation in land should feel the effects. Sales rose to $3,200,000 in 1831, to $4,000,000 in Speculation. 1833, to $5,000,000 in 1834, to $15,000,000 in 1835, and to $25,000,000 in 1836. In 1835 the President announced to Congress that the public debt was extin-

guished, and that some way of dealing with the surplus should be found. Calhoun's proposal, that after the year 1836 all revenue above $5,000,000 should be divided among the States as a loan, was adopted, though only one such loan was made. The States had already taken a hand in the general speculation by beginning works of public improvement. Foreign, particularly English, capital was abundant; and States which had been accustomed to seek a dozen times over a tax of a hundred thousand dollars now began to negotiate loans of millions of dollars and to appropriate the proceeds to the digging of canals and the construction of railroads. Their enterprises were badly conceived and badly managed, and only added to the confusion when the crash came. If the Federal Government and the States felt that they were rich, the imaginations of individuals ran riot. Every one wanted to buy; prices rose, and every one was growing rich on paper. The assessed value of real estate in New York city in 1832 was $104,000,000; in 1736 it had grown to $253,000,000. In Mobile the assessed value rose from $1,000,000 to $27,000,000. Fictitious values were the rule everywhere.

215. When Jackson (1833) ordered the Government revenues to be deposited elsewhere than in the Bank of the United States (§ 204), there was no Government agent to receive them. The secretary of the treasury selected banks at various points in which the revenue should be deposited by the collecting officers; but these banks were organized under charters from their States, as were all banks except that of the United States. The theory of the dominant party denied the constitutional power of Congress to charter a bank, and the States had not yet learned how

Corporations.

to deal with such institutions. Their grants of bank charters had been based on ignorance, intrigue, favoritism, or corruption, and the banks were utterly unregulated. The democratic feeling was that the privilege of forming banking corporations should be open to all citizens, and it soon became so. Moreover it was not until after the crash that New York began the system of compelling such deposits as would really secure circulation, which was long afterward further developed into the present national bank system. In most of the States banks could be freely organized with or without tangible capital, and their notes could be sent to the West for the purchase of Government lands, which needed to be held but a month or two to gain a handsome profit. "Wildcat banks" sprang up all over the country, and the "pet banks," as those chosen for the deposit of Government revenues were called by their rivals, went into speculation as eagerly as the banks which hardly pretended to have capital.

216. The Democratic theory denied the power of Congress to make anything but gold or silver legal tender. There have been "paper-money heresies" in the party but there were none such among The "specie circular." the new school of Democratic leaders which came in in 1829; they were "hard-money men." In 1836 Jackson's secretary of the treasury ordered land agents to take nothing in payment for lands except gold or silver. In the following spring full effects of the order became evident; they fell on the administration of Van Buren, Jackson's successor. Van Buren had been Jackson's secretary of state, the representative man of the new Democratic school, and, in the opinion of the opposition, the evil genius of the Jackson administration; and it seemed to

the Whigs poetic justice that he should bear the weight of his predecessor's errors. The "specie circular" turned the tide of paper back to the east, and, when it was presented for payment most of the banks suspended specie payment with hardly a struggle. There was no longer a thought of buying; every one wanted to sell; and prices ran down with a rapidity even more startling than that with which they had risen. Failures, to an extent and on a scale unprecedented in the United States,

Panic of 1837. made up the "panic of 1837." Many of the States had left their bonds in the hands of their agents, and, on the failure of the latter, found that the bonds had been hypothecated or disposed of, so that the States got no return from them except a debt which was to them enormous. Saddled suddenly with such a

Repudiation. burden, and unable even to pay interest, many of the States "repudiated" their obligations; and repudiation was made successful by the fact that a State cannot be sued except by its own consent (§ 65). Even the Federal Government felt the strain, for its revenues were locked up in suspended banks. A little more than a year after Congress had authorized the distribution of its surplus revenues among the States, Van Buren was forced to call it into special session to provide some relief for the Government itself.

217. Van Buren held manfully to the strictest construction of the powers of the Federal Government. He insisted that the panic would best right itself without Government interference, and, after a four years' struggle, he succeeded in making the "sub-treasury scheme"

Sub-treasury scheme. law (1840). It cut off all connection of the Government with banks, putting collecting and disbursing officers under bonds to hold money safely and to transfer it under orders from the treasury, and restricting payments to or by the United States to gold and silver. Its passage had been proceeded by another commercial crisis (1839), more limited in its field, but more discouraging to the people. It is true that Jackson, in dealing with the finances, had "simply smashed things," leaving his successor to repair damages; but it is far from certain that this was not the best way available at the time. The wisest scheme of financial reform would have had small chance of success with the land-jobbers in Congress; and Van Buren's firmness found the way out of the chaos.

218. Van Buren's firmness was unpopular; and the Whig party now adopted methods which were popular, if somewhat demagogical. It nominated Harrison in 1840; it contrasted his homely Election of 1840. frontier virtues with Van Buren's "ostentatious indifference to the misfortunes of the people" and with his supposed luxury of his life in the White House; and, after the first of the modern "campaigns" of mass meetings and processions, Harrison was elected. He died soon after his inauguration (1841), and the Vice-President, Tyler, became President. Tyler was of the extreme Calhoun school, which had shown some disposition to grant to Van Buren a support which it had refused to Jackson; and the Whigs had nominated Tyler to retain his faction with them. Now he was the nominal leader of the party, while his politics were opposite to theirs, and the real leader of the party, Clay, was ready to force a quarrel upon him. The quarrel took place; the Whig majority in Congress was not large enough to pass any measures over Tyler's veto; and the first two years of his administration were passed in barren conflict with his party. The "sub-treasury" law was repealed (1841);

the tariff of 1842 introduced a modified protection; and
there the Whigs were forced to stop.   Their dissensions
made democratic success comparatively easy,
Tariff of 1842.
and Tyler had the support of a Democratic
house behind him during the last two years of his term.

219. The success of the Democratic machinery, and
the reflex of its temporary check in 1840, with the influences brought to bear on it by the returning Calhoun
faction, were such as to take the control of the party out
of the hands of the leaders who had formed it.   They
had had high regard for political principle, even though
they were willing to use doubtful methods for its propa-
gation; these methods had now brought out new men,
who looked mainly to success, and to close connection
with the controlling political element of the south as
the easiest means of attaining success.   When the
Democratic convention of 1844 met it was expected to
renominate Van Buren.   A majority of the delegates
had been sent there for that purpose, but many of them
would have been glad to be prevented from doing so.
They allowed a resolution to be passed making a two-
thirds vote necessary for nomination; Van Buren was
unable to command so many votes; and, when his name
was withdrawn, Polk was nominated.   The Whigs nominated Clay.

220. Up to the beginning of the abolitionist movement in the United States, the establishment of the
Abolitionist *Liberator* (1831) and of the American Anti-
movement. Slavery Society (1833) "abolition" had
meant *gradual* abolition; it was a wish rather than a
purpose.   Garrison called for *immediate* abolition.   The
basis of the American system was in the reserved rights
of the States, and slavery rested on their will, which

was not likely to be changed. But the cry was kept up. The mission of the abolitionists was to force the people to think of the question; and, in spite of riots, assaults, and persecution of every kind, they fulfilled it manfully. It was inevitable that, as the northern people were brought unwillingly to think of the question, they should look with new eyes on many of its phases; while in the south many who might dislike slavery were disposed to resist the interferences with State rights which the new proposal involved. In truth, slavery was more and more out of harmony with the new economic conditions which were rapidly taking complete control of the north and west, but had hardly been felt in the south. Thus the two sections, north and south, were more and more disposed to take opposite views of everything in which slavery was involved, and it had a faculty of involving itself in almost everything. The status of slavery in the Territories had been settled in 1820 (§ 197); that of slavery in the States had been settled by the Constitution; but even in minor questions the intrusive element had to be reckoned with. The abolitionists sent their documents through the mails, and the south wished the Federal Government to interfere and stop the practice. The abolitionists persisted in petitioning Congress for the passage of various measures which Congress regarded as utterly unconstitutional; and the disposition of Congress to deny or regulate the right of petition in such matters excited the indignation of northern men who had no sympathy with abolition. But the first occasion on which the views of the two sections came into flat contrast was on the question of the annexation of Texas.

221. The United States had had a vague claim to

Texas until 1819, when the claim was surrendered to
Spain in part compensation for Florida.   On
Texas.
the revolt of Mexico, Texas became a part of
that republic.   It was colonized by Americans, mainly
southerners and slave-holders, and seceded from Mexico
in 1835, defeating the Mexican armies and establishing
its independence.   Southern politicians desired its annexation to the United States for many reasons.   Its
people were kindred to them; its soil would widen the
area of slavery; and its territory, it was hoped, could be
divided into several States, to reinforce the southern
column in the senate.   People in the north were either
indifferent or hostile to the proposal; Van Buren had
declared against it, and his action was the secret reason
for his defeat in the Democratic convention.   On the
other hand, there were indications that the
Oregon.
joint occupation of the Oregon country (§ 192)
could not last much longer.   American immigration into
it had begun, while the Hudson's Bay company, the English tenant of the soil, was the natural enemy of immigration.   To carry the sentiment of both sections, the
two points were coupled; and the Democratic convention
declared for the reannexation of Texas and the reoccupa-
tion of Oregon.

222. One of the cardinal methods of the political
abolitionists was to nominate candidates of their own
against a doubtful friend, even though this
Liberty party.
secured the election of an open enemy.   Clay's
efforts to guard his condemnation of the Texas annexation
project were just enough to push the Liberty party, the
political abolitionists, into voting for candi-
Election of 1844.
dates of their own in New York; on a close
vote their loss was enough to throw the electoral votes

of that State to Polk, and its votes decided the result. Polk was elected (November, 1844); and Texas was annexed to the United States in the following spring. At the next meeting of Congress (1845) Texas was admitted as a State.

Admission of Texas.

223. West of Texas the northern prolongation of Mexico ran right athwart the westward movement of American population; and, though the movement had not yet reached the barrier, the Polk administration desired further acquisitions from Mexico. The western boundary of Texas was undefined; a strip of territory claimed by Texas was settled exclusively by Mexicans; but the Polk administration directed Taylor, the American commander in Texas, to cross the Nueces river and seize the disputed territory. Collisions with Mexican troops followed; they were beaten in the battles of Palo Alto and Resaca de la Palma, and were chased across the Rio Grande. Taylor followed, took the city of Monterey, and established himself far within northern Mexico.

224. On the news of the first bloodshed, Congress declared war against Mexico, over the opposition of the Whigs. A land and naval force took possession of California, and a land expedition occupied New Mexico, so that the authority of Mexico over all the soil north of her present boundaries was abruptly terminated (1846). At the opening of 1847, Taylor fought the last battle in northern Mexico (Buena Vista), defeating the Mexicans, and Scott, with a new army, landed at Vera Cruz for a march upon the city of Mexico. Scott's march was marked by one successful battle after another, usually against heavy odds; and in September he took the capital city and held it

War with Mexico.
Conquest of Pacific coast.
Buena Vista.
Scott's campaign.
Peace.

until peace was made (1848) by the treaty of Guadalupe Hidalgo. Among the terms of peace was the cession of the present State of California and the Territories of Utah, Arizona, and New Mexico, the consideration being a payment of $15,000,000 by the United States and the assumption of some $3,000,000 of debts due by Mexico to American citizens. With a subsequent rectification of frontier (1853), this cession added some 500,000 square miles to the area of the United States; Texas itself made up some 375,000 square miles more. The settlement of the north-west boundary between Oregon and British Columbia (§ 221), giving its own share to each country (1846), with the Texas and Mexican cessions, gave the United States the complete territorial form retained until the annexation of Alaska in 1867.

225. In the new territory slavery had been forbidden under Mexican law; and its annexation brought up the Slavery in the question of its status under American law. new Territory. He who remembers the historical fact that slavery had never been more than a custom, ultimately recognized and protected by State law, will not have much difficulty in deciding about the propriety of forcing such a custom by law upon any part of a territory. But, if slavery was to be excluded from the new territory, the States which should ultimately be formed out of it would enter as free States, inclined to take an anti-slavery view of doubtful questions; and the influence of the south in the senate would be decreased. For the first time the south appears as a distinct *imperium in imperio* in the territorial difficulties which began in 1848.

226. The first appearance of these difficulties brought out in the Democratic party a solution which was so closely in line with the prejudices of the party, and

apparently so likely to meet all the wishes of the south, that it bade fair to carry the party through the crisis without the loss of its southern vote. This "Squatter was "squatter sovereignty," the notion that sovereignty." it would be best for Congress to leave the people of each Territory to settle the question of the existence of slavery for themselves. The broader and democratic ground for the party would have been that which it at first seemed likely to take, — the "Wilmot proviso," a condition proposed to be added to the Act authorizing acquisitions of territory, providing that slavery Wilmot proviso. should be forbidden in all territory to be acquired under the Act. In the end apparent expediency carried the dominant party off to "squatter sovereignty," and the Democratic adherents of the Wilmot proviso, with the Liberty party and the anti-slavery Whigs, united in 1848 under the name of the Free-Soil party. The Whigs had no solution to offer; their entire Free-Soil party. programme, from this time to their downfall as a party, consisted in a persistent effort to evade or ignore all difficulties connected with slavery.

227. Taylor, after the battle of Buena Vista, resigned and came home, considering himself ill-used by the administration. He refused to commit himself to any party; and the Whigs were forced to accept him as their candidate in 1848. The Democrats nominated Cass; and the Free-Soil party or "Free-Soil- Election of 1848. ers," nominated Van Buren. By the vote of the last-named party the Democratic candidate lost New York and the election, and Taylor was elected President. Taking office in 1849, he had on his shoulders the whole burden of the territorial difficulties aggravated by the discovery of gold in California and the sudden rise of popula-

tion there.   Congress was so split into factions that it
could for a long time agree upon nothing; thieves and
outlaws were too strong for the semi-military government
of California; and the people of that Territory, with the
approval of the President, proceeded to form a constitution and apply for admission as a State.   They had so
framed their constitution as to forbid slavery; and this
was really the application of the Wilmot proviso to the
richest part of the new Territory, and the south felt that
it had been robbed of the cream of what it alone had
fought cheerfully to obtain.

228.   The admission of California was not secured until
September, 1850, just after Taylor's sudden death, and
Admission of then only by the addition of a bonus to Texas,
California.   the division of the rest of the Mexican cession
into the Territories of Utah and New Mexico without
mention of slavery, and the passage of a Fugitive Slave
Law.   The slave trade, but not slavery, was forbidden in
the District of Columbia.   The whole was generally
known as the compromise of 1850.   Two of its features
Compromise of need notice.   As has been said, slavery was
1850.   not mentioned in the Act; and the status of
slavery in the Territories was thus left uncertain.   Congress can veto any legislation of a territorial legislature,
but, in fact, the two houses of Congress were hardly ever
able to unite on anything after 1850, and both these Territories did establish slavery before 1860, without a Congressional veto.   The advantage here was with the south.
Fugitive Slave The other point, the Fugitive Slave Law, was
Law.   a special demand of the south.   The Constitution contained clauses directing that ugitive criminals
and slaves should be delivered up, on requisition, by the
State to which they had fled (§ 124).   In the case of

criminals the delivery was directed to be made by the executive of the State to which they had fled; in the case of slaves no delivering authority was specified, and an Act of Congress in 1793 had imposed the duty on Federal judges or on local State magistrates. Some of the States had passed "personal liberty laws," forbidding or limiting the action of their magistrates in such cases; and the Act of 1850 transferred the decision of such cases to United States commissioners, with the assistance of United States marshals. It imposed penalties on rescues, and denied a jury trial. All the ill effects of the law were not felt until a year or two of its operation had passed (§ 244).

Personal liberty laws.

229. The question of slavery had taken up so much time in Congress that its other legislation was comparatively limited. The rates of postage were reduced to five and ten cents for distances less and greater than 300 miles (1845); and the naval school at Annapolis was established the same year. The military school at West Point had been established in 1794. When the Democratic party had obtained complete control of the government, it re-established the "sub-treasury," or independent treasury (1846), which is still the basis of the treasury system. In the same year, after an exhaustive report by Robert J. Walker, Polk's secretary of the treasury, the tariff of 1846 was passed; it reduced duties, and cut out all forms of protection. With the exception of a slight additional reduction of duties in 1857, this remained in force until 1861.

Tariff of 1846.

230. Five States were admitted during the last ten years of this period, — Florida (1845), Texas (1845), Iowa (1846), Wisconsin (1848), and California (1850).

The early entrance of Iowa, Wisconsin, and Florida had been due largely to Indian wars, — the Black Hawk war in Iowa and Wisconsin (1832), and the Seminole war

Admission of Florida, Iowa, and Wisconsin.

in Florida (1835–37), after each of which the defeated Indians were compelled to cede lands as the price of peace. The extinction of Indian titles in northern Michigan brought about the discovery of the great copper fields of that region, whose existence had been suspected long before it could be proved. Elsewhere settlement followed the lines already marked out, except in the new possessions on the Pacific coast, whose full possibilities were not yet

Railways and telegraphs.

known. Railroads in the Eastern States were beginning to show something of a connected system; in the south they had hardly changed since 1840; in the west they had only been prolonged on their original lines. The telegraph, which was to make man master of even the longest and most complicated systems, was brought into use in 1844; but it is not until the census of 1860 that its effects are seen in the fully connected network of railroads which then covers the whole north and west (§ 273).

231. The sudden development of wealth in the country gave an impetus to the spirit of invention. Goodyear's

Invention.

method of vulcanizing rubber (1839) had come into use. M'Cormick had made an invention whose results have been hardly less than that of the locomotive in their importance to the United States. He had patented a reaping-machine in 1834, and this, further improved and supplemented by other inventions, had brought into play the whole system of agricultural machinery whose existence was scarcely known elsewhere until the London " World's Fair " of 1851 brought it into notice. It was agricultural machinery that made western farms profitable and enabled the railroads to fill the west so rapidly (§ 278). A successful sewing-machine came in 1846; the power-loom and the surgical use of anæsthetics in the same year; and the rotary press for printing in 1847.

232. All the conditions of life were changing so rapidly that it was natural that the minds of men should change with them or become unsettled. This was the era of new sects, of communities, of fantastic proposals of every kind, of transcendentalism in literature, religion, and politics. Not the most fantastic or benevolent, but certainly the most successful, of these was the sect of Mormons or Latter-day Saints. They settled in the new Territory of Utah in 1847, calling *The Mormons.* their capital Salt Lake City, and spreading thence through the neighboring Territories. There they have become a menace to the American system; their numbers are so great that it is against American instincts to deprive them of self-government and keep them under a Congressional despotism; while their polygamy and submission to their hierarchy make it impossible to erect them into a State which shall have complete control of marriage and divorce.

233. The material development of the United States since 1830 had been extraordinary, but every year made it more evident that the south was not sharing in it. It is plain now that the fault was *The south.* in the labor system of the south: her only laborers were slaves, and a slave who was fit for anything better than field labor was *prima facie* a dangerous man. The process of divergence had as yet gone only far enough to awaken intelligent men in the south to the fact of its

existence, and to stir them to efforts as hopeless as they were earnest, to find some artificial stimulus for southern industries.   In the next ten years the process was to show its effects on the national field.

IX.

TENDENCIES TO DISUNION.

1850-61.

234. THE abolitionists had never ceased to din the iniquity of slavery into the ears of the American people. Calhoun, Webster, and Clay, with nearly all the other political leaders of 1850, had united Slavery and the sections.
in deploring the wickedness of these fanatics, who were persistently stirring up a question which was steadily widening the distance between the sections. They mistook the symptom for the disease. Slavery itself had put the south out of harmony with its surroundings, and still more out of harmony with the inevitable lines of the country's development. Even in 1850, though they hardly yet knew it, the two sections had drifted so far apart that they were practically two different countries.

235. The case of the south was one of arrested development. The south remained very much as in 1790; while other parts of the country had developed, it had stood still. The remnants of The "slave power."
colonial feeling, of class influence, which advancing democracy had wiped out elsewhere, retained all their force here, aggravated by the effects of an essentially aristocratic system of employment. The ruling class had to maintain a military control over the laboring class, and a class influence over the poorer whites. It had

even secured in the Constitution provision for its political power in the representation given to three-fifths of the slaves. The twenty additional members of the house of representatives were not simply a gain to the south; they were still more a gain to the "black districts," where whites were few, and the slave-holder controlled the district. Slave-owners and slave-holders together, there were but 350,000 of them; but they had common interests, the intelligence to see them, and the courage to contend for them. The first step of a rising man was to buy slaves; and this was enough to enroll him in the dominant class. From it were drawn the representatives and senators in Congress, the governors, and all the holders of offices over which the "slave power," as it came to be called, had control. Not only was the south inert; its ruling class, its ablest and best men, were united in defence of tendencies which were alien and hostile to those of the rest of the country.

236. Immigration into the United States was not an important factor in its development until about 1847. Immigration. The immigrants, so late as 1820, numbered but 8000 per annum; their number did not touch 100,000 until 1842, and then it fell for a year or two almost to half that number. In 1847 it rose again to 235,000, in 1849 to 300,000, and in 1850 to 428,000; all told, more than two and a quarter million persons from abroad settled in the United States between 1847 and 1854. Taking the lowest estimates, — eighty dollars each for the actual amount of money brought in by immigrants, and eight hundred dollars each for their industrial value to the country, — the wealth-increasing influence of such a stream of immigration may be calculated. Its political effects were even greater, and were all in

the same direction. Leaving out the dregs of the immigration, which settled down in the seaboard cities, its best part was a powerful nationalizing force. It had not come to any particular State, but to the United States; it had none of the traditional prejudices in favor of a State, but a strong feeling for the whole country; and the new feelings which it brought in must have had their weight not only on the gross mass of the people, but on the views of former leaders. And all the influences of this enormous immigration were confined to the north and west, whose divergence from the south thus received a new impetus. The immigration avoided slave soil as if by instinct. So late as 1880 the census reports that the Southern States, except Florida, Louisiana, and Texas, are "practically without any foreign element"; but it was only in 1850–60 that this differentiating circumstance began to show itself plainly. And, as the sections began to differ further in aims and policy, the north began to gain heavily in ability to ensure its success.

237. Texas was the last slave State ever admitted; and, as it refused to be divided, the south had no further increase of numbers in the senate. Until The sections in 1850 the admission of a free State had been Congress. so promptly balanced by the admission of a slave State that the senators of the two sections had remained about equal in number; in 1860 the free States had 36 senators, and the slave States only 30. As the representation in the house had changed from 35 free State and 30 slave State members in 1790 to 147 free State and 90 slave State in 1860, and as the electors are the sum of the numbers of senators and representatives, it is evident that political power had passed away from the south in

1850. If at any time the free States should unite they could control the house of representatives and the senate, elect the President and Vice-President, dictate the appointment of judges and other Federal officers, and make the laws what they pleased. If pressed to it, they could even control the interpretation of the laws by the Supreme Court. No Federal judge could be removed except by impeachment (§ 121), but an Act of Congress could at any time increase the number of judges to any extent, and the appointment of the additional judges could reverse the opinion of the court. All the interests of the south depended on the one question whether the free States would unite or not.

238. In circumstances so critical a cautious quiescence and avoidance of public attention was the only safe course Tendencies to for the "slave power," but that course had disunion. become impossible. The numbers interested had become too large to be subject to complete discipline; all could not be held in cautious reserve; and, when an advanced proposal came from any quarter of the slave-holding lines, the whole army was shortly forced up to the advanced position. Every movement of the mass was necessarily aggressive; and aggression meant final collision. If collision came, it must be on some question of the rights of the States; and on such a question the whole south would move as one man. Everything thus tended to disunion.

239. The Protestant churches of the United States had reflected in their organization the spirit of the political Sectarian divis- institutions under which they lived. Acting ion. as purely voluntary associations, they had been organized into governments by delegates, much like the "conventions" which had been evolved in the politi-

cal parties (§ 203). The omnipresent slavery question intruded into these bodies, and split them. The Baptist Church was thus divided into a northern and a southern branch in 1845, and the equally powerful Methodist Church met the same fate the following year. Two of the four great Protestant bodies were thus no longer national; it was only by the most careful management that the integrity of the Presbyterian Church was maintained until 1861, when it also yielded; and only the Episcopal and Roman Catholic Churches retained their national character. If the process of disruption did not extend to other sects, it was because they were already mainly northern or mainly southern.

240. The political parties showed the same tendency. Each began to shrivel up in one section or the other. The notion of "squatter sovereignty" attractive at first to the western democracy, and not repu- *Party changes.* diated by the south, enabled the Democratic party to pass the crisis of 1850 without losing much of its northern vote, while southern Whigs began to drift in, making the party continually more pro-slavery. This could not continue long without beginning to decrease its northern vote, but this effect did not become plainly visible until after 1852. The efforts of the Whig party to ignore the great question alienated its anti-slavery members in the north, while they did not satisfy its southern members. The Whig losses were not at first heavy, but, as the electoral vote of each State is determined by the barest plurality of the popular vote, they were enough to defeat the party almost everywhere in the presidential election of 1852. The Whigs nominated Scott *Election of 1852.* and the Democrats Pierce; and Pierce carried all but four of the thirty-one States, and was elected. This

revelation of hopeless weakness was the downfall of the Whig party; it maintained its organization for four years longer, but the life had gone out of it. The future was with the Free-Soil party, though it had polled but few votes in 1852.

241. During the administration of Taylor (and Vice-President Fillmore, who succeeded him) Clay, Webster, Changes in Calhoun, Polk, and Taylor were removed by leadership. death, and there was a steady drift of other political leaders out of public life. New men were pushing in everywhere, and in both sections they showed the prevailing tendency to disunion. The best of them were unprecedentedly radical. Sumner, Seward, and Chase came into the senate, bringing the first accession of recognized force and ability to the anti-slavery feeling in that body. The new southern men, such as Davis, and the Democratic recruits from the southern Whig party, such as Stephens, were ready to take the ground on which Calhoun had always insisted, — that Congress was bound not merely to the negative duty of not attacking slavery in the Territories, but to the positive duty of protecting it. This, if it should become the general southern position, was certain to destroy the notion of squatter sovereignty (§ 226), and thus to split the Democratic party, which was almost the last national ligament that now held the two fragments of the Union together.

242. The social disintegration was as rapid. Northern men travelling in the south were naturally looked upon Social diver- with increasing suspicion, and were made to gence. feel that they were on a soil alien in sympathies. Some of the worst phases of democracy were called into play in the south; and, in some sections, law openly yielded supremacy to popular passion in the cases

of suspected abolitionists. Southern conventions, on all sorts of subjects, became common; and in these meetings, permeated by a dawning sense of southern nationality, hardly any proposition looking to southern independence of the north was met with disfavor. In State elections a distinctly disunion element appeared; and, though it was defeated, the majority did not deny the right of secession, only its expediency.

243. Calhoun, in his last and greatest speech, called attention to the manner in which one tie after another was snapping. But he ignored the real peril Progress of disunion. of the situation — its dangerous facts: that the south was steadily growing weaker in comparison with the north, and more unable to secure a wider area for the slave system; that it was therefore being steadily forced into demanding active Congressional protection for slavery in the Territories; that the north would never submit to this; and that the south must submit to the will of the majority or bring about a collision by attempting to secede.

244. Anti-slavery feeling in the north was stimulated by the manner in which the Fugitive Slave Law (§ 228) was enforced immediately after 1850. The Fugitive Slave Law. chase after fugitive slaves was prosecuted in many cases with circumstances of revolting brutality, and features of the slave system which had been tacitly looked upon as fictitious were brought home to the heart of the free States. The added feeling showed Kansas-Nebraska Act. its force when the Kansas-Nebraska Act was passed by Congress (1854). It organized the two new Territories of Kansas and Nebraska. Both of them were forever free soil by the terms of the Missouri compromise (§ 197). But the success of the notion of squatter

sovereignty in holding the Democratic party together
while destroying the Whig party had intoxicated Douglas
and other northern Democrats; and they now applied the
doctrine to these Territories. They did not desire "to
vote slavery up or down," but left the decision to the
people of the two Territories.

245. This was the grossest political blunder in American
history. The status of slavery had been settled, by the
Constitution or by the compromises of 1820 or 1850, on
every square foot of American soil; right or wrong, the
settlement was made. The Kansas-Nebraska Act took a
great mass of territory out of the settlement and flung it
into the arena as a prize for which the sections were to
struggle; and the struggle always tended to force, as the
only arbiter. The first result of the Act was to throw
The "American parties into chaos. An American or "Know-
party." Nothing" party, a secret oath-bound organization, pledged to oppose the influence or power of foreign-
born citizens, had been formed to take the place of the
defunct Whig party. It had been quite successful in
State elections for a time, and was now beginning to have
larger aspirations. It, like the Whig party, intended to
ignore slavery, but, after a few years of life, the questions
complicated with slavery entered its organization and
divided it also. Even in 1854 many of its leaders in the
north were forced to take position against the Kansas-
Nebraska Act, while hosts of others joined in the opposition without any party organization. No American
party ever rose so swiftly as this latter; with no other
The Republican party name than the awkward title of "Anti-
party. Nebraska men," it carried the Congressional
elections of 1854 at the north, forced many of the former
Know-Nothing leaders into union with it, and controlled

the house of representatives of the Congress which met in 1855. The Democratic party, which had been practically the only party since 1852, had now to face the latest and strongest of its broad-constructionist opponents, one which with the nationalizing features of the Federal and Whig parties combined democratic feelings and methods, and, above all, had a democratic purpose at bottom. It acknowledged, at first, no purpose aimed at slavery, only an intention to exclude slavery from the Territories; but, under such principles, it was the only party which was potentially an anti-slavery party, the only party to which the enslaved laborer of the south could look with the faintest hope of aid in reaching the status of a man. The new party had grasped the function which belonged of right to its great opponent, and it seized with it its opponent's original title. The name Democrat had quite taken the place of that first used — Republican (§ 150), but the latter had never passed out of popular remembrance and liking at the north. The new party took quick and skilful advantage of this by assuming the old name, and early in 1856 the two great parties of the next thirty years — the Democratic and Republican parties — were drawn up against one another.

246. The foreign relations of the United States during Pierce's term of office were overshadowed by the domestic difficulties, but were of importance. In the Koszta case (1853) national protec- Koszta case. tion had been afforded on foreign soil to a person who had only taken the preliminary steps to naturalization. Japan had been opened to American inter- course and commerce (1854). But the ques- Japan. tion of slavery was more and more thrusting itself into foreign relations. A great southern republic, to

be founded at first by the slave States, but to take in gradually the whole territory around the Gulf of Mexico and include the West Indies, was soon to be a pretty general ambition among slave-holders, and its first phases appeared during Pierce's administration. Efforts were begun to obtain Cuba from Spain; and the three leading American ministers abroad, meeting at Ostend,

Ostend mani-　united in declaring the possession of Cuba to
festo.　　　be essential to the well-being of the United
Filibustering. States (1854). "Filibustering" expeditions against Cuba or the smaller South American states, intended so to revolutionize them as to lay a basis for an application to be annexed to the United States, became common, and taxed the energies of the Federal Government for their prevention. All these, however, yielded in interest and importance to the affairs in Kansas.

247. Nebraska was then supposed to be a desert, and attention was directed almost exclusively to Kansas.

Kansas　　No sooner had its organization left the matter of slavery to be decided by its "people" than the anti-slavery people of the north and west felt it to be their duty to see that the "people" of the Territory should be anti-slavery in sympathy. Emigrant associations were formed, and these shipped men and families to Kansas, arming them for their protection in the new country. Southern newspapers called for similar meas-ures in the south, but the call was less effective. South-ern men without slaves, settling a new State, were un-comfortably apt to prohibit slavery, as in California. Only slave-holders were trusty pro-slavery men; and such were not likely to take slaves to Kansas, and risk their ownership on the result of the struggle. But for the people of Missouri, Kansas would have been free soil at once. Lying across the direct road to Kansas, the Missouri settlers blockaded the way of free-state settlers, crossed into Kansas, and voted profusely at the first Territorial election. Their votes chose a Territorial legislature which gave a complete code of slave laws to the Territory. Passing to the north of Missouri the "free-state settlers" entered Kansas to find that their opponents had secured the first position. This brought out the fundamental difference between a Territory — under the absolute control of Congress and only privileged in certain branches of legislation — and a State with complete jurisdiction over its own affairs. Finding themselves cut off from control of the former, the free-state settlers determined to attempt to substitute the latter. They organized a State Free-state government (1855), and applied for admission by Congress. Such irregular erections of States had been known before; and, though they were confessedly not binding until confirmed by Congress, the Democratic party had always been tender with them, and prone to seek a compromise with them. A symptom of the process which had been making the Democratic party pro-slavery was seen in the attitude which the Democratic administration now took towards the inchoate State of Kansas. Never thinking of compromise, it pounced on the new organization, scattered it, arrested its leaders, and expressed a hesitating desire to try them for treason (1856). Nevertheless, the free-state settlers gave no further obedience to the Territorial Government, as the pro-slavery settlers refused to recognize the pseudo-state Government, and the struggle passed into a real civil war, the two powers mustering considerable armies, fighting battles, capturing towns,

and paroling prisoners. The struggle was really over in
1857, and the south was beaten. It could not compete
with the resources and enthusiasm of the other section;
its settlers were not unanimous, as their opponents were;
and the anti-slavery settlers were in a great majority.
There were, however, all sorts of obstacles yet to be
overcome before the new State of Kansas was recognized
by Congress, after the withdrawal of the senators of the
seceding States (1861).

248. In the heat of the Kansas struggle came the
presidential election of 1856. The Democrats nominated
Buchanan, declaring, as usual, for the strictest
limitation of the powers of the Federal Government on a number of points specified, and reaffirming
the principle of the Kansas-Nebraska Act — the settlement of slavery by the people of the Territory. The
remnant of the Whig party, including the Know-Nothings
of the north and those southern men who wished no
further discussion of slavery, nominated the President
who had gone out of office in 1853, Fillmore. The Republican party nominated Fremont; the bulk of its
manifesto was taken up with protests against attempts
to introduce slavery into the Territories; but it showed
its broad-construction tendencies by declaring for appropriations of public moneys for internal improvements.
The Democrats were successful in electing Buchanan;
but the position of the party was quite different from the
triumph with which it had come out of the election of
1852. It was no longer master of twenty-seven of the
thirty-one States; all New England and New York,
all the north-west, but Indiana and Illinois, all the free
States but five, had gone against it; its candidate no
longer had a majority of the popular vote, but was chosen

Election of 1856.

by a majority of the electoral votes; and it had before it a party with nearly as many popular votes as its own, the control of most of the strongest section of the Union, and an enthusiasm which was more dangerous still. For the first time in the history of the country a distinctly anti-slavery candidate had obtained an electoral vote, and had even come near obtaining the presidency. Fillmore had carried but one State, Maryland; Buchanan had carried the rest of the south, with a few States in the north, and Fremont the rest of the north and none of the south. If things had gone so far that the two sections were to be constituted into opposing political parties, it was evident that the end was near.

249. Oddly enough the constitutionality of the compromise of 1820 (§ 197) had never happened to come before the Supreme Court for consideration. The Dred Scott In 1856–57 it came up for the first time. decision. One Dred Scott, a Missouri slave who had been taken to the territory covered by the compromise, and had therefore sued for his freedom, was sold to a citizen of another State. Scott then transferred his suit from the State to the Federal courts, under the power given to them to try suits between citizens of different States, and the case came by appeal to the Supreme Court. Its decision was announced at the beginning of Buchanan's administration. It put Scott out of court on the ground that a slave, or the descendant of slaves, could not be a citizen of the United States or have any standing in Federal courts. The opinion of the chief-justice went on to attack the validity of the Missouri compromise, for the reasons that one of the constitutional functions of Congress was the protection of property; that slaves had been recognized as property by the Constitution;

and that Congress was bound to protect, not to prohibit, slavery in the Territories. The mass of the northern people held that slaves were looked on by the Constitution, not as property, but as " persons held to service or labor " by State laws; that the constitutional function of Congress was the protection of liberty as well as property; and that Congress was thus bound to prohibit, not to protect, slavery in the Territories. Another step in the road to disunion was thus taken, as the only peaceful interpreter of the Constitution was pushed out of the way. The north flouted the decision of the Supreme Court, and the storm of angry dissent which it aroused did the disunionists good service at the south. From this time the leading newspapers in the south maintained that the radical southern view first advanced by Calhoun, and but slowly accepted by other southern leaders, as to the duty of Congress to protect slavery in the Territories, had been confirmed by the Supreme Court; that the northern Republicans had rejected it; and that even the squatter sovereignty theory of northern Democrats could no longer be submitted to by the south.

250. The population of the United States in 1860 was over 31,000,000, an increase of more than 8,000,000 in ten years. As the decennial increase of population became larger, so did the divergence of the sections in population, and still more in wealth and resources. Two more free States came in during this period, — Minnesota (1858) and Oregon (1859), — and Kansas was clamoring loudly for the same privilege. The free and slave States, which had been almost equal in population in 1790, stood now as 19 to 12. And of the 12,000,000 in slave States, the 4,000,000 slaves and the 250,000 free blacks were not so much

Admission of Minnesota and Oregon.

a factor of strength as a possible source of weakness and danger. No serious slave rising had ever taken place in the south; but the sudden flaming out of John Brown's insurrection (1859), and the alarm John Brown's which it carried through the south, were raid. tokens of a danger which added a new horror to the chances of civil war. It was not wonderful that men, in the hope of finding some compromise by which to avoid such a catastrophe, should be willing to give up everything but principle and even to trench sharply upon principle itself, nor that offers of compromise should urge southern leaders farther into the fatal belief that "the north would not fight."

251. Northern Democrats, under the lead of Douglas, had been forced already almost to the point of revolt by the determination of southern senators to prevent the admission of Kansas as a free State, if not to secure her admission as a slave State. When the Division of Democratic convention of 1860 met at Charles- the Democratic ton, the last strand of the last national polit- party. ical organization parted; the Democratic party itself was split at last by the slavery question. The southern delegates demanded a declaration in favor of the duty of Congress to protect slavery in the Territories. It was all that the Douglas Democrats could then do to maintain themselves in a few northern States; such a declaration meant political suicide everywhere, and they voted it down. The convention divided into two bodies. The southern body adjourned to Richmond, and the northern and border State convention to Baltimore. Here the northern delegates, by seating some delegates friendly to Douglas, provoked a further secession of border State delegates, who, in company with the Rich-

mond body, nominated Breckinridge and Lane for President and Vice-President. The remainder of the original convention nominated Douglas and H. V. Johnson.

252. The remnant of the old Whig and Know-Nothing parties, now calling itself the Constitutional Union party,

Constitutional Union party. met at Baltimore and nominated Bell and Everett. The Republican convention met at

Republican party. Chicago. Its "platform" of 1856 had been somewhat broad constructionist in its nature and leanings, but a strong Democratic element in the party had prevented it from going too far in this direction. The election of 1856 had shown that, with the votes of Pennsylvania and Illinois, the party would then have been successful, and the Democratic element was now ready to take almost anything which would secure the votes of these States. This state of affairs will go to explain the nomination of Lincoln of Illinois, for President, with Hamlin, a former Democrat, for Vice-President, and the declaration of the platform in favor of a protective tariff. The mass of the platform was still devoted to the necessity of excluding slavery from the Territories. To sum up : the Bell party wished to have

The parties and slavery in the Territories. no discussion of slavery ; the Douglas Democrats rested on squatter sovereignty and the compromise of 1850, but would accept the decision of the Supreme Court; the Republicans demanded that Congress should legislate for the prohibition of slavery in the Territories ; and the southern Democrats demanded that Congress should legislate for the protection of slavery in the Territories.

253. No candidate received a majority of the popular vote, Lincoln standing first and Douglas second. But Lincoln and Hamlin had a clear majority of the elec-

toral vote, and so were elected, Breckinridge and Lane coming next. It is worthy of mention that, up to the last hours of Lincoln's first term of office, Congress would always have contained a majority opposed to him but for the absence of the members from the seceding States. The interests of the south and even of slavery were thus safe enough under an anti-slavery President. But the drift of events was too plain. Nullification had come and gone, and the nation feared it no longer. Even secession by a single State was now almost out of the question; the letters of southern governors in 1860, in consultation on the state of affairs, agree that no State would secede without assurances of support by others. If this crisis were allowed to slip by without action, even a sectional secession would soon be impossible. If secession were a right, it must be asserted now or never.

Election of 1860.

254. Some assurance of united action must have been obtained, for South Carolina ventured into secession. The Democratic revolution which, since 1829, had compelled the legislatures to give the choice of presidential electors (§ 119) to the people of the States had not effected South Carolina; her electors were still chosen by the legislature. That body, on the election day of November, 1860, having chosen the State's electors, remained in session until the telegraph had brought assurances that Lincoln had secured a sufficient number of electors to ensure his election; it then summoned a State convention and adjourned. The State convention, which is a legislative body chosen for a special purpose, met December 20, and unanimously passed an "ordinance of secession," repealing the Acts by which the State had ratified the Constitution and its

Secession.

amendments (§ 108), and dissolving "the Union now subsisting between South Carolina and other States, under the name of the United States of America." The convention took all steps necessary to make the State ready for war, and adjourned. Similar ordinances were passed by conventions in Mississippi (January 9, 1861), Florida (January 10), Alabama (January 11), Georgia (January 18), Louisiana (January 23), and Texas (February 1).

255. The opposition in the south did not deny the right to secede, but the expediency of its exercise. The argument for secession. Their effort was to elect delegates to the State conventions who would vote not to secede. They were beaten, says A. H. Stephens, by the cry that the States "could make better terms out of the Union than in it." That is, the States were to withdraw individually, suspend the functions of the Federal Government within their jurisdiction for the time, consider maturely any proposals for guaranties for their rights in the Union, and return as soon as satisfactory guaranties should be given. A second point to be noted is the difference between the notions of a State convention prevalent in the north and in the south. Action at the State conventions. The Northern State convention was generally considered as a preliminary body, whose action was not complete or valid until ratified by a popular vote. The Southern State convention was looked upon as the incarnation of the sovereignty of the State, and its action was not supposed to need a popular ratification. When the conventions of the seceding States had adopted the ordinances of secession, they proceeded to other business. They appointed delegates, who met at Montgomery, the capital of Alabama, Feb-

ruary 4, formed a provisional Constitution for the "Confederate States," chose a provisional President and Vice-President (Jefferson Davis and A. H. Stephens), and established an army, treasury, and other exec- The "Confederutive departments. The President and Vice- ate States." President were inaugurated February 18. The permanent Constitution, adopted in March, was copied from that of the United States, with variations meant to maintain State sovereignty, to give the cabinet seats in Congress, to prevent the grant of bounties or any protective features in the tariff or the maintenance of internal improvements at general expense, and to "recognize and protect" "the institution of negro slavery, as it now exists in the Confederate States."

256. Under what claim of constitutional right all this was done passes comprehension. That a State convention should have the final power of decision Constitutional on the question which it was summoned to rights. consider is quite as radical doctrine as has yet been heard of; that a State convention, summoned to consider the one question of secession, should go on, with no appeal to any further popular authority or mandate, to send delegates to meet those of other States and form a new national Government, which could only exist by warring on the United States, is a novel feature in American constitutional law. It was revolution or nothing. Only in Texas, where the call of the State convention was so irregular that a popular vote could hardly be escaped, was any popular vote allowed. Elsewhere, the functions of the voter ceased when he voted for delegates to the State convention; he could only look on helplessly while that body went on to constitute him a citizen of a new nation of which he had not dreamed when he voted.

257. The border States were in two tiers — North Carolina, Tennessee, and Arkansas, next to the seceding States, and Delaware, Maryland, Virginia, Kentucky, and Missouri next to the free States. None of these were willing to secede. There was, however, one force which might draw them into secession. A State which did not wish to secede, but believed in State sovereignty and the abstract right of secession, would be inclined to take up arms to resist any attempt by the Federal Government to coerce a seceding State. In this way, in the following spring, the original seven seceding States, were reinforced by four of the border States (§ 267), making their final number eleven.

The border States.

258. In the north and west surprisingly little attention was given to the systematic course of procedure along the Gulf. The people of these sections were very busy; they had heard much of this talk before, and looked upon it as a kind of stage-thunder, the inevitable accompaniment of recent presidential elections; and they expected the difficulty to be settled in some way. Republican politicians, with the exception of a few, were inclined to refrain from public declarations of intention. Some of them, such as Seward, showed a disposition to let the "erring sisters" depart in peace, expecting to make the loss good by accessions from Canada. A few, like Chandler, believed that there would be "blood-letting," but most of them were still doubtful as to the future. Democratic politicians were hide-bound by their repetition of the phrase "voluntary Union" (§ 180); they had not yet hit upon the theory which carried the War Democrats through the final struggle, that the sovereign State of New York could

Feeling in the north.

make war upon the sovereign State of South Carolina for the unfriendly act of secession, and that the war was waged by the non-seceding against the seceding States. President Buchanan publicly condemned the doctrine of secession, though he added a confession of his inability to see how secession was to be prevented if a State should be so wilful as to attempt it. Congress did nothing, except to admit Kansas as a free State and adopt the protective Morrill tariff (§ 276); even after its members from the seceding States had withdrawn, those who remained made no preparations for conflict, and, at their adjournment in March, 1861, left the Federal Government naked and helpless before its enemies.

Admission of Kansas.

Morrill tariff of 1861.

259. The only sign of life in the body politic, the half-awakened word of warning from the democracy of the north and west, was its choice of governors of States. A remarkable group of men, soon to be known as the "war governors," — Washburn of Maine, Fair-banks of Vermont, Goodwin of New Hamp-shire, Andrew of Massachusetts, Sprague of Rhode Island, Buckingham of Connecticut, Morgan of New York, Olden of New Jersey, Curtin of Pennsylvania, Dennison of Ohio, Morton of Indiana, Yates of Illinois, Blair of Michigan, Randall of Wisconsin, Kirkwood of Iowa, and Ramsey of Minnesota, — held the executive powers of the North-ern States in 1861–62. Some of these governors, such as Andrew and Buckingham, as they saw the struggle come nearer, went so far as to order the purchase of warlike material for their States on their private responsibility, and their action saved days of time. And at all times they were admirably prompt, methodical, clear-sighted, and intensely devoted to their one duty.

The "war gov-ernors."

260. The little army of the United States had been almost put out of consideration; wherever its detachments could be found in the south they were surrounded and forced to surrender and to be transferred to the north. After secession, and in some of the States even before it, the forts, arsenals, mints, custom-houses, shipyards, and public property of the United States had been

Seizure of United States property.

seized by the authority of the State, and these were held until transferred to the new Confederate States organization. In the first two months of 1861 the authority of the United States was paralyzed in seven States, and in at least seven more its future authority seemed of very doubtful duration.

261. Only a few forts, of all the magnificent structures with which the nation had dotted the southern coast,

Position of the remaining forts.

remained to it — the forts near Key West, Fortress Monroe at the mouth of Chesapeake Bay, Fort Pickens at Pensacola, and Fort Sumter in Charleston harbor. Both the last-named were beleaguered by hostile batteries, but the administration of President Buchanan, intent on maintaining the peace until the new administration should come in, instructed their commanding officers to refrain from any acts tending to open conflict. The Federal officers, therefore, were obliged to look idly on while every preparation was made for their destruction, and even while a vessel bearing supplies for Fort Sumter was driven back by the batteries between it and the sea.

262. The divergence between the two sections of the country had thus passed into disunion, and was soon to

Slavery and disunion.

pass into open hostility. The legal recognition of the custom of slavery, acting upon and reacted upon by every step in their economic development and every difference in their natural characteristics, sur-roundings, and institutions, had carried north and south further and faster apart, until the elements of a distinct nationality had appeared in the latter. Slavery had had somewhat the same effect on the south that democracy had had on the colonies. In the latter case the aristoc-racy of the mother country had made a very feeble struggle to maintain the unity of its empire. It remained to be seen, in the American case, whether democracy would do better.

THE CIVIL WAR.

1861-65.

263. SECESSION had taken away many of the men who had for years managed the Federal Government, and who understood its workings. Lincoln's party was in power for the first time; his officers were new to the routine of Federal administration; and the circumstances with which they were called upon to deal were such as to daunt any

Embarrassments of the Government.

spirit. The Government had become so nearly bankrupt in the closing days of Buchanan's administration that it had only escaped by paying double interest, and that by the special favor of the New York banks, which obtained in return the appointment of Dix as secretary of the treasury. The army had been almost broken up by the captures of men and material and by resignations of competent and trusted officers. The navy had come to such a pass that, in February, 1861, a house committee reported that only two vessels, one of twenty, the other of two guns, were available for the defence of the entire Atlantic coast. And, to complicate all difficulties, a horde of clamorous office-seekers crowded Washington.

264. Before many weeks of Lincoln's administration had passed, the starting of an expedition to provision Fort Sumter brought on an attack by the batteries around

the fort, and, after a bombardment of thirty-six hours, the fort surrendered (April 14, 1861). It is not necessary to rehearse the familiar story of the outburst of feeling which followed this event and the proclamation of President Lincoln calling for volunteers, the mustering of men, the eagerness of States, cities, and villages to hurry volunteers forward and to supply money to their own Government in its need. The 75,000 volunteers called for were supplied three or four times over, and those who were refused felt the refusal as a personal deprivation.

Surrender of Fort Sumter. Rising in the north.

265. There had been some belief in the south that the north-west would take no part in the impending conflict, and that its people could be persuaded to keep up friendly relations with the new nationality until the final treaty of peace should establish all the fragments of the late Union upon an international basis. In the spring months of 1861 Douglas, who had been denounced as the tool of the southern slave-holders, was spending the closing days of life in expressing the determination of the north-west that it would never submit to have "a line of custom-houses" between it and the ocean. The batteries which Confederate authority was erecting on the banks of the Mississippi were fuel to the flame. Far-off California, which had been considered neutral by all parties, pronounced as unequivocally for the national authority.

The north-west.

266. The shock of arms put an end to opposition in the south as well. The peculiar isolation of life in the south precluded the more ignorant voter from any comparisons of the power of his State with any other; to him it was almost inconceivable that his State should own or have a superior. The better

"Following the States."

educated men, of wider experience, had been trained to think State sovereignty the foundation of civil liberty, and, when their State spoke, they felt bound to "follow their State." The President of the Confederate States issued his call for men, and it was also more than met. On both sides of the line armed men were hurrying to a meeting.

267. Lincoln's call for troops met with an angry reception wherever the doctrine of State sovereignty had

The border States. a foothold. The governors of the border States (§ 257) generally returned it with a refusal to furnish any troops. Two States, North Carolina and Arkansas, seceded and joined the Confederate States. In two others, Virginia and Tennessee, the State politicians formed "military leagues" with the Confederacy, allowing Confederate troops to take possession of the States, and then submitted the question of secession to "popular vote." The secession of these States was thus accomplished, and Richmond became the Confederate capital. The same process was attempted in Missouri, but failed, and the State remained loyal. The politician class in Maryland and Kentucky took the extraordinary course of attempting to maintain neutrality; but the growing power of the Federal Government soon enabled the people of the two States to resume control of their governments and give consistent support to the Union. Kentucky, however, had troops in the Confederate armies; and one of her citizens, the late Vice-President, John C. Breckinridge, left his place in the senate and became an officer in the Confederate service. Delaware cast her lot from the first with the Union.

268. The first blood of the war was shed in the streets

of Baltimore, when a mob attempted to stop Massachusetts troops on their way to Washington (April 19). For a time there was difficulty Civil War. in getting troops through Maryland because of the active hostility of a part of its people, but this was overcome, and the national capital was made secure. The Confederate lines had been pushed up to Manassas Junction, about thirty miles from Washington. When Congress, called into special session by the President for July 4, came together, the outline of the Confederate States had been fixed. Their line of defence held the left bank of the Potomac from Fortress Monroe nearly to Washington; thence, at a distance of some thirty miles from the river, to Harper's Ferry; thence through the mountains of western Virginia and the southern part of Kentucky, crossing the Mississippi a little below Cairo; thence through southern Missouri to the eastern border of Kansas; and thence south-west through the Indian Territory and along the northern boundary of Texas to the Rio Grande. The length of the line, including also the Atlantic and Gulf coasts, has been estimated at 11,000 miles. The territory within it comprised about 800,000 square miles, with a population of over 9,000,000 and great natural resources. Its cotton was almost essential to the manufactories of the world; in exchange for it every munition of war could be procured; and it was hardly possible to blockade The blockade. a coast over 3000 miles in length, on which the blockading force had but one port of refuge, and that about the middle of the line. Nevertheless President Lincoln issued his proclamation announcing the blockade of the southern coast, a proclamation from President Davis appearing with it, offering letters of marque and reprisal against the commerce of the United States to private vessels. The news brought out proclamations of neutrality from Great Britain and France, and, according to subsequent decisions of the Supreme Court, made the struggle a civil war, though the minority held that this did not occur legally until the Act of Congress of July 13, 1861, authorizing the President, in case of insurrection, to shut up ports and suspend commercial intercourse with the inhabitants of the revolted district.

269. The President found himself compelled to assume powers never granted to the executive authority, trusting to the subsequent action of Congress to validate his action. He had to raise and support armies and navies; he even had to authorize seizures of necessary property, of railroad and telegraph lines, arrests of suspected persons, and Suspension of the suspension of the writ of *habeas corpus* in *habeas corpus.* certain districts. Congress supported him, and proceeded in 1863 to give the President power to suspend the writ anywhere in the United States, which he proceeded to do (§ 115). The Supreme Court, after the war, decided that no branch of the Government had power to suspend the writ in districts where the courts were open, — that the *privilege* of the writ might be suspended as to persons properly involved in the war, but that the writ was still to issue, the court deciding whether the person came within the classes to whom the suspension applied. This decision, however, did not come until "arbitrary arrests," as they were called, had been a feature of the entire war. A similar suspension of the writ took place in the Confederate States.

270. When Congress met (July 4, 1861), the absence of southern members had made it heavily Republican.

It decided to consider no business but that connected with the war, authorized a loan and the raising of 500,000 volunteers, and made confiscation of property a penalty of rebellion. While it was in session the first serious battle of the war — Bull Run, or Manassas — took place (July 21), and resulted in the defeat of the Federal army. Both armies were as yet so ill-trained that the victors gained nothing from their success. In the west the battle of Wilson's Creek, near Springfield, Mo. (August 10), was either a drawn battle or a Confederate victory; but here also the victors rather lost than gained ground after it. The captures of Fort Hatteras, N. C. (August 29), and Port Royal, S. C. (November 7), gave the blockading fleets two important harbors of refuge. The over-zealous action of a naval officer in taking the Confederate envoys Mason and Slidell out of a British mail-steamer sailing between two neutral ports almost brought about a collision between the United States and Great Britain in November. But the American precedents were all against the United States (§ 172), and the envoys were given up.

271. General McClellan, in the early months of the war, had led a force of western troops across the Ohio river, entered western Virginia, and beaten the Confederate armies in several battles. After the battle of Bull Run he was called to Washington and put in command of all the armies on the retirement of Scott. His genius for organization, and the unbounded confidence of the people in him, enabled him to form the troops at and near Washington into the first great army of the war — the army of the

Potomac. It was held, however, too much in idleness to
suit the eagerness of the people and the administration;
and the dissatisfaction grew louder as the winter of
1861–62 passed away without any forward movement
(§ 284).

272. If the army was idle, Congress was not. The
broad-construction tendencies of the party showed themselves more plainly as the war grew more serious; there
was an increasing disposition to cut every knot by legislation, with less regard to the constitutionality of the
legislation. A paper currency, commonly
known as "green-backs," was adopted and
made legal tender (February 25, 1862). The
first symptoms of a disposition to attack slavery appeared : slavery was prohibited in the District of Columbia and the Territories; the army was forbidden to
surrender escaped slaves to their owners : and slaves of
insurgents were ordered to be confiscated. In addition
to a Homestead Act, giving public lands to actual settlers
at reduced rates (§ 200), Congress began a further development of the system of granting public lands to railway
corporations.

Paper currency.

Slavery.

273. The railway system of the United States was but
twenty years old in 1850 (§ 230), but it had become to
assume some consistency. The day of short
and disconnected lines had passed, and the
connections which were to develop into railway systems
had appeared. Consolidation of smaller companies had
begun; the all-rail route across the State of New York
was made up of more than a dozen original companies at
its consolidation in 1853. The Erie railway was formed
in 1851; and another western route—the Pennsylvania
—was formed in 1854. These were at least the germs

Railways in 1850.

of great trunk lines (§ 312). The cost of American railways has been only from one-half to one-fourth of the cost of European railways; but an investment in a far western railway in 1850–60 was an extra-hazardous risk. Not only did social conditions make any form of business hazardous; the new railway often had to enter a territory bare of population, and there create its own towns, farms, and traffic. Whether it could do so was so doubtful as to make additional inducements to capital necessary. The means attempted by Congress in 1850, in the case of the Illinois Central Railroad, was to grant public lands to the corporation, reserving to the United States the alternate sections. The Land grants. expectation was that the railway, for the purpose of building up traffic, would sell lands to actual settlers at low rates, and that the value of the reserved lands would thus be increased. At first grants were made to the States for the benefit of the corporations; the Act of 1862 made the grant directly to the corporation.

274. The vital military and political necessity of an immediate railway connection with the Pacific coast was hardly open to doubt in 1862; but the necessity hardly justified the terms which were The Pacific railways. offered and taken. The Union Pacific Railroad was incorporated; the United States Government was to issue to it bonds; on the completion of each forty miles, to the amount of $16,000 per mile, to be a first mortgage; through Utah and Nevada, the aid was to be doubled, and for some 300 miles of mountain building to be trebled; and, in addition to this, alternate sections of land were granted. The land-grant system, thus begun, was carried on in the cases of a large number of other roads, the largest single grants being those of 47,000,000

acres to the Northern Pacific (1864) and of 42,000,000 to the Atlantic and Pacific line (1866).

275. Specie payments had been suspended almost everywhere towards the end of 1861; but the price of gold was but 102.5 at the beginning of 1862. About May its price in paper currency began to rise. It touched 170 during the next year, and 285 in 1864; but the real price probably never went much above 250. As gold rose, specie disappeared. Other articles felt the influence in currency prices. Mr. D. A. Wells, in 1866, estimated that prices and rents had risen ninety per cent. since 1861, while wages had not risen more than sixty per cent.

Prices in paper.

276. The duties on imports were driven higher than the Morrill tariff had ever contemplated (§ 258). The average rates, which had been eighteen per cent. on dutiable articles and twelve per cent. on the aggregate in 1860–61, rose, before the end of the war, to nearly fifty per cent. on dutiable articles and thirty-five per cent. on the aggregate. Domestic manufactures sprang into new life under such hothouse encouragement; every one who had spare wealth converted it into manufacturing capital. The probability of such a result had been the means of getting votes for an increased tariff; free-traders had voted for it as well as protectionists. For the tariff was only a means of getting capital into positions in which taxation could be applied to it, and the "internal revenue" taxation was merciless beyond precedent. The annual increase of wealth from capital was then about $550,000,000; the internal revenue taxation on it rose in 1866 to $310,000,000, or nearly sixty per cent. Even after the war the taxation was kept up unflinchingly,

Tariff and internal revenue taxation.

until the reduction of the national debt had brought it
to a point where it was evidently at the mercy of time
(§ 322).

277. The stress of all this upon the poor must have
been great, but it was relieved in part by the bond
system on which the war was conducted
(§ 322). While the armies and navies were   Bonds.
shooting off large blocks of the crops of 1880 or 1890,
work and wages were abundant for all who were competent for them. It is true, then, that the poor paid most
of the cost of the war; it is also true that the poor had
shared in that anticipation of the future which had been
forced on the country, and that, when the drafts on the
future came to be redeemed, it was done mainly by taxation on luxuries. The destruction of a northern railroad
meant more work for northern iron mills and their
workmen. The destruction of a southern road was an
unmitigated injury; it had to be made good at once, by
paper issues; the south could make no drafts on the
future, by bond issues, for the blockade had put cotton
out of the game, and southern bonds were hardly salable.
Every expense had to be met by paper issues; Paper issues in
each issue forced prices higher; every rise in   the south.
prices called for an increased issue of paper, with
increased effects for evil. *A Rebel War-Clerk's Diary*
gives the following as the prices in the Richmond
market for May, 1864: "Boots, two hundred dollars;
coats, three hundred and fifty dollars; pantaloons, one
hundred dollars; shoes, one hundred and twenty-five
dollars; flour, two hundred and seventy-five dollars per
barrel; meal, sixty to eighty dollars per bushel; bacon,
nine dollars per pound; no beef in market; chickens,
thirty dollars per pair; shad, twenty dollars; potatoes,

twenty-five dollars per bushel; turnip greens, four dollars per peck; white beans, four dollars per quart or one hundred and twenty dollars per bushel; butter, fifteen dollars per pound; lard same; wood, fifty dollars per cord." How the rise in salaries and wages, always far slower than other prices, could meet such prices as these, one must be left to imagine. It can only be said that most of the burden was really sustained by the women of the south.

278. The complete lack of manufactures told heavily against the south from the beginning. As men were drawn from agriculture in the north and west, the increased demand for labor was

Manufactures.

shaded off into an increased demand for agricultural machinery (§ 231); every increased percentage of power in reaping-machines liberated so many men for service at the front. The reaping-machines of the south — the slaves — were incapable of any such improvement, and, besides, required the presence of a portion of the possible fighting-men at home to watch them. There is an evident significance in the exemption from military duty in the Confederate States of "one agriculturist on such farm, where there is no white male adult not liable to duty, employing fifteen able-bodied slaves between ten and fifty years of age." But, to the honor of the enslaved race, no insurrection took place.

279. The pressing need for men in the army made the Confederate Congress utterly unable to withstand the growth of executive power. Its bills were

Confederate Congress and President.

prepared by the cabinet, and the action of Congress was quite perfunctory. The suspension of the writ of *habeas corpus*, and the vast powers granted to President Davis, or assumed by him under the plea of military necessity, with the absence of a watchful and well-informed public opinion, made the Confederate Government by degrees almost a despotism. It was not until the closing months of the war that the expiring Confederate Congress mustered up courage enough to oppose the President's will. The organized and even radical opposition to the war in the north, the meddlesomeness of Congress and its "committees on the conduct of the war," were no doubt unpleasant to Lincoln; but they carried the country through the crisis without the effects visible in the south.

280. Another Act of Federal legislation — the National Bank Act — should be mentioned here, as it was closely connected with the sale of bonds (February National bank-25, 1863). The banks were to be organized, ing system. and, on depositing United States bonds at Washington, were to be permitted to issue notes up to ninety per cent. of the value of the bonds deposited. As the redemption of the notes is thus assured, they circulate without question all over the United States. By a subsequent Act the remaining State bank circulation was taxed out of existence. The national banks are still in operation; but the disappearance of United States bonds threatens their continuance.

281. At the beginning of 1862 the lines of demarcation between the two powers had become plainly marked. The western part of Virginia had separated itself Admission of from the parent State, and was admitted as a West Virginia. State (1863) under the name of West Virginia. It was certain that Delaware, Maryland, Kentucky, and Missouri had been saved to the Union, and that the battle was to be fought out in the territory to the south of them. In the west Grant, commanding a part of Buell's gen-

eral forces, moved up the Tennessee river and broke the centre of the long Confederate line by the capture of
<small>Forts Henry and</small> Forts Henry and Donelson (February, 1862).
<small>Donelson.</small>   The collapse of the Confederate line opened the way for the occupation of almost all western Tennessee, including its capital, and the theatre of war was moved far forward to the southern boundary of the State, an advance of fully 200 miles into the heart of the Confederacy.   It had been shown already that the successful officers were to be those from West Point; but even they were getting their first experience in the handling of large masses of men.   Grant and Sherman owed a part of that experience to the military genius of the Confederate commander, Albert S. Johnston, whose sudden attack on
<small>Pittsburgh</small>   their army at Pittsburgh Landing (April 6)
<small>Landing.</small>   brought on the first great battle of the war. The Federal forces held out stubbornly until the arrival of Buell's advance guard relieved the pressure, and the Confederates were driven back to Corinth, with the heavy loss of their commander, who had been mortally wounded.   Steady advances brought the Union armies to
<small>Corinth.</small>   Corinth, an important railroad centre, in June; and the Mississippi was opened up as far as Memphis by these successes of the armies and by the hard fighting of the gunboats at Island Number Ten and other places.   At the northern boundary of the State of Mississippi the Union advance stopped for a time, but what had been gained was held.

282. At the same time the Mississippi was opened in part from below.   A great naval expedition under Farragut and Porter, with a land force under Butler, sailing from Fort Monroe, came to the mouth of the Mississippi. Farragut ran past the forts above the mouth of the river,

sank the ironclads which met him, and captured New Orleans (April 25). The land forces then took possession of it and the forts, while the fleet cleared the river of obstacles and Confederate vessels as far as Port Hudson and Vicksburg, where the Confederate works were situated on bluffs too high for a naval attack.

New Orleans.

283. The energy of the combatants had already brought ironclad vessels to the test which they had not yet met elsewhere, that of actual combat. Western ingenuity had produced a simple and excellent type of river ironclad by cutting down river steamers and plating them with railroad or other iron. The type needed for the rougher Eastern waters was different, and the Confederates converted the frigate " Merrimac," captured at Norfolk, into an ironclad of a more sea-going type. The battle between her and the " Monitor " (March 8), in Hampton Roads, was indecisive; but the " Merrimac " was driven back to Norfolk, the blockade and the cities of the Atlantic coast, which had seemed to be at its mercy, were saved, and the day of wooden war-vessels was seen to be over. Before the end of the following year there were 75 ironclads in the United States navy; the number of vessels had increased to 588, with 4443 guns, and 35,000 men.

The "Monitor" and "Merrimac."

284. The hundred miles between Washington and Richmond are crossed by numberless streams, flowing southeast, and offering strong defensive positions, of which the Confederates had taken advantage. McClellan (§ 271) therefore wished to move his army to Fort Monroe and attack Richmond from that point, on the ground of Cornwallis's campaign of 1781. He believed that such a movement would force the Confederate

The peninsula campaign.

armies away from Washington to meet him. The adminis-tration, believing that such a movement would only open the way for the enemy to capture Washington — a more valuable prize than Richmond — gave directions that a part of McClellan's force, under McDowell, should take the overland route as far as Fredericksburg, while the rest, under McClellan, were moving up the peninsula towards Richmond, and that, as the enemy withdrew to meet the latter, a junction of the two divisions should take place, so as to carry out McClellan's plans without uncovering Washington. But a month was spent in be-sieging Yorktown; when the attempt was made to form the junction with McDowell it involved the separation of the two wings by the little river Chickahominy; and in May the spring rains turned the little stream into a wide river, and the army was divided, Joseph E. Johnston, the Confederate commander, at once attacked the weaker Seven Pines and wing at Seven Pines and Fair Oaks, but was Fair Oaks. beaten, and was himself wounded and com-pelled to leave the service for a time. This event gave his place to Robert E. Lee, whose only military service in the war up to this time had been a failure in western Virginia. He was now to begin, in conjunction with Thomas J. ("Stonewall") Jackson, a series of brilliant campaigns.

285. From Staunton, one hundred miles west of Rich-mond, the Shenandoah valley extends north-east to the Jackson's raid. Potomac, whence there is an easy march of seventy-five miles south-east to Washington. Jackson struck the Union forces in the valley, drove them to the Potomac, and excited such alarm in Wash-ington that McDowell's troops were hastily withdrawn from Fredericksburg. Having thus spoiled McClellan's

plan of junction, and taken some 40,000 men from him, Jackson hurried to Richmond. Lee met him on the north side of the Chickahominy, and the two armies attacked McClellan's right wing at Gaines's Mill, and cut the connection between it and its base of supplies on the York river (June 26). Unable to reunite his wings and regain his base, McClellan was forced to draw his right wing south, and attempt to establish another base on the James river. Lee and Jackson followed hard on his retreat, and the "seven days' battles" were The "seven the most desperate of the war up to this days' battles." time, the principal battles being those of Savage's Station (June 29), Glendale (June 30), and Malvern Hill (July 1). The last ended the series, for McClellan had reached the James, and his army had fixed itself in a position from which it could not be driven.

286. Pope had succeeded McDowell, and Jackson attacked and beat him on the battle-ground of Bull Run (August 29), driving his army towards Wash- Pope's ington. McClellan was at once recalled to campaign. defend the capital. As he withdrew from the peninsula, Lee joined Jackson, and the whole Confederate army, passing to the north-west of Washington, began the first invasion of the north. As it passed through the mountains of north-western Maryland, the army of the Potomac, which had been brought up through Maryland in pursuit, reached its rear, and forced it to turn and fight the battle of Antietam, or Sharpsburg, Sep- Antietam. tember 17. Both sides claimed the victory, but Lee was compelled to recross the Potomac to his former position. McClellan was blamed for the slowness of his pursuit and was removed, Burnside becoming his successor. The only great event of his term

of command was his attempt to storm the heights behind
Fredericks-burg.
Fredericksburg (December 13) and the terrible slaughter of his defeat. Hooker was then put in his place. The year 1862 thus closed with the opposing armies in about the same positions as at the beginning of the war.

287. At the beginning of the war the people and leaders of the north had not desired to interfere with slavery, but circumstances had been too strong for them. Lincoln had declared that he meant to save the Union as he best could, — by preserving slavery, by destroying it, or by destroying part and preserving part of it. Just
The Emancipation Proclamation.
after the battle of Antietam he issued his proclamation calling on the revolted States to return to their allegiance before the following January 1, otherwise their slaves would be declared free men. No State returned, and the threatened declaration was issued January 1, 1863. As President, Lincoln could issue no such declaration; as commander-in-chief of the armies and navies of the United States, he could issue directions only as to the territory within his lines; but the Emancipation Proclamation applied only to territory outside of his lines. It has therefore been debated whether the proclamation was in reality of any force. It may fairly be taken as an announcement of the policy which was to guide the army, and as a declaration of freedom taking effect as the lines advanced. At all events, this was its exact effect. Its international importance was far greater. The locking up of the world's source of cotton-supply had been a general calamity, and the Confederate Government and people had steadily expected that the English and French Governments, or at least one of them, would intervene in the war for the purpose of

raising the blockade and releasing the southern cotton. The conversion of the struggle into a crusade against slavery made intervention impossible for Governments whose peoples had now a controlling influence on their policy, and intelligence enough to understand the issue which had now been made.

288. Confederate agents in England were numerous and active. Taking advantage of every loophole in the British Foreign Enlistment Act they built Confederate and sent to sea the "Alabama" and "Florida," privateers. which for a time almost drove American commerce from the ocean. Whenever they were closely pursued by United States vessels they took refuge in neutral ports until a safe opportunity occurred to put to sea again. Another, the "Georgia," was added in 1863. All three were destroyed in 1864, — the "Florida" by a violation of Brazilian neutrality, the "Georgia" after an attempt to transfer her to neutral owners, and the "Alabama" after a brief sea-fight with the "Kearsarge," off Cherbourg (June 19). Confederate attempts to have ironclads equipped in England and France were unsuccessful.

289. In the west (§ 281) Bragg, now in command of the Confederate forces, turned the right of the Union line in southern Tennessee, and began an invasion of Kentucky about the time when Lee was beginning his invasion of the north. Carrying off much booty, he retired into Tennessee. Towards the end of the year Rosecrans moved forward from Nashville to attack him. The armies met at Murfreesboro', and fought a drawn battle during the last day of the year Murfreesboro'. 1862 and the first two days of January, 1863. The western armies were now in four parts, — that of Rosecrans near Murfreesboro', that of Grant near Corinth, that of

Schofield in Missouri and Arkansas, and that of Banks in Louisiana. The complete opening of the Mississippi being the great object, the burden of the work fell to Grant, who was nearest the river. Vicksburg was the objective point, and Grant at first attempted to take it from the opposite or western bank of the river. Failing here, he moved south to a favorable point for crossing, and used the river fleet to transfer his army to the eastern bank. He was now on the Vicksburg side of the river. J. E. Johnston was north-east of him at Jackson, with a weaker army; the bulk of the Confederate forces was at or near Vicksburg, under Pemberton. Johnston wanted no siege of Vicksburg; Pemberton wanted no junction with Johnston, which might cost him the glory of defeating Grant; and Grant solved their difficulty for them. Moving north-east he struck Johnston's army near Jackson, beat it, and drove it out of any possibility of junction. He then turned westward, fighting several sharp battles as he went, and late in May he had Pemberton shut up in Vicksburg. His lines were maintained for six weeks, and then (July 4, 1863) the finest Confederate army in the west surrendered. Port Hudson surrendered to Banks five days later: the Mississippi was opened from end to end, and the Confederacy was cleft in twain. From this time communication between the two parts of the Confederate States became increasingly more difficult, and the transfer of supplies from the rich country west of the Mississippi was almost at an end. There was little further fighting to the west of the great river, except an intermittent guerilla warfare and the defeat of Banks's expedition against north-western Louisiana early in 1864. When the war ceased in the east, the isolated western half of the Confederacy fell with it.

290. While Grant was besieging Vicksburg, Rosecrans had begun to move from the eastern end of the Union line in Tennessee against Bragg at Chattanooga. He drove Bragg through the place, and a dozen miles beyond it, into Georgia. Here the Confederate army took position behind Chickamauga creek, and Chickamauga. inflicted a complete defeat upon the pursuing Union forces (September 19-20, 1863). Thomas covered the rear stubbornly, and secured a safe retreat into Chattanooga, but the possession of the mountains around the place enabled Bragg to cut off almost all roads of further retreat and establish a siege of Chattanooga. Bragg was so confident of success that he detached a part of his army, under Longstreet, to besiege Knoxville, in eastern Tennessee. Grant was ordered to take command at Chattanooga, and went thither, taking Sherman and others of the officers who had taken part in his Vicksburg campaign. He soon opened new routes of communication to the rear, supplied and reinforced his army, and began to prepare for the storming of the mountains before him. His assaults on Lookout Mountain and Missionary Ridge (November 23-25) were among the most dramatic Lookout Moun- and successful of the war. Bragg was driven tain and Mission- out of all his positions and back to Dalton, ary Ridge. where Davis was compelled by the complaints of his people to remove him, and appoint J. E. Johnston his successor. Longstreet broke up the siege of Knoxville, and made good his retreat across the mountains into Virginia to join Lee.

291. The army of the Potomac, under Hooker, kept its place near Fredericksburg (§ 286) until May, 1863. Hooker then began a movement across the Rapidan towards Richmond and was defeated in the battle of Chan-

cellorsville (May 2–3). The victorious army suffered the severest of losses in the death of Jackson, but this did not check Lee's preparations for a second invasion of the north, which began the next month. As his army moved northwards, very nearly on the route which it had followed the year before, the army of the Potomac held a parallel course through Maryland and into Pennsylvania. The Confederate forces penetrated farther than in 1862 ; their advance came almost to Harrisburg, and threw the neighboring northern cities into great alarm ; but the pursuing army, now under Meade, met Lee at Gettysburg (July 1–3) and defeated him. The Confederate army, assaulting its enemy in very strong positions, suffered losses which were almost irreparable, and it was never again quite the same army as before Gettysburg. Some northern cities were inclined to think that Lee's former successes had really been due to Jackson's genius, and that he had lost his power in losing Jackson. The campaign of 1864 was to prove the contrary. The customary retreat brought the two armies back to very nearly the same positions which they had occupied at the beginning of the war, the Rappahannock flowing between them. Here they remained until the following spring.

Chancellorsville.

Gettysburg.

292. The turning point of the war was evidently in the early days of July, 1863, when the victories of Vicksburg and Gettysburg came together. The national Government had at the beginning cut the Confederate States down to a much smaller area than might well have been expected ; its armies had pushed the besieging lines far into the hostile territory, and had held the ground which they had gained ; and the war

The current of success changes.

itself had developed a class of generals who cared less for the conquest of territory than for attacking and destroying the opposing armies. The great drafts on the future which the credit of the Federal Government enabled the north to make gave it also a startling appearance of prosperity; so far from feeling the war, it was driving production of every kind to a higher pitch than ever before. The cities began to show greater evidences of wealth, and new rich men appeared, many of them being the "shoddy aristocracy," who had acquired wealth by mis-serving the Government, but more being able men who had grasped the sudden opportunities offered by the changes of affairs.

293. The war had not merely developed improved weapons and munitions of war; it had also spurred the people on to a more careful attention to the welfare of the soldiers, the fighting men drawn from their own number. The Sanitary Commission, the Christian Commission, and other voluntary associations for the physical and moral care of soldiers received and disbursed very large sums. The national Government was paying an average amount of $2,000,000 per day for the prosecution of the war, and, in spite of the severest taxation, the debt grew to $500,000,000 in June, 1862, to twice that amount a year later, to $1,700,000,000 in June, 1864, and reached its maximum August 31, 1865, — $2,845,907,626. But this lavish expenditure was directed with energy and judgment. The blockading fleets were kept in perfect order and with every condition of success. The railroad and telegraph were brought into systematic use for the first time in modern warfare. Late in 1863 Stanton, the secretary of war, moved two corps of 23,000 men from Washington to Chattanooga, 1200 miles, in seven days.

A year later he moved another corps, 15,000 strong, from Tennessee to Washington in eleven days, and within a month had collected vessels and transferred it to North Carolina. Towards the end of the war, when the capacity of the railroad for war purposes had been fully learned, these sudden transfers of troops by the Federal Government almost neutralized the Confederate advantage of interior lines.

294. On the other hand, the Federal armies now held almost all the great southern through lines of railroad, except the Georgia lines and those which supplied Lee from the south (§ 296). The want of the southern people was merely growing in degree, not in kind. The

Conscription. conscription, sweeping from the first, had become omnivorous; towards the end of the war every man between seventeen and fifty-five was legally liable to service, and in practice the only limit was physical incapacity. In 1863 the Federal Government also was driven to conscription. The first attempts to carry it out resulted in forcible resistance in several places, the worst being the "draft riots" in New York (July), when the city was in the hands of the mob for several days. All the resistance was put down; but exemptions and substitute purchases were so freely permitted that the draft in the north had little effect except as a stimulus to the States in filling their quotas of volunteers by voting bounties.

295. Early in 1864 Grant (§ 290) was made lieutenant-general, with the command of all the armies. He went

Grant and Sher- to Washington to meet Lee, leaving Sherman
man. to face Johnston at Dalton. Events had thus brought the two ablest of the Confederate generals opposite the two men who were the best product of the war on

the northern side. It remained to be seen whether Lee, with his army of northern Virginia, could resist the methods by which Grant and Sherman had won almost all the great table-land which occupies the heart of the country east of the Mississippi. And it remained to be seen, also, whether the reputation which Grant had won at a distance from the political atmosphere of Washington would not wither in his new position. It was necessary for him to take the overland route to Richmond, or meet McClellan's fate. He did not hesitate. Early in May, 1864, with about twice as many men (125,000) as Lee, he entered the " Wilderness " on the other side of the Rapidan. At the same time he sent 30,000 men, under Butler, up the James river ; but this part of his plan proved of comparatively little service.

296. Two weeks' hard fighting in the Wilderness and at Spotsylvania Court House (May 5-18), and four days more at North Anna (May 23-27), with flank "Wilderness" movements as a means of forcing Lee out of campaign. positions too strong to be taken from the front, brought the army of the Potomac to Cold Harbor, in the immediate defences of Richmond. One assault, bloodily repulsed, showed that there was no thoroughfare in this direction. Lee had so diligently prepared that his position became stronger as he was driven into greater concentration ; and Grant began to move along the eastern face of the line of Confederate fortifications, striking at them as he passed them, but finding no weak spot. As he crossed the James river and reached Petersburg, he came at last into dangerous proximity to the railroads which brought Lee's supplies from Petersburg. the south — the Weldon Railroad, running directly south, the Danville Railroad, running south-west, and

the Southside Railroad, running west.   At this end of his line, therefore, Lee kept the best part of his troops, and resisted with increasing stubbornness Grant's efforts to carry his lines farther to the south-west or to reach the railroads.   Resorting to the plan which had been so effective with McClellan, he sent Early on a raid up the Shenandoah valley to threaten Washington (July).   But Early was not Jackson, and he returned with no more success than the frightening of the authorities at Washington.   Grant put Sheridan in command in the valley, and he beat Early at Cedar Creek (October), scattering his army for the remainder of the war.   In August Grant succeeded in seizing a few miles of the Weldon Railroad; but Lee brought his supplies in wagons round that portion held by Grant.   Late in the year this was stopped by the destruction of some twenty miles of the road.   Here Grant was himself stopped for the time. Lee had so taken advantage of every defensive position that Grant could not reach the nearer of the other two railroads without an advance of fifteen miles, or the further one without a circuit of about forty miles.   The two armies remained locked until the following spring. Grant, however, was operating still more successfully elsewhere through Sherman.

297. Sherman (§ 295) had moved on the same day as Grant (May 5). Johnston's retreat was skilfully conducted; every position was held to the last moment; and it was not until the middle of July that Sherman had forced him back to his strongest lines of defence — those around Atlanta.   The Confederate forces could not retreat much beyond Atlanta, for the great central table-land here begins to fall into the plains which stretch to the Atlantic.   Sherman had

Johnston's retreat.

now been brought so far from his base that the two armies were much more nearly on an equality than in May; and Johnston was preparing for the decisive battle when Davis made Sherman's way clear. A feature in Davis's conduct of the war had been his extraordinary tendency to favoritism. He had been forced to take Johnston as commander in Georgia; and the widespread alarm caused by Johnston's inexplicable persistence in retreating gave him the excuse he desired. He removed Johnston (July 17), naming Hood, a "fighting general," as his successor. Before the end of the month Hood had made three furious attacks on Sherman and been beaten in all of them. Moving around Atlanta, as Grant was doing around Petersburg, Sherman cut the supplying rail- Atlanta. roads, and at last was able to telegraph to Washington (September 2), "Atlanta is ours, and fairly won."

298. Hood, by the direct command of Davis, then adopted a course which led to the downfall of the Confederacy in the following spring. Moving from between Sherman and the open coun- Nashville. try, he set out for Tennessee, expecting to draw Sherman after him. Sherman sent Thomas to Nashville, called out the resources of the north-west to support him, and left Hood to his march and his fate. Hood reached Nashville; but in the middle of December Thomas burst out upon him, routed his army, and pursued it so vigorously that it never again reunited. One of the two great armies of the Confederacy had disappeared; and Sherman, with one of the finest armies of the war, an army of 60,000 picked veteran troops, stood on the edge of the Georgia mountains, without an organized force between him and the back of Lee's army in Virginia.

299. In the meantime the presidential election of 1864 had taken place, resulting in the re-election of Lincoln, with Andrew Johnson as Vice-President.

Election of 1864. The Democratic convention had declared that, after four years of failure to restore the Union by war, during which the Constitution had been violated in all its parts under the plea of military necessity, a cessation of hostilities ought to be obtained, and had nominated McClellan and Pendleton. Farragut's victory in Mobile Bay (August 5), by which he sealed up the last port, except Wilmington, of the blockade-runners, and the evidently staggering condition of the Confederate resistance in the east and the west, were the sharpest commentaries on the Democratic platform; and its candidates carried only three of the twenty-five States which took part in the election. The thirty-sixth State — Nevada — had been admitted in 1864.

Admission of Nevada.

300. Sherman began (November 16, 1864) the execution of his own plan, — to "send back his wounded, make a wreck of the railroad, and, with his effective army, move through Georgia, smashing things to the sea." He had been drawing supplies from a point 500 miles distant, over a single railroad. He now destroyed the railroad and the telegraph, cut off his communication with the north, and moved towards the Atlantic coast. The sea was reached on December 12, and Savannah was taken on the twentieth. He had threatened so many points, and kept the enemy in so much doubt as to his objects, that there had hardly been men enough in his front at any one time to make a skirmish line. On January 15, 1865, the army moved north from Savannah, through Columbia, to Fayetteville,

Sherman's march through Georgia and the Carolinas.

N.C. The march had forced the evacuation of Charleston and the other coast cities, and their garrisons had been put by Davis under command of Johnston as a last hope. Wilmington, which had been captured by a land and sea force on the day when Sherman left Savannah, was an opening for communication with Washington; and it would have been possible for Sherman, with Wilmington as a base, to crush Johnston at once. All that he cared to do was to hold Johnston where he was while Grant should begin his final attack on Lee.

301. During the opening days of March, 1865, Sheridan, with a body of cavalry, moved from the Shenandoah valley along the James river to a junction with Grant (§ 296). On the way he had ruined the canal and railroad communication directly west from Richmond, and had reduced Lee to dependence on the two railroads running south-west. Grant resumed his attempts to work his lines further round to the south of Petersburg; and, with each successful advance, Lee was compelled to lengthen his thin line of men. Sheridan was put in command on the extreme left; he pushed forward to Five Forks, destroyed the Southside Railroad Five Forks. (April 1), and held his ground. Giving Lee time to lengthen his line to meet this new danger, Grant gave the signal for a general advance the next day. It was successful everywhere; Petersburg was taken, and Richmond the next day; Davis and the other political leaders fled to North Carolina; and Lee retreated westward, hoping to join Johnston. The pursuit was too hot, and he surrendered (April 9). All the Surrender of Lee. terms of surrender named by Grant were generous: no private property was to be surrendered; the men were even to retain their horses, "because they would need

them for the spring ploughing and farm-work "; and both officers and men were to be dismissed on parole, not to be disturbed by the United States Government so long as they preserved their parole and did not violate the laws. It should be stated, also, to Grant's honor that, when the politicians afterwards undertook to repudiate some of the terms of surrender, he personally intervened and used the power of his own name to force an exact fulfil-

Surrender of ment. Johnston surrendered on much the Johnston. same terms (April 26), after an unsuccessful effort at a broader settlement. All organized resistance had now ceased; Union cavalry were ranging the south, picking up Government property or arresting leaders; but it was not until May that the last detached parties of Confederates, particularly beyond the Mississippi, gave up the contest.

302. Just after Lee's surrender President Lincoln died by assassination (April 15), the theatrical crime of a half-crazed enthusiast. Even this event Death of Lincoln. did not impel the American people to any vindictive use of their success for the punishment of individuals. In the heat of the war, in 1862, Congress had so changed the criminal law that the punishment of treason and rebellion should no longer be death alone, but death or fine and imprisonment. Even this modified punishment was not inflicted. There was no hanging for treason; some of the leaders were imprisoned for a time, but were never brought to trial. The leader and President of the Confederate States is living (1889) quietly at his home in Mississippi; and the Vice-President, before his death, had returned to the Congress of the United States as an efficient and respected member.

303. The armies of the Confederacy are supposed to

have been at their strongest (700,000) at the beginning
of 1863; and it is doubtful whether they con- The opposing
tained 200,000 men in March, 1865. The dis- armies.
satisfaction of the southern people at the manner in
which Davis had managed the war seems to have been
profound; and it was only converted into hero-worship
by the ill-advised action of the Federal Government in
arresting and imprisoning him. Desertion had become
so common in 1864, and the attempts of the Confederate
Government to force the people into the ranks had become so arbitrary, that the bottom of the Confederacy,
the democratic elements which had given it all the success it had ever obtained, had dropped out of it before
Sherman moved northward from Savannah; in some
parts the people had really taken up arms against the
conscripting officers. On the contrary, the numbers of
the Federal armies increased steadily until March, 1865,
when there were a few hundreds over a million. As
soon as organized resistance ceased, the disbanding of
the men began; they were sent home at the rate of
about 300,000 a month, about 50,000 being retained in
service as a standing army. The debt reached
its maximum August 31, 1865, amounting to Cost of the war.
$2,845,907,626.56. Some $800,000,000 of revenue had
also been spent mainly on the war; States, cities, counties, and towns had spent their own taxation and accumulated their own debts for war purposes; the payments
for pensions will probably amount to $1,500,000,000 in
the end; the expenses of the Confederacy can never be
known; the property destroyed by the Federal armies
and by Confederate armies can hardly be estimated;
and the money value ($2,000,000,000) of the slaves
in the south was wiped out by the war. Altogether

while the cost of the war cannot be exactly calculated, $8,000,000,000 is a moderate estimate.

304. In return for such an expenditure, and the death of probably 300,000 men on each side, the abiding gain Results of the war. was incalculable. The rich section, which had been kept back in the general development by a single institution, and had been a clog on the advance of the whole country, had been dragged up to a level with the rest of the country. Free labor was soon to show itself far superior to slave labor in the south; and the south was to reap the largest material gain from the destruction of the Civil War (§ 314). The persistent policy of paying the debt immediately resulted in the higher taxation falling on the richer north and west; and the new wealth of the south will forever escape the severe taxation which the other sections have been compelled to feel. As a result of the struggle the moral stigma of slavery was removed. The power of the nation, never before asserted openly, had made a place for itself; and yet the continuing power of the States saved the national power from a development into centralized tyranny. And the new power of the nation, guaranteeing the restriction of government to a single nation in central North America, gave security against any introduction of international relations, international armament, international wars, and continual war taxation into the territory occupied by the United States. An approach for four years to the international policy of Europe had given security against its future necessity. Finally, democracy in America had certainly shown its ability to maintain the unity of its empire.

XI.

THE RECONSTRUCTED NATION.

1865–87.

305. THE Federal Government had begun the war with an honest expression of its determination not to interfere with slavery; the progress of the war had The 13th forced it into passing the 13th amendment amendment. in 1865, abolishing slavery in the United States forever. In much the same way circumstances were driving it into interference with what had always been regarded as the rights of the States. In the latter case the process was certain to find an obstacle in Lincoln's successor, Johnson. He had been elected, like Pres. Johnson Tyler, to the comparatively unimportant office and the Republican party. of Vice-President in order to gain the votes of War Democrats; and now the dominant party found itself with a President opposed to its fundamental views of the powers of the Federal Government. The case was worse for Johnson, since the war had built up a new party. Until 1861 the Republican party had been a mixture of a strong Whig element and a weak Democratic element; now it was a real party, and demanded complete loyalty from its leaders, not skilful compromises between its two elements. Just as in the cases of Seward, Sumner, Trumbull, and very many of its original leaders, the party was now ready to repudiate its leaders if they did not come up to its ideas.

306. The universal idea in 1861 had been that the States were to be forced to return with all their rights un-

Presidential re-construction. impaired. This original notion was seriously limited by the Emancipation Proclamation of 1862–63; as soon as the President opened a door, by demanding a recognition of the abolition of slavery as a condition precedent to the return of a State, the way was just as open for the imposition of whatever conditions Congress as well should think essential to an abiding peace. But Congress was not called to face the difficulty for some time. President Lincoln went on to reorganize civil government in Virginia, Tennessee, Arkansas, and Louisiana, by giving amnesty to such voters as would swear to support the Government of the United States and the abolition of slavery, and recognizing the State officers elected by such voters. When Johnson succeeded to the presidency in April, 1865, he had a clear field before him, for Congress was not to meet until December. Before that time he had reorganized the governments of the seceding States; they had passed the 13th amendment (§ 125); and they were ready to apply for readmission to Congress. Tennessee was readmitted in 1866 by Congress; but the other seceding States were refused recognition for a time.

307. It was not possible that slave-owners should pass at one step from the position of absolute masters to that of political equality with their late slaves. Their State legislation assumed at once a very paternal character. Every means was taken, in the passage of contract and vagrant laws, and enactments of that nature, to force the freedmen to work; and the legislation seemed to the northern people a re-establishment of slavery under a new name. Johnson had a very unhappy disposition for

such a state of affairs ; he had strong convictions, great
stubbornness, and a hasty, almost reckless, Quarrel between
habit of speech. As soon as it became clear Congress and the
that Congress did not intend to readmit the President.
Southern States at once he began (February, 1866) to
denounce Congress in public speeches as "no Congress"
so long as it consisted of representatives from but part
of the States. The quarrel grew rapidly more bitter;
the Congressional elections of 1866 made it certain that
the Republicans would have a two-thirds majority in
both houses through the rest of Johnson's term of office;
and the majority passed over the veto (§ 113) every bill
which Johnson vetoed. Thus were passed the Freedmen's
Bureau Bill (1866) for the protection of the Admission of
emancipated negroes, the Act for the admis- Nebraska.
sion of Nebraska, with equal suffrage for blacks and
whites (1867), the Tenure of Office Bill making the
assent of the senate necessary to removals, which had
always been regarded as within the absolute power of
the President (1867), and the Reconstruction Acts (1867).
The increasing bitterness of the quarrel be- Impeachment of
tween the President and the majority in Con- the President.
gress led to the impeachment of the President in 1868
for removing Stanton, the secretary of war, without the
assent of the senate ; but on trial by the senate a two-
thirds majority for conviction could not be obtained, and
Johnson served out his term.

308. The Reconstruction Acts divided the seceding
States into military districts, each under command of a
general officer, who was to leave to the State Governments then in existence such powers as he should not
consider to be used to deprive the negroes of their rights.
The State Governments of the seceding States were to

be considered provisional only, until conventions, elected without the exclusion of the negroes, but with the exclusion of the leading Confederates, should form new or "reconstructed" State Governments, on a basis of manhood suffrage, and their legislatures should ratify the

The 14th amendment. 14th amendment to the Constitution (§ 125). This amendment, passed by Congress in 1866, was in five sections, but had three main divisions. (1) All persons born or naturalized in the United States were declared citizens of the United States and of their States, and the States were forbidden to abridge the "privileges or immunities" of such citizens. This was to override the Dred Scott decision (§ 249). (2) The representation of the States in Congress was to be reduced in proportion to the number of persons whom they should exclude from the elective franchise. This was to *induce* the States to adopt negro suffrage. On the other hand, specified classes of Confederate office-holders were excluded from office until Congress should remove their disabilities. (3) The war debts of the Confederacy and the seceding States were declared void forever, and the war debt of the United States was guaranteed. Congress was given power to enforce all these provisions by "appropriate legislation."

309. The presidential election of 1868 sealed the process of reconstruction. The Democrats opposed it, and Election of 1868. nominated Seymour and Blair; the Republicans endorsed it, and nominated Grant and Colfax. Virginia, Mississippi, and Texas were the only States of the late Confederacy which were excluded from this election; all the rest had been reconstructed, and re-admitted by Congress in June, 1868; and the Republican candidates carried twenty-six of the thirty-four voting

States, and were elected. The legislatures of the reconstructed States, representing mainly the negroes freed by the war, were devoted supporters of the new order of things; and their ratifications secured the necessary three-fourths of the States to make the 14th amendment a part of the Constitution (1868). Congress went on to propose a 15th amendment, forbidding the United States, The 15th or any State, to limit or take away the right amendment. of suffrage by reason of race, color, or previous condition of servitude. This was ratified by the necessary number of States and became a part of the Constitution (1870).. Ratification of it was imposed as an additional condition on Virginia, Mississippi, and Texas, which had rejected the original terms of readmission. They accepted it, and were readmitted (1870). It was not until January 30, 1871, that all the States were once more represented in Congress.

310. The foreign affairs of the United States during this period took on a new appearance. The country's promptness in disarming at the end of the war put it under no disadvantage in dealing with other nations; power and pacific intentions were united in the act. The successful completion of the Atlantic cable (1866) gave a celerity and directness to diplomacy which was well suited to American methods. The tone of American complaint at the continued presence of French soldiers in Mexico grew more emphatic as the success of Mexico. the war became assured; and, at the end of the war, significant movements of troops to the Mexican frontier led the French emperor to withdraw his support of Maximilian. Alaska was purchased from Alaska. Treaty Russia in 1867. The treaty of Washington of Washington. (1871) provided for the settlement by arbitration of the " Alabama " disputes, of the north-western boundary,

and of the claims of Canada for damages for use of the shore by American fishermen. The capture by a Spanish man-of-war of the "Virginius,"

The "Virginius" case.

a vessel claiming American nationality, and

The Chinese.

the execution of a part of her crew (1873), threatened to interrupt friendly relations with Spain; but the rupture was averted by proof that the vessel's papers were false. Chinese immigration had grown largely on the Pacific coast. There were riotous attacks on the Chinese by worthless white men; and many others did not feel that they were a desirable political addition to the population of the United States. A treaty with China was obtained (1880), by which the limitation of Chinese immigration was allowed.[1] So, also,

"Dynamiters."

the raising of money in the United States to assist the destruction of private and public buildings in England by some of the more desperate of the Irish people (1885) gave England reason for discontent. But the American Government had no power in the premises. The matter was under the exclusive jurisdiction of the State Governments; and, as soon as these began to apply the common law to the case, the "dynamite subscriptions" disappeared. Further difficulties made their appearance as to the Canadian fisheries (1886–

The Canadian fisheries.

87). When American fishing-vessels bought ice or bait in Canadian ports, the Canadian Government seized and condemned them, on the ground that such purchases were acts "preparatory to fishing in Canadian waters." Retaliatory measures were sug-

[1] After rigorous legislation in 1882 and 1884 by Congress under the provisions of this treaty, the expected ratification by China of a new treaty that had been long negotiating fell through in 1888, and Congress passed a law absolutely prohibiting the immigration of Chinese laborers.

gested, but no full retaliatory system has been adopted, nor has the dispute yet been settled.

311. The prosperity of the United States knew no cessation. It had been found that gold was not confined to California. In 1858 it had been discovered in Colorado, at Pike's Peak. It has since been found in most of the Pacific States and Territories. Silver, a metal hardly known hitherto in the United States, was discovered in Nevada (1858); and this metal also has been found to be widely scattered over the Pacific coast. Petroleum was found in north-western Pennsylvania (1859), and the enormous drain of this oil from the earth still continues without apparently affecting the reservoir. The coal-fields of the country began to be understood clearly. Taylor, in 1848, thought that the coal-area of the United States amounted to 133,000 square miles; it was estimated in 1883 at over 200,000 square miles. Natural gas has since come into use, and has made production of many kinds cleaner, more effective, and cheaper. Manufactures and every variety of production have increased with cumulative rapidity. In 1860 the largest flouring-mill in the United States was in Oswego, N. Y., the next two in Richmond, Va., and the fourth in New York city; and the capacity of the largest was only 300,000 barrels a year. In 1887 the flour production of Minneapolis, almost unknown in 1860, is 100,000 barrels a week or 5,000,000 barrels a year. The absolute free trade which prevails between the States has resulted in a constant shifting of centres of production, a natural arrival at the best conditions of production, and an increasing development. Mulhall, perhaps safer as a foreign authority,

Gold.

Silver.

Petroleum.

Coal.

Natural gas.

Manufactures.

gives the total manufactures of the United States as £682,000,000 in 1870 and £888,000,000 in 1880, Great Britain coming next with £642,000,000 in 1870 and £758,000,000 in 1880. He estimates the accumulated

Wealth.

wealth of Great Britain at £8,310,000,000 in 1870 and £8,960,000,000 in 1880, an increase of £650,000,000; and that of the United States at £6,320,-000,000 in 1870 and £7,880,000,000 in 1880, an increase of £1,560,000,000. If he had followed the American census returns his value for 1880 would have been twenty-five per cent. larger. In 1870 the United States stood third in wealth; in 1880 they had passed France in the race, and stood at least second. The country whose population has been developed within 280 years does already one-third of the world's mining, one-fourth of its manufacturing, and one-fifth of its agriculture; and at least one-sixth of the world's wealth is already concentrated in the strip of territory in central North America which is the home of the United States.

312. Of the 290,000 miles of railroad in the world, probably 135,000 are in the United States. Of the

Railways.

600,000 miles of telegraph lines, more than a fourth are in the United States; and the American telephone lines are probably still longer in the aggregate. The new development of the American railways began in 1869, when Vanderbilt consolidated the Hudson River and New York Central Railroads and formed a trunk line to the west. It was undoubtedly hastened by the completion of the Central Pacific line in that year, and it has resulted in a universal tendency to consolidation of railways and the evolution of "systems," under combined managements (§ 273). The coincident introduction of Bessemer steel rails, the steady increase of weight carried by trains, and concentrated competition have reduced railway freight rates through the whole of this period. The average rates per ton per mile were 1.7 cents in New York in 1870, and 0.8 in 1880; 2.4 cents in Ohio in 1870, and 0.9 in 1880. The persistent effects of such a process on the industries of so large a country can hardly be described.

313. The extraordinary stimulus given to a new territory, if it has any basis for production, by the introduction of a new railway, is also quite beyond Railways in the description. Most of the western railways west. have had to build up their own traffic; the railway has been built, and the sales of lands have afterward brought into existence the towns and even States which are to support it. Nebraska was described in the Government reports of 1854 as a desert country, hopelessly unfitted for agriculture, and the maps of the time put it down as a part of the "Great American Desert." It is now one of the leading agricultural States of the Union, with a population of a million; and Dakota is waiting only for the legal form of admission[1] to become a State. The profits of railway construction, the opportunities for skilful management in the development of territory, and the spice of gambling which permeated the whole were great temptations to Americans to embark in the business. The miles of railway constructed per annum, which had been from 1000 to 3000 (averaging about 1500 miles) for the period 1859–68, rose to 4615 miles in 1869, to 6070 miles in 1870, and to 7379 miles in 1871. Masses of laborers were brought into situations from which they could not easily escape; and masses of capi-

---

[1] See notes, pp. 58 and 96.

tal were locked up in railways which were finally unpro-
ductive, and resulted only in total loss. The result was
Financial   the financial crisis of 1873, from which the
crisis of 1873.   country has hardly yet fully recovered.

314. For the first time in the history of the United
States, the south has taken a normal part in all this
Progress of the development (§ 304), though it was not until
south.   about 1885 that southern progress was fully
understood by the rest of the country. Staggering under
a load of poverty and discouragement which might have
appalled any people, with the addition of social problems
which no other country has solved with any great satisfaction, the southern people began to feel for the first
time the healthy atmosphere of free labor. The former
slave is a free laborer, and the white man has gone to
work; white labor produced ten per cent. of the cotton
crop of 1860 and fifty-five per cent. of that of 1886.
The last eighteen slave-labor crops of cotton amounted
to 51,000,000 bales; the first eighteen free-labor crops
amounted to 75,000,000 bales. And the latter figures
are deceptive from the fact that, in their period, the
south had turned a large percentage of its labor and
capital into industries which had not been possible, only
longed for, under the slave system. Cotton-seeds were
waste under slavery: 600,000 tons of them were crushed
in 1886, giving an entirely new production of $12,000,000
per annum of cotton-seed oil. Southern railways, which
had made but a meagre comparison with those of the
north and west in 1860, began to assume something of
the network appearance of the latter; they too began to
concentrate into "systems," to reduce rates and improve
service, and to develop new territory. Southern manufactures began to affect northern markets; cotton-mills

in the south began to reap the advantages of their immediate contiguity to their raw material. Pennsylvania iron-masters were startled as their product was undersold in the Philadelphia markets by southern iron; and the great mineral fields of Tennessee and northern Georgia, Alabama, and Mississippi, over which Sherman's and Hood's men had so lately been tramping and fighting, were brought into notice and development. Wonderful as the general progress of the United States has been during this period, the share of the new south under free labor has been one of the most remarkable phases in it.

315. The population rose from 31,443,321 in 1860 to 38,558,371 in 1870, and 50,155,783 in 1880. At the normal rate of increase up to 1860 — one- Increase of population.
third for each ten years — the increase from
1860 to 1870 should have been about ten and a half millions, instead of seven millions. The difference represents the physical influences of the civil war. This influence was shown most plainly in the Southern States, notably in South Carolina and Alabama, which had hardly any increase, and a real decrease in adult males. It should also be noticed that natural checks on the increase of population are plainly perceptible in the Atlantic States in 1880, and were probably in operation, to a less extent, in 1860–70, though they were made indistinguishable by the war. The increase in 1870–80 at the former normal rate should have been a little over a million more than it was. The tendency will be more evident in future, but it ought to be allowed for in 1860–70.

316. The material prosperity of the country brought its own disadvantages. The sudden development of wealth gave the country for the first time a distinct wealthy class, not engaged in production of any kind,

and very often having none of the characteristics of the people who are the real strength of the country. The

The era of speculation and corruption. inevitable extravagance of Government man-agement, aggravated by a period of civil war, when the people were disposed to excuse almost any error of detail for which good motives could be shown, had its reflex influence on the people, as well as on the Governments of the nation, the States, and the cities. An era of legal tender paper currency (§ 272), legally unvarying in value, but showing its effects in the constant shiftings of price in every other thing, brought uncertainty as to every article, price, and transaction. The people had learned that "unhappy lesson — that there is an easier way to make a dollar than by working for it"; and it was not long before speculation among the people called out its correlative of dishonesty among Government officials. Money was lavished on the navy; in expenditures on that branch of the service the United States stood third or fourth among the nations, while the

"Rings." effective results were discouraging. "Rings" of politicians obtained control of the larger cities. The "Tweed ring" in New York city was over-thrown in 1872; but New York was not the only city of corruption: Philadelphia, Chicago, and almost every city large enough to have fat opportunities for fraud and to deprive universal suffrage of the general acquaintance of neighbors, each fell under control of its "ring," and was plundered without mercy. Corruption even attacked the judiciary; for the first time American judges were found who were willing to prostitute their positions, and the members of the "Erie ring" were able to hold their ill-gotten railroads because they owned the necessary judges. A "whiskey ring" of distillers and Govern-

ment employees (1874) assumed national proportions, and robbed the Government of a large percentage of its internal taxation on spirits. The "star routes," in which the contracts for mail trans- *"Star routes."* portation were altered at the discretion of the contractor and the Government after the competition for the contracts had been decided, gave rise to as great scandals through the connivance of Government agents with dishonest contractors. No one who lived in this period will wonder at the pessimistic tone of the public speeches which marked the hundredth year of the republic (1876).

317. The republic had life and vigor in it, and its people showed no disposition to despair before the mass of corruption which confronted them. The newspapers attacked the star-route contractors, and drove the Government into an attack upon the ring, which broke it up. The efforts of private individuals, backed by newspapers, broke up the Tweed ring, banished or imprisoned its members, expelled the corrupt judges from the bench, and carried destruction into the widespread whiskey ring. Local rings were attacked in city after city, were broken up and revived again, but always found the struggle for existence more and more desperate. The people have shown themselves almost vindictive in driving out of public life any who have been proved dishonest: when the "Credit Mobilier," the construction com- *"Credit Mobilier."* pany of the Central Pacific Railroad, was shown to have bribed or influenced members of Congress to vote for it, there is ground for believing that the punishment was distributed more widely than justice demanded; and it has come to be recognized as a decided disadvantage for a public man to be known as **shrewd** rather than honest.

318. The completion of reconstruction in 1870, and the adoption of the 15th amendment (§ 125), made negro
The reconstruct- suffrage the law of the land, even in the South-
ed Government. ern States.   The southern whites were the tax-payers; the negroes were the majority; and the negro legislatures proved hopelessly corrupt.   In one or two States the whites recovered control of their States by hiring their negroes to remain at home on election day, or by threatening them with discharge for voting.   Failing in this line of action in other States, the whites fell into a steady tendency towards violence.   A widespread
"Ku-Klux- secret society, the "Ku-Klux-Klan," beginning
Klan." with the effort to overawe the negro population by whipping and arson, was rapidly driven into political murders.   The reconstructed Governments resisted as best they could.   They tried to use the force of the State against the offenders; but the best part of the force of the State was the white element, which was most deeply involved in the resistance to the legal Government. On the application of the legislature of a State, or of the governor if the legislature cannot be summoned, the President may send Federal troops to suppress rebellion (§ 125).   The reconstructed Governments called on President Grant for such aid, and received it.   But the whites were the stronger race, struggling for property, and knowing well the letter of the law.   They refused to resist the smallest atom of Federal authority : a large force of them, mainly old Confederates and excellent fighting men, who had seized the city of New Orleans and overturned the reconstructed Government (1874), retired quietly before a detachment of United States troops, and allowed the State Government to be restored.   The little United States army in the south was kept busy.   Wherever it appeared, resist-

ance ceased at once, breaking out at the same time elsewhere. The whites had to gain but a single victory; as soon as they secured a majority in a State legislature they so arranged the election laws and machinery that a negro majority was thenceforth impossible. The legislatures and governors, with nearly all the local officers, were then Democrats: calls for Federal troops ceased at once ; and the Republicans of the north, the dominant party of the nation, were reduced to the necessity of seeing their southern vote disappear, without the ability to do anything to check the process. As the election of 1876 drew near, the reconstructed Governments of all the seceding States, except Florida, South Carolina, and Louisiana, had become Democratic.

319. Congress, which was controlled by the Republicans, had not been idle. The Civil Rights Act (1870) provided that fines and damages should be imposed for any attempt to violate or evade *Civil Rights Act.* the 15th amendment or for conspiracy to deprive the negroes of the right of suffrage. The Election Act (1870) exercised for the first time the right to alter or amend State laws as to Federal *Election Act.* elections which the Constitution had given to Congress. This was strengthened by another Act in the following year. The Force Act (1871) went farther than the instincts of the American people could follow *Force Act.* Congress. It provided that any conspiracy or combination strong enough to deprive the negroes of the benefits of the 14th amendment should be evidence of a "denial by the State of the equal protection of the laws" to all its citizens; that the President should be empowered to use the army, navy, and militia to suppress such combinations; that, when any combination should appear in

arms, the act should be a rebellion against the United States; and that, in such case, the President should have power to suspend the writ of *habeas corpus* in the rebellious Territory (§ 305).

320. It was plain that the southern whites meant to govern their States with little present regard to the last two amendments, and that it was impossible to defeat their purpose without cutting up the State system in the south by the roots. Even in 1872 a strong element of the Republican party thought that the party policy had gone too near the latter course. It held a convention of Liberal Repub- its own, under the name of the Liberal Repub-lican party. lican party, and nominated Greeley and Brown. The Democratic party, anxious to save local government and State rights in the south, but completely discredited by its opposition to the war, accepted the Liberal Republican platform and nominations. Its action was in one sense a failure; Greeley had been one of the bitterest and angriest critics of the Democratic party, and so many of the Democrats refused to vote for him that his defeat was hardly ever doubtful. The Republicans Election of 1872. renominated Grant, with Henry Wilson for Vice-President; and they received the votes of 286 of the 349 electors, and were elected. The action of the Democratic party in adopting the Liberal Republican platform, and thus tacitly abandoning its opposition to reconstruction, brought it back into the lines of political conflict and made it a viable party.

321. The election of 1876 was the first really contested election since 1860. The Democrats nominated Tilden and Hendricks, and the Republicans Election of 1876. Hayes and Wheeler. The platforms showed no distinct grounds of party struggle, except that of

the ins and the outs. The election turned on the votes of the Southern States in which the reconstructed Governments still held their own or claimed to do so; and the extra-constitutional device of an electoral commission resulted in a decision in favor of Hayes and Wheeler. As a part of the result, some arrangement had been made for the settlement of the southern difficulties, for Grant immediately withdrew the troops from Florida, South Carolina, and Louisiana, and the reconstructed Governments of those States surrendered without a struggle. All the Southern States were now Democratic; the negroes had every right but that of voting; and even this was permitted to a sufficient extent to throw a veil over the well-understood general state of affairs. Colorado, the thirty-eighth State (and the last up to 1887), was admitted in 1876 and took part in this election. Admission of Colorado.

322. The Hayes administration was a welcome period of calm. The main subject of public interest was monetary, and much of it was due to the change of conditions during and since the war. In order to sell bonds during the war it had been necessary, not only to make the interest very high (in some cases seven and three-tenths per cent.), but to sell them for the Government's own depreciated paper. The Act of 1869, to restore the public credit, pledged the faith of the United States that the bonds should be paid in coin. This had seemed very inequitable to some, but was acquiesced in. When the price of silver had fallen, in July, 1876, to 94 cents, a ratio for gold and silver of 20 : 1, and Demonetization of silver. it was found that an Act of 1873 had dropped the silver dollar from the coinage, the people jumped to the conclusion that this was a trick of the bondholders to secure a

further advantage in the payment of their bonds in the
more valuable metal only. It was useless to urge that
for forty years before 1873 the silver dollar had been
token money, and that its average coinage had been
only about $150,000 a year; the current was too strong
to be resisted, and Congress passed (1878) an Act to
restore the silver dollar to the coinage, to compel the
coinage of at least $2,000,000 in silver per month, and to
make the silver dollar legal tender to any amount. The
Act is still (1887) in force, in spite of the recommendations of successive Presidents and Secretaries of the
Treasury for its repeal. The operation of
Refunding. refunding had been begun under the Act of
July 14, 1870, authorizing the issue of five, four and a
half, and four per cent. bonds, to take the place of those
at higher interest which should be payable. This first
refunding operation was completed in the year of the re-
sumption of specie payments (1879). The issues were
$500,000,000 at five per cent., $185,000,000 at four and
one-half, and $710,345,950 at four, reducing the annual
interest charge from $81,639,684 to $61,738,838. One
secret of the success of the Government and its high
credit was the persistence of the people in urging the
payment of the national debt. The work was begun as
soon as the war was ended; before all the soldiers had
Reduction of been sent home $30,000,000 of the debt had
national debt. been paid, and hardly a month has passed
since without some reduction of the total amount.
Between 1865 and 1880 the debt fell from $2,850,000,000
to about $2,000,000,000; and, as it decreased, the ability
of the Government to borrow at lower interest increased.
About $200,000,000 of six per cent. bonds fell due in
1881, and the Secretary of the Treasury (Windom) took

the responsibility of allowing the holders of them to exchange them for three and one-half per cent. bonds, redeemable at the pleasure of the Government. This privilege was extended to about $300,000,000 of other bonds, giving a saving of $10,000,000 interest. The four and one-half per cent. bonds of 1870–71 ($250,000,000) are not redeemable until 1891, and the four bonds ($738,000,000) until 1907. Roughly stated, the whole debt, deducting cash in the treasury, is under $1,400,-000,000, about $1,100,000,000 being interest bearing, the remainder non-interest bearing paper currency of different kinds.

323. In 1880 the Republicans nominated Garfield and Arthur, and the Democrats Hancock and English. Again there was no great distinction between the party principles advocated. The Democrats, Election of 1880. naturally a free-trade party, were not at all ready to fight a battle on that issue; and the Republicans, turning the contest to the point on which their opponents were divided, succeeded in electing their candidates. They were inaugurated in 1881; and the scramble for office which had marked each new administration since 1829 followed (§ 202). The power of the senate to confirm the President's nominations had brought about a practice by which the appointments in each State were left to the suggestion of the administration senators from that State. The senators from New York, feeling aggrieved at certain appointments in their State, and desiring the prestige of a re-election by their legislature, resigned. Unfortunately for them the legislature took them at their word, and began to ballot for their successors. Their efforts to be re-elected, the caucuses and charges of treachery or corruption, and the newspaper comments

made up a disgraceful scene. In the midst of it a disappointed applicant for office shot the President (July 2),
Assassination of Garfield. and he died two months later. Vice-President Arthur succeeded him (§ 117), and had an uneventful administration. The death of President Garfield called general attention to the abominations of the system under which each party, while in office, had paid its party expenses by the use of minor offices for *Civil service reform.* its adherents. The President's power of appointment could not be controlled; but the Pendleton Act (1883) *permitted* the President to make appointments to designated classes of offices on the recommendation of a board of civil service commissioners. President Arthur executed the law faithfully, but its principle could hardly be considered established until it had been put through the test of a Democratic administration; and this consideration undoubtedly *Election of 1884.* had its influence on the next election (1884). The Republicans nominated Blaine and Logan, and the Democrats Cleveland and Hendricks. A small majority for the Democratic candidates in the State of New York gave them its electoral votes and decided the election in their favor. They were inaugurated (1885), and for the first time in more than fifty years no general change of office-holders took place. The Pendleton Act was obeyed; and its principle was applied to very many of the offices not legally covered by it. There have been, however, very many survivals of the old system of appointment, and each of them has been met by a general popular disapproval which is the best proof of the change of public sentiment. At least, both parties are committed to the principle of civil service reform. There is a growing desire to increase the number of offices to

which it is to be applied; and the principle is making its way into the administration of States and cities.

324. At home and abroad there is not a cloud on the political future of the United States. The economic conditions are not so flattering; and there are indications that a new era of struggle is opening before the country, and that it must meet even greater difficulties in the immediate future. The seeds of these may perhaps be found in the way in which the institutions of the country have met the new economic conditions which came in with the railway in 1830.

325. Corporations had existed in the United States before 1830, but the conditions, without the railway or telegraph, were not such as to give them pronounced advantages over the individual. All this was changed under the new régime; the corporation soon began to show its superiority. In the United States at present there are many kinds of business in which, if the individual is not very highly endowed, it is better for him to take service with a corporation. Individual success is growing more rare; and even the successful individual is usually succeeded by a corporation of some sort. In the United States, as in England, the new era came into a country which had always been decided in its leanings to individual freedom; and the country could see no new departure in recognizing fully an individual freedom of incorporation (§ 215). Instead of the old system under which each incorporation was a distinct legislative act, general provisions were rapidly adopted by the several States, providing forms by which any group of persons could incorporate themselves for any purpose. The first Act of the kind was passed in Connecticut in

Corporations in the United States.

Freedom of Incorporation.

1837, and the principle of the English Limited Liability Act of 1855 was taken directly from it. The change was first embodied in New York in its constitution of 1846, as follows : " Corporations may be formed under general laws, but shall not be created by special Act, except for municipal purposes and in cases where, in the judgment of the legislature, the objects of the corporation cannot be attained under general laws." The general laws were for a long time merely directions to the corporators as to the form of the certificate and the place where it was to be deposited. The New York provision was only a development of the principle of a statute of 1811 applying to manufacturing, but it is an instance of what was taking place all over the country.

326. The consequent freedom of corporations was also influenced by the law, as expounded by the Supreme Court of the United States in the "Dartmouth College case" (1819), whose principle has always been the object of vigorous but unsuccessful criticism. The States are prohibited by the Constitution from passing any laws which shall alter the obligation of contracts. This decision held that a charter was a contract between the State and the corporation created by it, and therefore unalterable except by consent of the corporation. The States were careful thereafter to insert in all charters a clause giving the State the right to alter the charter; but the decision has tended to give judges a bias in favor of the corporations in all fairly doubtful cases. Corporations in the United States thus grew luxuriantly, guarded by the Constitution, and very little trenched upon by the States.

327. American corporations have usually been well managed, and very much of the extraordinary develop-

ment of the wealth of the United States has been due
to them. But a corporation which holds $400,000,000 of
property, owns more than one State legisla-
ture, and has a heavy lien on several others, Corporate power.
is not an easy creature to control or limit. Wars of
rates between rival corporations claiming great stretches
of territory as "their own," into which other corporations must not intrude, are startling things to any people. The rise of a corporation, built upon the ruins·
of countless individual business concerns, and showing
that it can reduce railway corporations to an obedience
which they refuse to the State, is too suggestive of
an *imperium in imperio* to be pleasant to a democracy.
The States, to which the whole subject legiti- Inter-State
mately belongs, confess their inability to deal Commerce Act.
with it by leaving Congress to pass the Inter-State
Commerce Act (1887), intended to stop the encroach-
ments of railway corporations on individual rights
(§ 106); but the success of even this measure is still
quite doubtful.

328. Still more unhappy have been some of the effects
of the new régime on the relations between employers
and employed. The substitution of a corpo- Corporations as
ration for an individual as an employer could employers.
not but affect such relations unhappily, at least for a
time; but the freedom and power of the corporate
employers strained the relations farther than was at all
necessary. The first clumsy attempts to control the
corporations, by limiting the percentage of their profits,
led to the artifice of "watering," or unnecessarily increasing their stock. In good years the nominal dividends were thus kept down to an apparently normal
percentage. When bad years, or increasing competition,

began to cut down the dividends, the managers were often forced to attack the wages, or increase the duties, of their employees. The "bad years" began to be more numerous and constant after the financial crisis of 1873 had set in; and the first serious effects appeared in the "railroad strikes of 1877."

329. For many years past, the drift of population had been towards an urban life. Taking the town of 8000 Concentration inhabitants as the lower limit of urban popu- of population. lation, we find that 3.3 per cent. of the population was to be classed as urban in 1790, and that the percentage had risen to 22.5 in 1880. If towns of 4000 inhabitants had been taken as the lower limit, the urban population in 1880 would have been 13,000,000, or more than twenty-five per cent. It may be thought that the policy of protection, of abnormal stimulation of manufactures, had something to do with this tendency; but it is noteworthy that the increase during the generally free-trade period of 1840–60, from 8.5 to 16.1, was the greatest of any twenty years, unless we take the period 1850–70, half free-trade and half protective, when the percentage rose from 12.5 to 20.9. Whatever may have been the cause, the tendency is indubitable, and its effects in increasing the facility of organization among the employees of corporations, whose fields of operation are generally urban, are as easily to be seen.

330. Some of the corporations were controlled by men who were believed, in some cases on the best of evidence, Popular to have gained their control by the defects of feeling towards American corporation law, particularly by the corporations. privilege of the majority of stock-holders to use the whole stock almost at their discretion, even for the wrecking of the road and its repurchase on terms

ruinous to the minority's interests. Disrespect for "property rights" thus acquired was apt to extend to other corporate property, acquired legitimately; in the railroad strikes of 1877, there were cases in which citizens usually law-abiding watched with hardly concealed satisfaction the destruction of such property as belonged to corporations. Further, the neutral position of the United States had brought about the transfer of considerable English and other foreign capital to the United States to be invested, under corporate privileges, in cattle-ranges or other industries connected with western agriculture. The American managers of these corporations, feeling little responsibility to any power except their foreign employers, permitted themselves to take liberties with individual settlers and their rights which arrayed a large part of the agricultural population of the west against corporate property. Finally, the differential rates made in private, even secret, contracts, by railway corporations all over the country, had gathered up passions of all sorts against the corporate "monopolies." The anchor of agricultural conservatism, usually a safe reliance in the United States, had ceased to be of service in this matter. An order, the "Patrons of Husbandry," said to number 1,500,000 "Patrons of members in 1874, had been formed with the Husbandry." avowed object of checking the common corporate enemy; and, though its prominence was short-lived, its influence remained.

331. The growing power of corporations, and that at a time when the democracy had just shown its strength most forcibly and to its own satisfaction; the Anti-economic evident tendency of the corporations, espe- influences. cially in the protected industries and in transportation,

to further combinations, such as "pools" and "trusts"; the consequent partial disappearance of that competition which had seemed to be a restriction on the power of the corporations over the individual; the power and disposition of corporations to cut wages down whenever dividends made it necessary to do so; the half-understood, but heartily dreaded, weapon known as the "black list," by which combinations of employers, especially of corporations, drove employees inclined to "agitation" out of employment; the general misgivings as to the wisdom or honesty of the State legislatures, in which the power over corporations was vested; the unhappy influences of the increase of urban population over the jury system; the complicated systems of appeals which had grown up in American law, with their opportunities for delay or perversion of justice by wealthy and determined corporations; the altered character of American labor, which was now largely made up of a mass of immigration hardly yet fully digested, and more apt than American labor had once been to seek help in something else than individual effort,—all these influences made up a mass of explosives which became seriously dangerous after 1880. It was no longer so easy for the individual to defend himself against corporate aggression; if it had been, the American working man was no longer so apt to trust to an individual defence; and laborers began to turn to combinations against corporations, though these combinations were even more prompt and successful in attacking individual employers than in attacking corporations.

332. The trade unions, which retained most of the conservative influences of their generally beneficiary nature, were not radical enough; and a local Philadelphia society, the "Knights of Labor," was

Trade unions.

developed into a national organization, following the usual American system of local "assemblies," with delegates to State and national conventions.   " Knights of With but 52,000 members in 1883, it claimed   Labor." 630,000 in October, 1886, and 1,000,000 at the beginning of 1887. Its general object was the union of all classes and kinds of labor into one organization, so that, "an injury to one being the concern of all," the oppression of even the humblest and weakest individual might be answered by the sympathetic action of more important and, if necessary, of all classes of labor. The "boycott," an imported idea, was its most   The " boycott." successful weapon; the firm or corporation which oppressed its employees was to be brought to terms by a refusal of all members of the national organization to buy its productions, or to deal with any one who bought or sold them. Such a scheme was directly subversive of all social protection or security; and yet it had gone on for nearly two years before it came plainly to public notice (January, 1886). Boycotts increased in num-   Anti-social ber; local assemblies, intoxicated by their   results. sudden success, went beyond the control of the well-intentioned head of the order; the passive obedience on the part of the members, which was a necessary feature of the system, evolved a class of local dictators, or "rings," which were irresponsible as well as tyrannical; and the business of the country was very seriously threatened all through the years 1886 and 1887.

333. Law has begun to pronounce distinctly against both the black list and the boycott, as well as against the systems based upon them. There can be no doubt of the cruel tyranny which the new system of labor organization tends to erect not only over its enemies, the class of

employers and those working men who are not of the order, but over its own members. But the demonstration of the illegality and tyranny does not alter the conditions of the problem, of which it is but a single phase. How are the English common law, its statutory development, and its jury system, to exist, when a great mass of the population is discontented, distrustful, and under the dominion of a secret public opinion, and when the way does not seem to be open for a removal of their discontents except by the serious curtailment of the corporate system which has been so powerful an agent in American development and wealth? The great American republic,

The new era. then, seems to be entering upon a new era, in which it must meet and solve a new problem — the reconciliation of democracy with the modern conditions of production.

BIBLIOGRAPHY.

———◦◦———

The works treating of the various phases of the history of the United States are so numerous that only the names of the leading authorities can be given: The histories of the United States by Bancroft (to 1783), Pitkin (to 1797), Ramsay (to 1814), Hildreth (to 1820), Bradford (to 1840), Tucker (to 1840), Spencer (to 1857), Bryant and Gay, Schouler, Von Holst, Higginson; M'Master, *History of the American People;* Gilman, *History of the American People;* Winsor, *Narrative and Critical History;* Williams, *Statesman's Manual;* H. H. Bancroft, *History of the Pacific Coast; The American Commonwealth Series;* Force, *Tracts relating to the Colonies* and *American Archives;* Poore, *Federal and State Constitutions;* Hazard, *Historical Collections;* Neill, *English Colonization in America;* Dodge, *English Colonies in America;* Doyle, *English Colonies in America;* Burke, *English Settlements in America;* Holmes, *Annals of America;* Graham, *History of the United States;* Marshall, *History of the Colonies;* Palfrey, *History of New England;* Parkman's *Works;* Gordon, *History of the Independence of the United States;* Winsor, *Reader's Handbook of the Revolution;* Carrington, *Battles of the Revolution;* Ludlow, *War of American Independence;* Frothingham, *Rise of the Republic;* Story, *Commentaries;* Chalmers, *Annals of the Colonies,* and *Revolt of the Colonies;* Scott, *Consti-*

tutional Liberty in the Colonies; Journals of Congress,
1774–89; *Annals of Congress,* 1789–1824; *Register of
Debates in Congress,* 1824–37; *Congressional Globe,* 1833–
72; *Congressional Record,* 1872–87; *American State
Papers* (to 1815); Benton, *Abridged Debates of Congress*
(to 1850); *United States Statutes at Large; Revised
Statutes of the United States;* Niles, *Weekly Register,*
1811–36; *Tribune Almanac,* 1838–87; Appleton, *Annual
Cyclopædia,* 1861–86; Spofford, *American Almanac,*
1878–87; M'Pherson, *Political Manuals;* Greeley, *Political
Text-Book,* 1860; Cluskey, *Political Cyclopædia,* 1860;
Hamilton, *Republic of the United States;* Benton, *Thirty
Years' View;* Young, *American Statesman;* Johnston,
History of American Politics; Stanwood, *History of Pres-
idential Elections;* Porter, *Constitutional History;* Story,
Commentaries on the Constitution; Kent, *Commentaries
on American Law;* Wharton, *Commentaries;* Duer, *Con-
stitutional Jurisprudence;* Brownson, *American Republic;*
Mulford, *The Nation; The Federalist;* Jameson, *Consti-
tutional Convention;* "Centz," *Republic of Republics;*
Tucker, *Blackstone's Commentaries;* Curtis, *History of
the Constitution;* Bancroft, *History of the Constitution;*
Elliot, *Debates;* Cooley, *Constitutional Limitations, Taxation,* and *Constitutional Law;* Sedgwick, *Statutory and
Constitutional Law;* Bump, *Notes of Constitutional Decisions;* Wilson, *Congressional Government;* Fiske, *American Political Ideas;* M'Crary, *Election Laws;* Rorer, *Inter-
State Law;* Lamphere, *American Government; Counting
the Electoral Vote,* 1787–1876; M'Knight, *Electoral System;* Dillon, *Municipal Corporations;* Morse, *Citizenship;*
Lalor, *Political Cyclopædia;* Burnet, *Settlement of the
North-West Territory,* 1847; Flint, *Geography and History of the Mississippi Valley,* 1828; Histories of the

various States; Bishop, *History of American Manufactures;* Seybert, *Statistical Annals;* Pitkin, *Statistical View,* 1816; De Bow, *Industrial Record of the South and West,* 1852; *Eighty Years' Progress of the United States,* 1861; *First Century of the Republic,* 1876; *Compendium of the Census,* for 1850, 1860, 1870, and 1880; Walker, *Statistical Atlas,* 1874; Scribner's *Statistical Atlas,* 1884; *Reports of the Bureau of Statistics,* 1866–87; Lyman, *Diplomacy of the United States;* Trescot, *Diplomacy of the Revolution,* and *Diplomatic History,* 1797–1801; Baker, *Diplomatic History,* 1861–65; *Reports of the Secretary of the Treasury;* Cooper, *History of the Navy* (to 1853); Emmons, *History of the Navy* (to 1853); Preble, *History of the American Flag;* Rossevelt, *Naval History of the War of 1812;* Boynton, *History of the Navy,* 1861–65; Porter, *Naval History of the Civil War;* Williams, *History of the Negro Race;* Wilson, *Rise and Fall of the Slave Power;* Goodell, *Slavery and Anti-Slavery;* Hurd, *Law of Freedom and Bondage;* Hammond and others, *The Pro-Slavery Argument;* Stephens, *War between the States;* Blaine, *Twenty Years in Congress;* *Official Records of the Civil War;* *Rebellion Record;* Personal Narratives of Grant, Sherman, McClellan, J. E. Johnston, Hood, and Beauregard; *Reports of the Committee on the Conduct of the War;* Scribner, *Campaigns of the Civil War;* *Battles and Leaders of the Civil War;* Comte de Paris, *History of the Civil War in America;* Greeley, *American Conflict;* Draper, *History of the Civil War;* Pollard, *Lost Cause;* Davis, *Rise and Fall of the Confederate Government;* *American State Papers on Finance* (to 1828); Bolles, *Financial History of the United States;* Sumner, *History of American Currency;* Gouge, *Paper Money in the United States;* Spalding, *Legal Tender*

Paper Money; Knox, *United States Notes;* H. C. Adams, *Public Debts;* Gibbons, *Public Debt of the United States; Reports of the Secretary of the Treasury;* Wells, *Internal Revenue Commission Report,* 1866; Taussig, *Protection to Young Industries,* and *History of the Present Tariff,* 1860–83; Young, *Tariff Legislation of the United States,* 1870; Hadley, *Railroad Transportation;* Poor, *Railroad Manual;* Adams, *Railroads: their Origin and Problems;* Hudson, *Railways and the Republic;* Ely, *Labor Movement in America; Reports* of the Bureaus of Statistics of the various States.

INDEX.